Palgrave Studies in the History of Subcultures and Popular Music

Series Editors
Keith Gildart
University of Wolverhampton, Wolverhampton, UK

Anna Gough-Yates
University of West London, London, UK

Sian Lincoln
Liverpool John Moores University, Liverpool, UK

Bill Osgerby
London Metropolitan University, London, UK

Lucy Robinson
University of Sussex, Brighton, UK

John Street
Vancouver, British Columbia
Canada

Peter Webb
University of the West of England
Cambridge, UK

Matthew Worley
University of Reading, UK

From 1940s zoot-suiters and hepcats through 1950s rock 'n' rollers, beatniks and Teddy boys; 1960s surfers, rude boys, mods, hippies and bikers; 1970s skinheads, soul boys, rastas, glam rockers, funksters and punks; on to the heavy metal, hip-hop, casual, goth, rave and clubber styles of the 1980s, 90s, noughties and beyond, distinctive blends of fashion and music have become a defining feature of the cultural landscape. The Subcultures Network series is international in scope and designed to explore the social and political implications of subcultural forms. Youth and subcultures will be located in their historical, socio-economic and cultural context; the motivations and meanings applied to the aesthetics, actions and manifestations of youth and subculture will be assessed. The objective is to facilitate a genuinely cross-disciplinary and transnational outlet for a burgeoning area of academic study.

More information about this series at
http://www.springer.com/series/14579

Pamela Thurschwell
Editor

Quadrophenia
and Mod(ern) Culture

palgrave
macmillan

Editor
Pamela Thurschwell
University of Sussex
Falmer, UK

Palgrave Studies in the History of Subcultures and Popular Music
ISBN 978-3-319-64752-4   ISBN 978-3-319-64753-1   (eBook)
https://doi.org/10.1007/978-3-319-64753-1

Library of Congress Control Number: 2017949452

© The Editor(s) (if applicable) and The Author(s) 2018
This work is subject to copyright. All rights are solely and exclusively licensed by the Publisher, whether the whole or part of the material is concerned, specifically the rights of translation, reprinting, reuse of illustrations, recitation, broadcasting, reproduction on microfilms or in any other physical way, and transmission or information storage and retrieval, electronic adaptation, computer software, or by similar or dissimilar methodology now known or hereafter developed.
The use of general descriptive names, registered names, trademarks, service marks, etc. in this publication does not imply, even in the absence of a specific statement, that such names are exempt from the relevant protective laws and regulations and therefore free for general use.
The publisher, the authors and the editors are safe to assume that the advice and information in this book are believed to be true and accurate at the date of publication. Neither the publisher nor the authors or the editors give a warranty, express or implied, with respect to the material contained herein or for any errors or omissions that may have been made. The publisher remains neutral with regard to jurisdictional claims in published maps and institutional affiliations.

Cover illustration: QUADROPHENIA: Jimmy and Brighton pier. Photograph by Ethan Russell. Copyright © Ethan Russell. All rights reserved

Printed on acid-free paper

This Palgrave Macmillan imprint is published by Springer Nature
The registered company is Springer International Publishing AG
The registered company address is: Gewerbestrasse 11, 6330 Cham, Switzerland

Acknowledgements

I have a great many thanks to give, starting with all the participants from the conference, *Here by the Sea and Sand: A Symposium on Quadrophenia* that took place at the University of Sussex in July, 2014, and spawned this book. Special thanks go out to Franc Roddam, Alan Fletcher, Paolo Hewitt, and James Wood. Thanks go to the aptly named Centre for Modernist Studies at the University of Sussex for funding the original conference, along with the Centre for Visual Fields and the Centre for Research into Childhood and Youth, also at Sussex. Thanks to the Subcultures Network editors and to all the people on the Subcultures, Popular Music and Social Change Facebook page who have supplied me with information and inspiration. Enormous thanks go to Franc Roddam, Ethan Russell, Robert Rosenberg, and the Who, all of whom have been generous with time, permissions, words, and images.

Big thanks, and love, to Jim Endersby who read my article and introduction, formatted my book, saved the index, and my life. Also for input and readings along the way, thanks goes to Geoff Gilbert, Keith Gildart, and Matt Worley. Suzanne Canally has seen me through all my Mod moments and supplied me with old copies of *Mojo* and *Uncut* when I needed them. My brothers, Adam and Eric Thurschwell, introduced me to the album and took me to see the movie for the first time, and for that I am grateful. Thanks to the mini-Mods in my life, Max and Katya Endersby. Thanks, obviously, to Pete Townshend and the Who, without whom, well, there wouldn't be a bleeding book, would there?

Contents

1 Introduction: Dressed Right for a Beach Fight   1
Pamela Thurschwell

Part I   *Quadrophenia* in its Histories

2 Brighton Rocked: Mods, Rockers, and Social Change During the Early 1960s   13
Bill Osgerby

3 "Who (the Fuck) Are You?": Out with the In-Crowd in *Quadrophenia*   35
Ben Winsworth

4 Discovering the Who's Mod Past: The American Reception of *Quadrophenia*   51
Christine Feldman-Barrett

5 Heatwave: Mod, Cultural Studies, and the Counterculture   67
Sam Cooper

Part II The Mobility of Mod: Class, Culture, and Identity

6 Class, Youth, and Dirty Jobs: The Working-Class and
   Post-War Britain in Pete Townshend's *Quadrophenia*   85
   Keith Gildart

7 Quad to Run: The Crucible of Identity as Represented
   in *Quadrophenia* and *Born to Run*   119
   Suzanne Coker

8 Taking the 5:15: Mods, Social Mobility,
   and the Brighton Train   131
   Tom F. Wright

Part III Reading *Quadrophenia*: Genre, Gender, Sexuality

9 "What are You Gonna Do Tonight?" "Wait
   for a Phone Call I Suppose": Girls, Mod Subculture,
   and Reactions to the Film *Quadrophenia*   151
   Rosalind Watkiss Singleton

10 "Poofs Wear Lacquer, Don't They,
   Eh?": *Quadrophenia* and the Queerness
   of Mod Culture   173
   Peter Hughes Jachimiak

11 The Drowning Machine: The Sea and the Scooter
   in *Quadrophenia*   199
   Brian Baker

12 "You Were Under the Impression, that When
   You Were Walking Forwards, that You'd End up
   Further Onwards, but Things Ain't Quite
   that Simple": Time Travelling
   and *Quadrophenia*'s Segues   217
   Pamela Thurschwell

13 **Interview with Franc Roddam** 235
    Pamela Thurschwell

14 **Interview with Ethan Russell** 251
    Pamela Thurschwell and Keith Gildart

Index 263

Editor and Contributors

About the Editor

Pamela Thurschwell teaches at the University of Sussex. Her books include *Literature, Technology and Magical Thinking, 1880–1920* (2001), *Sigmund Freud* (2000), *Literary Secretaries/Secretarial Culture* (2005) co-edited with Leah Price, and *The Victorian Supernatural* (2004) co-edited with Nicola Bown and Carolyn Burdett. She has also published widely on pop music, including articles on Billy Bragg, The Smiths, Bob Dylan, and Elvis Costello.

Contributors

Brian Baker is a senior lecturer in English and Creative Writing at Lancaster University. He works on science fiction, masculinities, and post-war British and American fiction, having published monographs on *Masculinities in Fiction and Film 1945–2000* (2006), *Iain Sinclair* (2007), *Contemporary Masculinities in Fiction, Film and Television* (2015), and also *The Reader's Guide to Essential Criticism in Science Fiction* (2014).

Suzanne Coker lives and works near Birmingham, Alabama. While she has published a small amount of poetry, this is her first prose publication.

Sam Cooper is the author of *The Situationist International in Britain* (2016). His research examines British engagements with continental avant-garde movements through the twentieth century.

Christine Feldman-Barrett is a lecturer in Sociology at Griffith University. Her work examines the histories of youth and popular music. She is author of *"We Are the Mods": A Transnational History of a Youth Subculture* (2009), the first scholarly book to focus exclusively on Mod culture.

Keith Gildart is Professor of Labour and Social History at the University of Wolverhampton, UK. He is an editor of the *Dictionary of Labour Biography* (Palgrave) and his most recent book is *Images of England through Popular Music: Class, Youth and Rock 'n' Roll, 1955–1976* (Palgrave, 2013).

Peter Hughes Jachimiak contributes to *Subbaculture zine*, reviews for *Vive Le Rock!* magazine, and co-wrote the booklet that accompanied the four-CD *Millions Like Us—The Story of the Mod Revival, 1977–1989* (2014). He is also the author of *Remembering the Cultural Geographies of Home* (2014) and "The Politics of Mod" chapter in *Mojo Talkin'— Under the Influence of Mod* (2017).

Bill Osgerby is Professor of Media, Culture, and Communications at London Metropolitan University. He has published widely on twentieth-century British and American cultural history. His books include *Youth in Britain Since 1945, Playboys in Paradise: Youth, Masculinity and Leisure-Style in Modern America*, and *Youth Media*.

Rosalind Watkiss Singleton lectures at the University of Wolverhampton. Publications include "Off the back of a Lorry" in *Solon* (2014); '"Doing your Bit": National Savings Movement' in *The Home Front in Britain: Images, Myths and Forgotten Experiences*: "Today I Met the Boy I'm Gonna Marry" in *Youth Acts, Riots, Rucks and Rock 'n' Roll*.

Ben Winsworth is a senior lecturer in English at the University of Orléans in France where he teaches classes on the history and analysis of "pop" and youth subcultures in the United Kingdom. He has published a variety of articles on contemporary fiction and more recently on the Beatles and the Jam. He is particularly interested in psychoanalysis and literature and all things related to Mod.

Tom F. Wright is a senior lecturer in American Literature at the University of Sussex in the United Kingdom, where he specializes in transatlantic literary and cultural history. He is the author of *Lecturing the Atlantic: Speech, Print and an Anglo-American Commons* (2017) and editor of *The Cosmopolitan Lyceum* (2013).

List of Figures

Fig. 2.1	"That is Brighton, my sons!"	14
Fig. 6.1	Jimmy's bedroom	94
Fig. 6.2	Jimmy's Battersea is largely untouched by post-war affluence	101
Fig. 8.1	He gets pilled up and takes the train to Brighton	133
Fig. 10.1	Jimmy in his sopping wet Levi's	180
Fig. 10.2	Jimmy topping up his eyeliner on the train	185
Fig. 11.1	Jimmy's smashed-up scooter: not a symbol of affluence or mobility	209
Fig. 12.1	The punk not quite meeting the godfathers, in front of the Hammersmith Odeon	225
Fig. 12.2	"Under the breakfast, the beach!"	228

CHAPTER 1

Introduction: Dressed Right for a Beach Fight

Pamela Thurschwell

At the final ceremony of the British summer Olympics in London, in 2012, fifty Mods revved into the O2 stadium on their Lambrettas and Vespas, delivering Kaiser Chief, Ricky Wilson to centre stage to perform the Who's "Pinball Wizard." The ceremony closed with the Who themselves performing "My Generation," "Baba O'Riley," and "See Me, Feel Me" from *Tommy*. The display at the Olympics, as Simon Wells has pointed out, showcases Mod as one of *the* cultural signifiers of British identity.[1] Sleeker, less threatening, and harder to make fun of than punk, more definitively British (while simultaneously stolen from Europe, America, and the West Indies) than Goth, Mod is a style that seems timelessly cool, even as it is also embedded in the very specific economic and cultural history of post-war Britain. As Richard Weight writes in his celebratory, *Mod: A Very British Style*, "Formed against a backdrop of American global supremacy and European decline, Mod was a uniquely British amalgam of American and European culture."[2]

It is arguable that Mod is the only twentieth-century style to spawn its own academic discipline. One of the founding texts of British subcultural

P. Thurschwell (✉)
University of Sussex, Brighton, UK
e-mail: p.thurschwell@sussex.ac.uk

© The Author(s) 2018
P. Thurschwell (ed.), *Quadrophenia and Mod(ern) Culture*,
Palgrave Studies in the History of Subcultures and Popular Music,
https://doi.org/10.1007/978-3-319-64753-1_1

studies, Dick Hebdige's *Subculture: The Meaning of Style* is directly indebted to the stealthy manoeuvres of 1960s' Mods, whose complex relation to the dominant discourses of their day made them ripe for analysis, while also revealing them to be savvy and creative manipulators of their own image: "The mods invented a style which enabled them to negotiate smoothly between school, work and leisure, and which concealed as much as it revealed."[3] Hebdige's work on subculture took off from the energized, political, emerging field of Cultural Studies that developed in the late 1960s, which, as Sam Cooper, argues in his chapter in this book, "believed that politics happened on the dancefloor, in the café and in front of the television."[4] Thinking through and with Mod allowed Hebdige, Stanley Cohen, and the critics who followed them to reflect on a huge number of pressing social issues: changes to working-class culture and family relations; European influence in postwar British society; gender and sexuality (as refracted through Mod style that made men fashion arbiters and gave women chic short haircuts); the politics of resistance and compliance; race (in Mod's debts to black style and music); drugs; motor bikes; and crucially, juvenile criminality and rebellion. The beachfront battles during the bank holiday weekends of 1964, carried out by the Mods and Rockers at Brighton, Hastings, Bournemouth, Margate, and Clacton, made them into household names: "Sawdust Caesars" in the words of the judge in Margate who sentenced them.[5] It's more than a little ironic that at the 2012 Olympics Mods charged in on scooters celebrating their style as a proud signifier of British identity, when in the early sixties Mod was seen as a threat to the established order, a harbinger of the corruption of youth, and the potential downfall of civilisation: teenagers transformed into well-dressed "folk devils" sparked off a moral panic in the early 1960s at a moment when traditional British culture was in the midst of rapid change.[6] By the 2012 Olympics, Mod had definitively lost its menace, and, although the not very Mod amalgam of songs played at the ceremony doesn't indicate it, a large part of that journey to the centre of British culture was due to the ongoing effects felt from the album and film *Quadrophenia*.

Mod, as an identity is a treasure trove of cultural paradoxes, a chocolate box for academics who like sharp suits and soul songs mixed in with their Pierre Bourdieu. What has been less acknowledged is the many ways in which the continuing circulation of the idea of Mod in contemporary culture has relied on its most potent and brilliant representation: the soundtrack, story, and film that charts it all out. The Who's 1973 album *Quadrophenia* and Franc Roddam's 1979 cult classic film based on the album are now inseparable from Mod identity, and in part responsible for the style's staying power. If Mod as a style has been central to the development of cultural and subcultural studies in Britain, then *Quadrophenia*—the album and the film—is Mod's canon. *Quadrophenia* brought Mod to the consciousness of the greater public and the world, and the cult status of the film means that it continues to introduce Mod style to subsequent generations. From Paul Weller and the Jam's influence on the late 1970s' Mod revival in Britain that was already in train when the film was released, to Mod's more recent and continuing influence on subcultures in Germany, Sweden, and Japan, Mod revives and persists.[7] If you tap "Mod images" into a Google search you find a plethora of photos of contemporary scooters and rallies and advertisements for Mod all-nighters, as well as the old photos, target signs, stills from the film, early photos of the Who, and shots from the album's evocative photographs. Mod identity and *Quadrophenia* continue to work together. *Quadrophenia* has escaped its moorings in the album and film, and has become, as the film's tag line suggests, a way of life.

This collection of essays, then, returns to the album and the film to uncover a contested canon of Mod history. The legendary persnicketiness (or perhaps we should say, attention to detail) of Mod devotees has assured that both Pete Townshend's representation of the trials and tribulations of the every-Mod Jimmy, and Franc Roddam's filmic version, have been subject to unstinting criticisms about their authenticity and faithfulness to their source material.[8] The contributors to this volume are, on the whole, less concerned with some ideal of authenticity than they are with the ways Mod history interacts with its fictional representations, and with the ways in which *Quadrophenia* has created new ways of telling and retelling Mod myths and truths. *Quadrophenia* is, of course, about topics beyond Mod as well. Contributors to this volume analyse the film and album through numerous contexts: the history of the Who's reception and influences, the 1970s' cultural and social landscape into which the album and film emerged, the adolescent novel of development (the *bildungsroman*), adolescent angst, 1970s' socialist politics, trains, glam rock, Brighton, and Bruce Springsteen are but a few topics that arise alongside Mod stories here.

There is also another story running in a subterranean way through many of the scholarly essays in this book—the story of what it means to be a fan and critic together. My own history with *Quadrophenia* began in 1978, when I lay on a couch for three years getting through the worst of my adolescence by never having it off the turntable. *Quadrophenia*, the Who's dark, elusive, 1973 conceptual double album, was the follow-up to *Who's Next*, the record that introduced me to the possibility that my own teenage waste land could be made bearable by turning the music up loud. I loved the fact that *Quadrophenia* told a story. Jimmy, the pilled-up, emotional, occasionally violent, Mod teenager, seemed both representative of every adolescent in his ur-teenage activities (like fighting with his parents) and—a very specific case—a kid with bipolar disorder enmeshed in the exacting style and requirements of his demanding Mod subculture at his specific historical moment. Jimmy's dilemmas spoke to me through all the paradoxes of adolescence: desperately wanting a crowd of friends to ratify you, to shelter you, but also desperately needing to be an individual, a unique identity. As Jimmy says in the line in the film that makes everybody laugh: "I don't want to be the same as everyone else. That's why I'm a mod, see?"[9] The album played out as a wailing plea for love and understanding, from the younger to the older generation, from the young to anyone who will listen, from the young to the crashing sea. Set against the remote (for me) historical and geographical backdrop of the Mods and Rockers' encounter in the locale of Brighton, England, 1964, it was impossibly exotic and absolutely familiar. I fell in love with it.

This collection is in part dedicated to the ways in which an artwork gets under your skin and lodges there. As a teenager I examined the album in detail. The cover of *Quadrophenia* shows the brooding back of a boy on a massive scooter with multiple side mirrors each reflecting the face of one member of the Who. Open the album and you find the story Townshend wrote for the inside cover along with Ethan Russell's compelling book of black-and-white photographs depicting, in what seemed like brutal realism, the hero's (or anti-hero's) life. *Quadrophenia* was a treasure trove of information from a world I didn't recognise; it was smoke signals sent up from somebody else's much more interesting adolescence. I remember wondering what a parka was. I couldn't believe there was such a thing as an Eel and Pie shop. *Quadrophenia* might have been the first time I genuinely became interested in history; listening to "The Punk and the Godfather" was the moment I remember first trying to interpret a text. When Franc Roddam's glorious, sad, and funny film of *Quadrophenia* came to America it fleshed out the story for me;

it felt at the time like a documentary of a way of life I needed to know more about. Phil Daniels seemed lifted from his life as Jimmy and parachuted into the film.[10] With its gritty realist feel, and punk-related stars, such as Toyah and Sting, it brought the earlier story of the album into the now of late 1970s punk. *Quadrophenia* was then, and has remained, a rich text, much like *Middlemarch* or *The Golden Bowl*. It bears repeat listenings and watchings; it is worth thinking with and through. The chapters in this book have helped me see *Quadrophenia* as a window into late twentieth-century British social history including subcultural styles and sexualities, the history of Brighton, and class politics, amongst many other topics. I hope they will help you as well.

In Part 1, "*Quadrophenia* in its Histories," Bill Osgerby's "Brighton Rocked: Mods, Rockers, and Social Change During the Early 1960s" sets the stage by unpacking the 1960s' mythologies of youth, affluence, and social change that underpin the storyline of *Quadrophenia*, showing the ways in which the furore that surrounded the Mod "invasions" of British seaside resorts in 1964 was indebted to the growing social significance of youth culture after the Second World War, together with the profound transformations taking place in working-class life as a consequence of shifting patterns of employment and the growing impact of consumerism. National angst about youth culture was given an especially sharp inflection in Brighton as the town navigated its way through a period of change in its economy and social make-up. Ben Winsworth's "Who (the Fuck) are You?: Out with the In-Crowd in *Quadrophenia*" considers the ways in which *Quadrophenia* reflects, anticipates, and interacts with some of the key theoretical work on subcultures published in the 1970s. Considering the historical and cultural context of the album's release, including glam and punk, it looks at how Pete Townshend's revisiting of the past was also an attempt to carry the Who forward and show the pre-punk generation how subcultures had—and still have—the power to effect significant changes within both individuals and society at large. Christine Feldman-Barrett's "Discovering the Who's Mod Past: The American Reception of *Quadrophenia*" argues that the Who's arena rock band reputation in America was changed by the release of the film *Quadrophenia* in 1979, when for the first time, many of the Who's American fans learned about the band's Mod past. This chapter chronicles the Who's initial reception in the United States, their hard-rocking reputation there throughout the 1970s, and the way in which *Quadrophenia* helped American fans reimagine the band. It also considers how the film became the catalyst for a new Mod scene in the United States. Sam Cooper's "Heatwave: Mod, Cultural Studies, and the Counterculture" considers the history of Mod's reception by two different activist traditions in 1960s Britain: the counterculture, focussed on West London, and Cultural Studies, developed in Birmingham's Centre for Contemporary Cultural Studies (CCCS). It considers how underground, proto-Situationist avant-garde groups, as well as Birmingham School academics (including Richard Hoggart, Stuart Hall, and Dick Hebdige), recognised that Mod was a measure of epistemic shifts in class and social relations in the post-war period, arguing that Mod, perhaps more than any other movement within the youth revolt of the 1960s, was a product of its historical conditions and simultaneously a critique of those conditions.

Part 2, "The Mobility of Mod: Class, Culture, and Identity" opens with Keith Gildart's "Class, Youth, and Dirty Jobs: The Working-Class and Post-War Britain in Pete Townshend's *Quadrophenia*," which examines the way *Quadrophenia* depicts continuity and change in the lives of the British working class in the period that the album documents (1964/1965), the political milieu in which it was written (1972/1973), and the legacy of the concept that was later depicted on screen (1978/1979). The album is both a social history of an element of youth culture in the mid-1960s and a reflection on contemporary anxieties relating to youth, class, race, and national identity. It argues that *Quadrophenia* is a significant historical source for reading these pivotal years providing a sense of how musicians were both reflecting and dramatizing a sense of "crisis," "continuity," and "change" in working-class Britain. Suzanne Coker's article "Quad to Run: The Crucible of Identity as Represented in *Quadrophenia* and *Born to Run*" explores a fan's relationship to two favourite albums of the 1970s. The similarities between Bruce Springsteen's and the Who's albums are striking, both focusing on young men's journey toward adulthood. Both centre on the fantasies of place and escape they engender, the bikes they use to get away, their relationships with women, with male friends, and with work. Each paints a portrait of a particular group identity, London's Mods of the 1960s and New Jersey teens of the 1970s, whose differences only underline their similarities. Tom F. Wright's "Taking the 5:15: Mods, Social Mobility, and the Brighton Train" explores *Quadrophenia*'s powerful theme of mobility, both literal and social. By considering the key song "5:15" and moment in the album and film's narrative that it dramatizes, it argues that the image of Jimmy aboard the Brighton train is a symbolic moment that lets the album, film, and Alan Fletcher's novel explore the connections between transport, identity, and the meanings of Mod. Initially contextualising these themes of mobility within ideas of the post-war affluent worker, the chapter proceeds to pick apart the things that each medium does with this train scene, relating this to the broader literary and cinematic history of the railway carriage as arena of class drama and broader debates over youth subcultures and social mobility.

Part 3, "Reading *Quadrophenia*: Genre, Gender, Sexuality" opens with Rosalind Watkiss Singleton's "'What are you gonna do tonight?' 'Wait for a phone call I suppose': Girls, Mod Subculture, and Reactions to the Film *Quadrophenia*." Watkiss Singleton argues that the film's portrayal of young women Mods as little more than accessories within another male-dominated subculture, less important than the haircuts, sharp suits, or Vespas—"pillion fodder" is both accurate and inaccurate. The chapter uses autobiographies and oral testimony to examine the reality of the relationship between Mod "boys" and their "girls." Focusing on the testimonies of West Midlands Mods, it attempts to ascertain whether the experiences of the Mods in the provinces were different to those who lived and worked in "Swinging London" and to establish the parameters of female involvement in the Mod subculture. Peter Hughes Jachimiak's "'Poofs wear lacquer, don't they, eh?': *Quadrophenia* and the Queerness of Mod Culture" examines the homosocial and homoerotic nature of Mod subculture in *Quadrophenia* and beyond it. It offers a critical queer reading of *Quadrophenia* that aids our deeper understanding of Pete Townshend's apparently macho opus not only within Mod, but also in wider social and cultural structures.

Brian Baker's "The Drowning Machine: The Sea and the Scooter in *Quadrophenia*" interprets *Quadrophenia* through the image of the drowned scooter on the back cover of the album, comparing the presentation of the scooter in the album artwork and in the film. It offers a reading of the importance of the scooter to Mod masculinity through cultural and historical context, and then develops an analysis of Jimmy's Vespa GS as a form of "armoured" masculinity that defends the masculine subject against the pressures (and pleasures) of de-individuation. Through the work of Klaus Theweleit, Mod masculinity is read as a late re-articulation of a clean, healthy, hygienic male body and subjectivity proposed by modernity and Modernism. Pamela Thurschwell's "'You were under the impression, that when you were walking forwards, that you'd end up further onwards, but things ain't quite that simple': Time Travelling and *Quadrophenia*'s Segues" argues that through its segues and soundscape, the album *Quadrophenia* represents clashes between its two historical moments, the early 1960s and the early 1970s. If the ending of *Quadrophenia* is notoriously ambiguous in its flirtation with suicide and its unanswered questions about Jimmy's future, it may be that it is instead more productive to linger with the impasses that *Quadrophenia* dramatizes. *Quadrophenia*'s representation of Jimmy's fraught relationship to Mod subculture, class, masculinity, sex, work, and the existential angst of the teenager, creates a dead-end for him in terms of one kind of narrative, the narrative of development, but opens up other possibilities that are enacted through *Quadrophenia*'s sometimes jarring leaps and transitions across space and time, its anachronisms, its nostalgia, its orientation toward a different kind of future.

The book finishes with two interviews, from Franc Roddam, the director of *Quadrophenia*, and Ethan Russell, the photographer of the book of photographs in the original album, who both generously gave their time and assistance to the project.

Notes

1. Simon Wells, *Quadrophenia—A Way of Life (Inside the Making of Britain's Greatest Youth Film)* (London: Countdown Books, 2014), 17.
2. Richard Weight, *Mod: A Very British Style* (London: The Bodley Head, Random House, 2013), 5.
3. Dick Hebdige, *Subculture: The Meaning of Style* (London: Methuen & Co., 1979), 52.
4. Sam Cooper, "Heatwave: Mod, Cultural Studies, and the Counterculture," 68.
5. See Bill Osgerby's article in this book, and Thurschwell, "Lure of the Mods remains strong 50 years on from the battle on the beach" *The Conversation*, May 19, 2014. http://theconversation.com/lure-of-the-mods-remains-strong-50-years-on-from-the-battle-on-the-beach-25349.
6. Stanley Cohen, *Folk Devils and Moral Panics: The Creation of Mods and Rockers* (London: Routledge, 2011 (1972)), quoted in Hebdige 96–97.
7. See Christine Feldman, *We are the Mods: A Transnational History of a Youth Subculture* (New York: Peter Lang, 2009) and Robin Ekelund's work on Swedish Mod culture.
8. Stephen Glynn's excellent short book on the film *Quadrophenia* (New York: Columbia University Press, 2014) includes a list of the errors fans

have spotted over the years and a spirited defense of Franc Roddam's anachronisms (57–67).
9. Townshend says in the BBC documentary *Can You See the Real Me?* "I like to be subsumed in a gang"… "I felt safer in a gang of Mods than I did in the band." (Matt O'Casey (director) *Quadrophenia: Can you see the Real Me?* BBC Four documentary, 2012).
10. Of course this was mistaken. Phil had been to film school in Islington.

Bibliography

Cohen, Stanley. *Folk Devils and Moral Panics: The Creation of Mods and Rockers*. London: Routledge, 2011 (1972).
Feldman, Christine. *We are the Mods: A Transnational History of a Youth Subculture*. New York: Peter Lang, 2009.
Glynn, Stephen. *Quadrophenia*. New York: Wallflower Press, 2014.
Hebdige, Dick. *Subculture: The Meaning of Style*. London: Methuen & Co., 1979.
O'Casey. Matt. (director) *Quadrophenia: Can you see the Real Me?* BBC Four documentary, 2012.
Thurschwell, Pamela. "Lure of the Mods remains strong 50 years on from the battle on the beach" *The Conversation*, May 19, 2014. http://theconversation.com/lure-of-the-mods-remains-strong-50-years-on-from-the-battle-on-the-beach-25349.
Weight, Richard. *Mod: A Very British Style*. London: The Bodley Head, Random House, 2013.
Wells, Simon. *Quadrophenia: A Way of Life*. London: Countdown Books, 2014.

PART I

Quadrophenia in its Histories

CHAPTER 2

Brighton Rocked: Mods, Rockers, and Social Change During the Early 1960s

Bill Osgerby

"That Is Brighton, My Sons!"

Brighton—Britain's popular holiday resort, fifty miles south of London—provides a charismatic backdrop to *Quadrophenia*. The Who's 1973 rock opera and Franc Roddam's subsequent (1979) film adaptation both feature Brighton as a setting for pivotal narrative sequences. But, in the movie version especially, the seaside town also has symbolic importance. Set in May 1964, the film begins as diehard, West London Mod Jimmy Cooper (Phil Daniels) and his friends are building up to the excitement of a bank holiday in Brighton. Jimmy pays off his new, tailor-made suit ("Three buttons, side vents, 16-inch bottoms"), gets a razor-sharp haircut and, with mates in tow, trawls around London for a weekend's supply of Purple Hearts. Then, as dawn breaks, a phalanx of scooter-riding Mods heads south, with Jimmy leading the way. As the ranks of Lambrettas and Vespas crest the Downs (the bucolic hills overlooking the sea), Jimmy pulls up to take in the view. "Look at that! That is Brighton, my sons!" Jimmy crows, as he gazes down at the seaside town. Laid out

B. Osgerby (✉)
London Metropolitan University, London, UK
e-mail: bill@osgerby.co.uk

© The Author(s) 2018
P. Thurschwell (ed.), *Quadrophenia and Mod(ern) Culture*,
Palgrave Studies in the History of Subcultures and Popular Music,
https://doi.org/10.1007/978-3-319-64753-1_2

like an alluring, Mod-*esque* version of Shangri-La, the town is a vision of enticing possibilities. Offering liberating escape from the workaday world of drudgery and obligation, Brighton seems to symbolise the Mod ideals of high living and non-stop hedonism (Fig. 2.1).

Indeed, following Whitsun 1964, Brighton has had a special place in Mod folklore. The "Battle of Brighton" that took place that weekend—an episode central to *Quadrophenia*'s storyline—has anchored the town in Mod mythology. Tales of the Mod "invasion" of Brighton, and images of beachside battles between Mods and Rockers, have become key motifs in the popular history of Mod subculture and have seen Brighton immortalised as a Mod mecca. And this enshrinement certainly has some justification. The events that unfolded were undoubtedly spectacular and were a major news story. They also played a significant part in the development of Mods and Rockers as discrete, distinctive groups with clear-cut styles and identities.

At the same time, however, sociologists and historians have pointed to the way the "Battle of Brighton" was exaggerated and distorted by the press of the time. Magnified and misrepresented by a fevered media, the "Battle of Brighton" was presented as emblematic of seismic social and cultural changes that were transforming the nation; changes in which young people and youth culture were configured as the strident

Fig. 2.1 "That is Brighton, my sons!"

vanguard. It is, then, important to recognise the "mythological" dimensions to the Mod bank holiday mayhem; and the way *Quadrophenia* both portrays this process of mythologisation and is, itself, constituent in the myth-making.

Unpacking the mythologies that lie behind *Quadrophenia*'s storyline requires attention to their historical context. To understand why the Mod "invasion" of Brighton was such a newsworthy event, the episode must be seen in relation to the wider patterns of social change that characterised Britain during the early 1960s. Particular recognition must be given to the way the mythologies surrounding the "Battle of Brighton" were rooted in the growing social significance of youth culture after the Second World War; together with the profound transformations taking place in working-class life as a consequence of shifting patterns of employment and the growing impact of consumerism. But a longer historical context also deserves recognition. Brighton's Mod fracas of Whitsun 1964 and the media uproar that followed were, in many respects, just the latest instalment in a long history of controversy that surrounded the town's "invasion" by raucous groups of working-class youngsters.

"London by the Sea"

Brighton's status as a haven for leisure and pleasure dates from the 1750s when the town was one of many declining fishing ports revived by the fashionable elite's enthusiasm for coastal resorts. During the nineteenth century, gradual increases in disposable income and annual holidays brought more working-class visitors, especially with the completion of a railway link with London in 1841. Initially, rail fares to "London by the sea" (as Brighton became known) were prohibitive; but by the 1860s, third-class travel and low-priced excursion trains had made regular seaside jaunts a possibility for most working people and popular weekends saw nearly 150,000 Londoners descend southwards as "To Brighton and back for three shillings" became a household phrase in the capital.

Renowned as a place where the staid and the serious gave way to the ribald and the risqué, Brighton attracted throngs of working-class visitors out for a taste of fun and excitement. This loosening of restraint, however, was always a site of tension. Fear of the unleashed lower orders plagued respectable Victorians, and high-minded essayists hotly condemned the holidaying crowd's dress, morality and—especially—their propensity for debauched excess. In 1860, for example, one anonymous author (identifying himself as simply "A Graduate of the University of London") bemoaned Brighton's "scenes of vice and temptation", the outraged writer reserving particular ire for young visitors from the capital. That year, the critic lamented, reduced fares on Sunday excursion trains had seen the arrival of thousands of young Londoners who were responsible for the "disgraceful scenes which were enacted in many parts of the town":

> Towards the evening, the Queen's Road swarmed with drunken and disorderly persons, who set aside all decency, and whose conduct was an offence against public morals. Many of them got too drunk to make their way to the station in time, and were left behind. The carriages were filled with young men and women, in too many cases inflamed with strong drink, whose conversation was disgusting enough to shock every sense of propriety.[1]

Brighton's reputation for licentious leisure endured and, during the inter-war period, was complemented by an aura of small-time villainy. This was largely indebted to the rival turf gangs of the 1920s and 1930s who feuded at the race track and on the promenade, reputedly slashing their enemies with cut-throat razors—events that were the inspiration for Graham Greene's 1938 novel, *Brighton Rock*.[2] Greene's teenage anti-hero, "Pinkie" Brown, was a fictional character, but the aspiring gangster and his cronies were closely based on the criminals that frequented Brighton's inter-war race meetings. The gangs were finally broken up in June 1936 after a fight at the nearby Lewes Races. A thirty-strong East London gang known as the Hoxton Mob descended on the event, planning to attack a local bookmaker; but police had anticipated the raid and a violent mêlée ensued. The Londoners were "tooled-up" with iron bars, billiard cues, and knuckle dusters, but most were eventually arrested and jailed.

After the Second World War, Brighton rode high on a post-war holiday boom, but by the 1960s its prosperity was looking shaky. In 1961 *The Economist* was warning that Brighton was "on the rocks," the town depending on a short peak of seasonal trade centred on the August bank holiday.[3] The 1963 summer season, however, was Brighton's most unsuccessful in twelve years and the local Entertainment Managers' Association lamented "the appalling situation which the whole of Brighton and Hove is suffering by the lack of visitors and the almost complete emptiness of the town."[4] But it was not simply the numbers of visitors that prompted concern. The attitude and behaviour of those who *did* visit the resort also provoked unease. Victorian distaste for working-class leisure-seekers found echoes in the angst of Brighton's post-war grandees who, like local author Hector Bolitho, bemoaned the "fish–and–chip–minded people who hurry down from London," turning the town into "a shabby trippers' resort."[5] And, as in the nineteenth century, it was younger visitors who attracted the fiercest ire. This time, however, the concerns were felt even more keenly as traditional anxieties about youth running wild were given added impetus by patterns of social and economic change that had pushed young people into the national spotlight.

"The Teenage Town"

For some, young people in post-war Britain were a bright prospect. As historians Selina Todd and Hilary Young show, many working-class parents encouraged their children to enjoy more adventurous lives amid the newfound economic security of the 1950s and early 1960s.[6] Indeed, many young people faced social and economic opportunities unknown to previous generations. A decline in heavy industry, movement of capital into lighter forms of production (especially consumer goods) and the expansion of production-line technologies created a demand for flexible, though not especially skilled, labour power—and young people (because they were cheaper to employ than adults) were ideally suited to the role. As a consequence, the 1950s and early 1960s saw buoyant levels of youth employment and young people's spending power steadily grew.

Indeed, the equation of "youth" with "affluence" became a prevalent post-war theme. During the late 1950s and early 1960s, market research conducted for the London Press Exchange by Mark Abrams helped popularise the notion that youth, more than any other social group, had prospered since 1945.[7] Widely cited in an array of official reports (and a welter of books, magazines and newspaper articles), Abrams' data suggested that since the war young people's real earnings had risen by 50% (roughly double that of adults), while youth's "discretionary" spending had risen by as much as 100%—representing an annual expenditure of around £830 million.[8] Abrams maintained, moreover, that this spending was concentrated in particular consumer markets (representing, for example, 44% of total spending on records and 39% of spending on motorcycles), which, he concluded, represented the rise of "distinctive teenage spending for distinctive teenage ends in a distinctive teenage world."[9]

Abrams' research was—and continues to be—frequently cited as an index of young people's soaring post-war prosperity. Room exists, however, to qualify some of his contentions. For example, Abrams' definition of teenagers as "those young people who have reached the age of fifteen but are not yet twenty-five years of age and are unmarried" would have undoubtedly disguised differences of earnings and expenditure within this group; while his discussion of *total* expenditure and *average* earnings would, again, have concealed differences and disparities.[10] Moreover, less well-known research contrasted with Abrams' more spectacular claims. For instance, in 1967, Pearl Jephcott's study of Scottish youngsters found that 59% of 15–17½-year-olds had less than £1 a week spending money and 81% of 17½–19-year-olds had less than £3; while in 1966, Cyril Smith's study of youth in the northern town of Bury found that only 5.5% of fifteen- to eighteen-year-olds spent more than £2 per week, with 61.5% spending less than 15s.[11] "The popular picture of affluent teenagers," Smith concluded, "grossly simplifies the very real differences in income among them."[12] And in Brighton, too, research painted a more modest picture of teenage spending. In 1959, the town council's Education Committee tasked themselves with investigating the social and economic needs of local youngsters (a decision that, itself, testifies to the salience of "youth issues" during the period), and the ensuing report recorded that most local boys spent les than £2 a week, while most girls spent between £1 and £1.10s—roughly half the levels calculated by Abrams.[13]

Nevertheless, while Abrams' claims (and the publicity surrounding them) may have exaggerated the scale of "teenage affluence," it was not pure illusion. Figures produced by the Department of Employment and Productivity confirm that young people's weekly earnings rose steadily in the post-war era and show that, whereas male manual workers younger than 21 years-old received only 31% of their older workmates' earnings in 1935, by 1965 this had risen to 68%. Similarly, whereas female manual workers younger than 18 years-old received only 45% of older women's earnings in 1935, this had risen to 68% by 1965.[14] Teenage wallets, then, may not have been bulging, but they were certainly increasingly replete, and—as Brighton's Education Committee concluded in 1959—there was "obviously some justification for the claim that young people today have comparatively much more money to spend."[15]

It was, moreover, a spending power of increasing importance to Brighton. The local elite may have been aghast, but the town's businesses increasingly orientated to the youth market as older visitors drifted away. As journalist Dan Farson observed in his introduction to "Living For Kicks," an ITV documentary profiling local teenagers in 1960:

> Brighton—a favourite place for almost everything, including retirement. But today it's also known as "the teenage town" because of the large number of amusements there.[16]

The same point was made in 1959 by a young Brightonian, who explained to readers of *New Statesman* that:

> ... if there's one thing better than being a Teenager in Love, it's being a teenager in Brighton. ... There are numerous cinemas with adequate snogging facilities, pubs that are tolerant of under eighteenish types ... and above all there are innumerable coffee bars, each with a character of its own.[17]

Enthusiasm for teenage culture, however, was hardly universal. As Dick Hebdige argues, a recurring duality has characterised popular debate about youth. For Hebdige, contrasting images of "youth-as-fun" and "youth-as-trouble" have regularly served as motifs around which dominant interpretations of social change have been constructed.[18] In these terms, young people have been *both* celebrated as the exciting precursor to a prosperous future *and* vilified as the most deplorable evidence of social decline. Hence, alongside the breathless celebrations of teenage consumption, post-war Britain also saw many more fearful accounts that cast juvenile delinquency and commercial youth culture as depressing indices of social decline. During the 1950s the anxieties coalesced around the spectre of the Teddy Boy.

It was around 1954 that the Teddy Boy was first identified by the media in the working-class neighbourhoods of south London. His style of a long, drape jacket and drainpipe trousers was sometimes interpreted as an adaptation of Edwardian fashion—hence the sobriquet "Teddy Boy"—but it was really a variant of the American—influenced styles that had become popular among many working-class youngsters in Britain during the 1940s. And, as historian Geoffrey Pearson shows, longstanding anxieties that cast working-class youth "as the harbinger of a dreadful future" were given especially sharp inflection in responses to the Ted, who was cast as the villainous culprit responsible for a surge in crime and violence.[19] The Teddy Boy was presented as a new, uniquely vicious menace stalking streets and dancehalls all over the country. Not least in Brighton, where existing concerns about working-class "trippers" were given additional force by the alarm that increasingly surrounded the styles, tastes and attitudes of "affluent youth."

Throughout the 1950s and early 1960s Brighton saw a spate of anxieties about young visitors and their impact on the town. In 1954, for example, the local press blamed London Teddy Boys for a stabbing at the town's Regent dancehall; while in 1956 seafront traders, outraged at obscene graffiti, held "Teddy boy trippers" responsible.[20, 21] Critics argued that particular problems were posed by the train from London that arrived in Brighton early on Sunday mornings. The cheap fares available on the service were said to attract "Teddy Boy gangs and skiffle groups travelling to Brighton for a day by the sea"; and the "Trouble Tram" (as it was dubbed) became known for its "skiffling Edwardians and their teen-age 'molls' who terrorize the passengers."[22] One incident saw fourteen youths detained and sent back to London after smashing windows and fighting with fire extinguishers, while on another occasion the local press reported that a "noisy cargo of London skifflers out on a spree" was greeted by a squad of more than thirty police officers who were "standing by to scatter the skifflers if they had decided to play rough."[23]

Other groups of youngsters also drew hostility from Brighton officialdom. Particular enmity was directed towards neo-bohemian beats or beatniks—or "beachniks" as they were dubbed in the town. During the early 1960s, hundreds of young visitors spent summer nights sleeping on the stretch of beach between Brighton's two piers and, speaking to "a young man in a thick black jersey and jeans and embryo beard," a *Times* journalist discovered that most of the group were "youths between 16 and 22 looking for a good time – but a good time which costs as little as possible," the bemused reporter observing that on Sunday mornings the seafront was:

> … more like a dormitory than a beach. Groups of young men trailing their bedrolls over their shoulders, carrying their transistor radios … and recounting their night's adventures are a common sight. Wherever shelter from the biting night breezes offers itself one may expect to come on a beachnik.[24]

But seafront traders, town politicians and the local press were appalled. One town councillor, for instance, suggested that sleeping beachniks should be roused with fire hoses, while colleagues speculated that bulldozing sections of the beach might be a better deterrent.[25]

National concerns, then, were given especially sharp inflection in Brighton. Since the Victorian era the town had wrestled with anxieties about the behaviour of working-class visitors and, during the 1950s and early 1960s, the fears became more pronounced as Brighton struggled to adjust to changes in its traditional holiday trade. And, amid the wave of national unease about youth culture, Brighton's young visitors were regularly configured as both a source and a symptom of the resort's problems. Initially, Teddy Boys and "beachniks" were cited as principal threats. But events in 1960 foreshadowed a new phase of dread. That March Brighton's press reported that the town centre had seen a "running battle" between local lads and a gang of London youths, twenty-strong and armed with broken bottles and a hatchet.[26] This time, however, the Londoners had not travelled by train. They had arrived on scooters.

"You've Got to Be Somebody"

The pack of young scooterists who arrived in Brighton during 1960 were indicative of changes in British youth style. The late 1950s saw the Ted's drape jacket and greasy quiff gradually give way to the chic, Italian-inspired flair associated with the Mods.[27] Italian aesthetics wielded a general influence on British design throughout the period, popularised by films such as *Roman Holiday* (dir. William Wyler, 1953) and *La Dolce Vita* (dir. Frederico Fellini, 1960) and, by the late 1950s, the smoothly tailored lines of Italian fashion were increasingly sported by the "Modernists"—the hip cliques of young West Londoners immortalised in Colin MacInnes's 1959 novel, *Absolute Beginners*.[28] The "Modernist" look of short, "bum-freezer" jackets and tapered trousers quickly spread through London's working-class housing estates where youngsters' taste for exquisitely cut suits took them to tailors such as John Stephen in Carnaby Street; which, itself, was transformed into the throbbing heart of the Mod universe. Other Mod haunts included Soho nightclubs such as the Scene and the Flamingo where white, British Mods got down to the sounds of black, American soul music and rhythm and blues (the latter emulated by "Mod" groups like the Who and the Small Faces), together with early Jamaican ska and bluebeat. The scene was fuelled by amphetamine pills—Purple Hearts, French Blues, Black Bombers—while mobility was provided by gleaming Italian Vespa and Lambretta scooters, sometimes turned into wondrous, two-wheeled sculptures through the addition of a profusion of chrome accessories and superfluous wing mirrors. And long, "fishtail" parkas (courtesy of American army surplus) protected the Mods' all-important suits from engine oil and the vagaries of the British weather.

Mod, according to social theorists such as Phil Cohen, was spawned from broader changes in the fabric of working-class culture. After 1945, Cohen argues, the institutions that had once formed the bedrock of working-class life—the extended family, traditional employment structures and the ecology of neighbourhood communities—were increasingly undermined by the trajectory of social and economic trends. Specifically, the redevelopment and re-housing schemes of the 1950s and 1960s destabilised traditional communities and kinship networks, while the decline of traditional industries, post-war affluence, and the rise of consumerism steadily recast working-class identities and values. Although the impact of these changes was felt by the working class as a whole, Cohen argues it was the young who experienced their most significant consequences as their life experiences were transformed by the changing world of work, leisure and "the new ideology of consumption."[29]

It is a thesis to which *Quadrophenia* eloquently subscribes. Mod hero Jimmy Cooper is portrayed as being at the sharp end of the changes reconfiguring British working-class life. He is a child of West London's housing estates, but he is a world away from his parents. Working as a mail clerk in an advertising agency, Jimmy is part of the new, burgeoning universe of 1960s affluence and consumerism. And he finds his identity not in work, family and the local neighbourhood but in style, image, and hedonism. Jimmy, moreover, personifies the sense of defiance that cultural critic Dick Hebdige sees as characteristic of the Mod's sense of self. The archetypal Mod, Hebdige explains, "was determined to compensate for his relatively low position in the daytime status-stakes over which he had no control, by exercising complete dominion over his private estate – over his appearance and choice of leisure pursuits."[30] Again, the thesis is neatly echoed in *Quadrophenia*. Explaining to his childhood pal, Kevin (Ray Winstone), his fanaticism for being a Mod, Jimmy emphasises the powerful sense of individuality and self-worth he derives—"I don't want to be like everyone else; that's why I'm a Mod!" "You've got to be somebody," Jimmy insists, "otherwise you might as well jump in the sea and drown."

Jimmy's passion for Mod starkly contrasts to Kevin's ardour for the trappings of an "older" teen cult. A hard-line Mod, Jimmy favours sharp suits, short hair, an Italian scooter. But his old school mate is rooted in the Rocker styles popularised during the 1950s—leather jacket, dirty jeans, greasy quiff, powerful motorcycle.[31] And, in their singing duel at the public bath-house, Jimmy gives an emphatic (albeit tuneless) rendition of a Kinks number, while Kevin opts for a 1950s Gene Vincent rock 'n' roll standard. The contrast neatly embodies Cohen's view of 1960s youth style as emblematic of the transitions reconfiguring the British working class. Jimmy, the Mod, personifies the new horizons of working-class life—affluence, consumerism, style consciousness. But Kevin, the Rocker, is the incarnation of a style that harks back to working-class values of the past—rugged, tough, and avowedly blue collar. In *Quadrophenia* the differences are intensely felt and present Jimmy with his first moral dilemma of the film, as he chooses to turn his back on his old friend when Kevin is ambushed and beaten to a pulp by a gang of Jimmy's Mod brethren.

Social differences between Mods and Rockers were also noted at the time. According to sociologists Paul Barker and Alan Little, court data collected after a "Mods and Rockers" fracas in Margate in 1964 showed that most offenders were working class—but the typical rocker was an unskilled manual worker, while the typical Mod was a semi-skilled or clerical worker.[32] As Hebdige notes, however, "whether the Mod/rocker dichotomy was ever really essential to the self-definition of either group remains doubtful."[33] Indeed, while youth styles of the early 1960s may well have been generated by shifts in the landscape of working-class life, the intensity of the Mod/rocker polarity was at least partly indebted to the media coverage of the "riots" that rocked through British seaside resorts during the early 1960s—an episode expertly dissected by Stanley Cohen in his classic sociological study, *Folk Devils and Moral Panics*, originally published in 1972.

"Battle of Brighton"

According to Cohen, press reports of the first recorded Mod/rocker clash set the scene for, and gave shape to, the events that followed. The opening skirmish took place at the Essex resort of Clacton in March

1964. Like Brighton, Clacton had long been a destination for leisure-seeking, working-class youngsters. But that weekend was cold and wet, and the town's facilities for young people were limited. With little to do, minor scuffles broke out between local lads and the visiting Londoners, a few beach huts were vandalised and some windows broken. But, in the absence of other newsworthy material, reporters from national newspapers seized upon the relatively innocuous events and conjured up visions of wholesale havoc. As Cohen described:

> On the Monday morning following the initial incidents at Clacton, every national newspaper, with the exception of *The Times* (fifth lead on main news page) carried a leading report on the subject. The headlines are self-descriptive: "Day of Terror By Scooter Groups" (*Daily Telegraph*), "Youngsters Beat Up Town – 97 Leather Jacket Arrests" (*Daily Express*), "Wild Ones Invade Seaside - 97 Arrests" (*Daily Mirror*). The next lot of incidents received similar coverage on the Tuesday and editorials began to appear, together with reports that the Home Secretary was being "urged" (it was not usually specified exactly by *whom*) to hold an enquiry or to take firm action.[34]

For Cohen, the media furore was an exercise in hyperbole and angst-ridden distortion, or what he termed a "moral panic." Newspaper text was peppered with overblown phrases such as "riot," "siege," "orgy" and "screaming mob"; and this, combined with wild exaggerations of the numbers involved, resulted in the perception that events were considerably more violent than was the case. As a consequence, Cohen argued, events began to escalate as journalists, police and young people all expected "Mods and Rockers" trouble at Whitsun, the next bank holiday. Anticipated and vigilantly watched for at a number of seaside towns—including Margate, Eastbourne and (of course) Brighton—"Mods and Rockers" violence was duly spotted by the police and vigorously dealt with. As a consequence, arrest rates soared and magistrates (keen to show they were "getting tough" with the tearaways) imposed harsher penalties. Indeed, as historian Richard Grayson shows, even the government were worried by the episode, and nervous ministers pondered possibilities for new, more punitive legislation to deal with the Mods and Rockers "problem."[35]

But, as Stanley Cohen points out, this was a classic case of self-fulfilling prophecy. Media attention and exaggerated press reports fanned the sparks of an initially trivial incident, creating a self-perpetuating "amplification spiral" that steadily heightened the social significance of the events. It also "breathed life" into the opposing camps of Mods and Rockers. The "Mods and Rockers," Cohen argued, had initially been fairly ill-defined youth styles, but were given greater form and substance in the sensational news stories. And the two groups steadily polarized as youngsters throughout Britain began to identify themselves as members of either faction—the Mods or the Rockers.

Cohen's "moral panic" thesis clearly filters into *Quadrophenia*'s representation of events. Elements of media exaggeration, expectation and self-fulfilling prophecy figure clearly in the build-up to the Mods' Brighton foray. As Jimmy wakes on bank holiday morning, he gazes above his head at his collection of histrionic newspaper clippings reporting the earlier "Mods and Rockers" furore at Clacton. A radio news broadcast, meanwhile, anticipates further trouble that day:

> Shopkeepers in the Brighton area, fearing a reoccurrence of disturbances caused by gangs of rival youths in other resorts, were putting up shutters last night. A spokesman said that, while they weren't expecting any trouble, they were going to be prepared.

As *Quadrophenia*'s narrative unfolds, however, elements of mythology become more central. When Jimmy's Mods arrive in Brighton, it is as if the town has fallen to a conquering army. A legion of scooters roll down the seafront and parka-clad teenagers swarm through the town as chants of "We are the Mods!" resound through the streets. Tasting Mod's collective power, Jimmy is exhilarated. Pilled-up and pumping, he hits the dancefloor in a Mod-packed nightclub, and is cheered on as, precariously, he climbs the balcony's balustrade and heroically struts his stuff to The Kingsmen's "Louie Louie." The next morning more thrills flow. Joining the Mod throng, Jimmy helps rout a pack of hapless Rockers, stampeding across the pebbly beach and trading punches with the hard-pressed police. As the riot spreads from the seafront into the town's backstreets, the Mods are hemmed in by the law. But Jimmy strikes lucky. Together with Steph (Leslie Ash)—a gorgeous Mod belle over whom Jimmy has been hungrily lusting—he escapes down a back alley and, as the tumult continues in the road behind them, Jimmy and Steph have a furtive (but fervid) "quickie."

Stumbling back into the fracas, Jimmy is collared by the police. But even this cannot dim his spirits. In the back of the Black Maria, Jimmy's devotion to Mod is bolstered by comradeship with stylish *über*-Mod, "Ace Face" (Sting). And, as the beaten and bruised Mods are paraded in court, Jimmy is energised by Ace's brazen defiance. As the magistrate castigates the young prisoners, Ace affects boredom and glances theatrically at his watch. Hit with a hefty fine, Ace is unfazed. Reaching into his pristine leather raincoat he pulls out a chequebook and responds nonchalantly, "I'll pay now, if you don't mind." Then, to laughs and cheers from the Mod ranks, Ace turns to the dour magistrate and cheekily asks, "Haven't got a pen have you, your honour?"

The courtroom exchange was inspired by actual events. In the aftermath of the Mods and Rockers "invasion" of Margate, the press widely reported that a young miscreant had told local magistrates that he would pay his £75 fine (then a sizeable sum) with a cheque. As Cohen observes, however, while the story was true enough, what few newspapers bothered explaining (though they were well aware of it) was that the lad's offer was an act of mischievous bravado. Three days later he admitted that not only did he not have the £75, but he did not even have a bank account and had never signed a cheque in his life. His admission, however, went largely unreported and, Cohen notes, the "£75 cheque story" was still widely cited years later "to illustrate the image of the Mods and Rockers as affluent hordes whom "fines could not touch.""[36] And, indeed, it was given a new lease of life in *Quadrophenia*.

The "£75 cheque story," Cohen argues, was indicative of the general dimensions of exaggeration and distortion that characterised press coverage of the 1964 seaside "invasions." In the case of Brighton, national newspapers conjured with images of a resort laid waste by marauding teens. The *Daily Sketch*, for instance, featured a large photo of battling Mods and Rockers and reported that Brighton police had arrested thirty-five "rioting teenagers",[37] while equally lurid images graced the front page of the *Daily Mirror* alongside a melodramatic account of "all the fury and hate of the scrap-happy Whitsun Wild Ones."[38] Local press reports were in a similar vein. The banner headline "Battle of Brighton," for instance, was emblazoned across the *Evening Argus* as the paper breathlessly related how the town had seen "fierce seafront clashes" and a "tidal wave of shouting youths had knocked people from the pavements."[39] For some it seemed the events were another nail in the coffin of Brighton's economic fortunes. "These Vermin Ruined Whit" and "Town With Teenage Plague" ran further headlines in the *Evening Argus*, the paper relating how local traders laid the blame for a decline in trade squarely on the crowds of riotous youngsters.[40]

Somewhat passed over in the reports, however, was the fact that holiday-makers may well have been deterred by the previous night's heavy rain and the cold, breezy weather on the day itself. Moreover, for some observers, the "Battle of Brighton" had been rather more prosaic than headlines suggested. Writing for the sociological journal *New Society*, Paul Barker sought to lay out "what really happened at Brighton on Whit Monday." Witnessing events first-hand, Barker explained how the Mod "invasion" had certainly been an impressive spectacle:

> Teenagers were perched everywhere – about a couple of thousand of them. Their get-up was chic as always: the boys in razor-cuts, short jackets and narrow trousers; the girls mostly in nylon anoraks and stretch slacks, their hair varying from long and ragged to closer-cropped than the boys.[41]

The crowd was huge but, Barker reported, for the most part "was totally passive, seeking only to be entertained."[42] As photographs and archival film footage testify, there *were* sporadic fights that sent deck chairs (and a few teenagers) flying. But Barker's account suggests the level of violence was small. Relatively few Rockers had actually come to the town and, in their absence, the Mod crowd had turned on a small group of unfortunate beats camped by the beachside paddling pool. Yet, even here, Barker depicts the "Battle of Brighton" as something of a damp squib:

> In fact, only seven or eight actually fought. We all scattered when the fight came rolling our way. It didn't last long (because the Beats won), but it was very un-Queensbury while it lasted. One Beat went to hospital after being hit on the head by an eel-shop sign.[43]

And a glance through the list of cases brought against twenty-seven reprobates in the aftermath of Brighton's Mod "invasion" suggests something less than a scene of carnage. A few charges, admittedly, seem reasonably serious. Five youths were accused of possessing offensive weapons, four with throwing missiles and one with assault on a policeman. Other cases, however, appear rather less grave. Eleven youths were charged with using threatening or insulting behaviour, two with stealing milk and one with wilful damage to a deck chair.[44]

Nevertheless, after Whitsun 1964, the notion of Mods and Rockers as malicious and menacing "folk devils" became fixed in the public mind. The image had such resonance because it condensed a much wider set of concerns that preoccupied Britain during the early 1960s. Configured by the press as "the neurosis of the affluent society,"[45] Mods and Rockers served as a focus for a broad sense of unease about cultural trends and the general state of the nation. Or, as Cohen eloquently puts it, they "touched the delicate and ambivalent nerves through which post-war social change in Britain was experienced."[46] And, as Cohen notes, the concerns were especially pronounced in a seaside resort like Brighton, which "had not yet come to terms with the fact that the old type of summer visitors and day-trippers were no longer coming … but spending their holidays on package trips to the Costa Brava."[47] The Mods and Rockers, then, were a symbolic vehicle; a powerful metaphor that articulated more general fears about cultural decline, both nationally and at a local level.

At the same time, however, there was—as Hebdige argues—always a Janus-like quality to representations of youth culture. Alongside fearful depictions of "youth-as-trouble" there were also enthused portrayals of "youth-as-fun" and, while Mods were reviled as the *bête noire* of the affluent society, they could also be fêted as pacesetters of 1960s social dynamism. Well dressed and clean-cut, the Mods' passion for style could be easily incorporated in notions that cast Britain as moving forward into a new era of exciting progress and modernity. Indeed, just three months after the "Battle of Brighton," the *Sunday Times Magazine* (then an arbiter of fashionable chic) featured a sumptuous, eight-page photo-spread spotlighting the Mods' sartorial flair.[48]

"I've Had Enough"

Quadrophenia masterfully captures the mood of Britain during the early 1960s. The film is an accomplished depiction of a world undergoing profound transformation; a world whose social, economic and cultural changes are tinged with both optimism and apprehension. Above all, *Quadrophenia* delivers a compelling portrayal of the "mythologies" of Mod—a youth movement pilloried by its detractors as the baleful index of national decline, but championed by its participants as a font of pulsating energy and the zenith of cutting-edge style.

By the mid-1960s, however, the Mod tide was ebbing. Influenced by the peacock panache of "swinging London," Mod's more flamboyant elements steadily morphed into a fashionable offshoot of the late 1960s hippy scene. Mod's "hard" constituency, meanwhile, gradually segued into the robust machismo of skinhead style, which, as cultural theorist John Clarke observes, can be read as an attempt to symbolically re-animate a "lost" working-class identity and "re–create through the 'mob' the traditional working class community, as a substitution for the *real* decline of the latter."[49] The shift was reflected in Brighton. Concerns about bank holiday violence spluttered on through the decade; but, while the local press continued to refer to young troublemakers as "Mods," by the mid-1960s newspaper photographs clearly show the shaved heads, boots and braces of embryonic skinheads.

Nevertheless, the intensity of local concerns about young "invaders" gradually subsided. Nationally, moral panics about youth and crime were sustained as the media projected a demonology of malevolent youth—stretching from the skinheads of late 1960s to the punks of the late 1970s—as a crystallisation of Britain's social ills. But in Brighton, postwar anxieties about "invasions" by out-of-town low-life steadily diminished as the resort adapted to the changing cultural landscape. Evading the clutches of tawdry, "fish–and–chip–minded" day-trippers, Brighton successfully repositioned itself as a centre for arts and culture with (from the mid-1960s) the expansion of its two universities, the opening of major conference and exhibition venues and the launch of one of Britain's largest annual arts festivals.

In contrast, *Quadrophenia*—in its film incarnation, at least—ends in pronounced uncertainty. Jimmy's soaring highs amid the "Battle of Brighton" are short-lived. Returning to London, the young Mod's life fragments. He loses his job and is thrown out of the family home. More crushingly, he is cold-shouldered and ridiculed by his erstwhile friends and is rejected by a spiteful Steph. Desperate to rediscover his earlier confidence and self-esteem, Jimmy returns to Brighton. But his hopes quickly turn to disillusion. The drizzle-soaked town now seems disconsolate and empty, while Jimmy spots the valiant Ace Face working as a humble bell boy, bowing and scraping to well-heeled hotel guests.

In its rock opera iteration, *Quadrophenia* closes enigmatically, with Jimmy stealing a boat and heading out to sea. The film version, however, sees a more melancholic conclusion. Wracked with disappointment and despair, Jimmy steals Ace's gleaming scooter and heads out of town. Reaching the deserted clifftops of Beachy Head (a renowned suicide spot), he rides perilously close to the sheer drop. The scooter then catapults over the cliff's edge, smashing dramatically on the rocks below. And, in the background, we hear the Who's "I've Had Enough," with Roger Daltrey singing that he's "had enough of street fights ... I'm finished with the fashions and acting like I'm tough." It is a powerful closing scene. The more so because the audience is left with the nagging feeling that—despite a beguiling "flashback" at the film's opening, which sees the young Mod walking away from the cliff—somewhere, off camera, a desperate Jimmy may have followed the ill-fated scooter. Nevertheless, the symbolism is fairly clear. Hit with the cold light of reality, Jimmy has seen through the myths that he once found so exhilarating and seductive.

And, like the rest of the film, *Quadrophenia*'s conclusion weaves into its narrative "mythologised" elements of actual events. Martin Stellman, the screenwriter (with Dave Humphries) of the film, was a former journalist and, in preparation for the movie, diligently went through library press cuttings in London and Brighton. Of course, we cannot be sure of exactly what Stellman saw in the clippings, but it is more than likely he stumbled across the story of seventeen-year-old Mod, Barry Prior. A trainee accountant from Finchley in north London, Prior had ridden down to Brighton for Whitsun bank holiday in 1964. At the end of the weekend, Prior and his friends had left town and pitched camp for the night on a high clifftop. In the morning, however, Prior was missing and his friends soon spotted his body sprawled on rocks a hundred feet below. In the bleak photo that accompanied the *Evening Argus* coverage, a huddle of Prior's parka-clad friends can be seen standing disconsolately next to the dead boy's scooter—a brand-new, scarlet Vespa.[50] The circumstances of Prior's fall were uncertain, and a verdict of "death by misadventure" was ultimately given at the Coroner's inquest. It was the most tragic of stories. And was, somehow, made all the more so by the fact that—while the overblown saga of the "Battle of Brighton" made national news headlines—the account of Barry Prior's death was relegated to the back pages of Brighton's local paper.

Notes

1. A Graduate of the University of London, *Brighton As It Is: Its Pleasures and Pastimes, With a Short Account of the Social and Inner Life of Its Inhabitants, Being a Complete Guide Book for Residents and Visitors* (Brighton: George Smart, 1860), 98.
2. Graham Greene, *Brighton Rock* (Harmondsworth: Penguin, 1938).

3. *The Economist*, "Brighton on the Rocks," 26 August 1961, 12–13.
 4. *Brighton and Hove Herald*, 27 July 1963.
 5. *Brighton and Hove Herald*, 6 June 1959.
 6. Selina Todd and Hilary Young, "Baby-Boomers to 'Beanstalkers': Making the Modern Teenager in Post-War Britain," *Cultural and Social History* 9, no. 3 (2012): 451–467.
 7. Mark Abrams, *The Teenage Consumer* (London: Press Exchange, 1959); Mark Abrams, *Teenage Consumer Spending in 1959* (London: Press Exchange, 1961).
 8. Abrams, *Teenage Consumer*, 9.
 9. Ibid., 10.
10. Abrams, *Teenage Consumer Spending*, 3.
11. Pearl Jephcott, *Time of One's Own: Leisure and Young People* (London: Oliver and Boyd, 1967).
12. Cyril Smith, *Young People at Leisure: A Report on Bury* (Manchester: University of Manchester, 1966), 17.
13. Brighton Education Committee, *Report of the Commission of Enquiry into the Needs of Youth in Brighton* (Brighton: Brighton and Hove Council, 1959), 8–9.
14. Department of Employment and Productivity, *British Labour Statistics Historical Abstract, 1886–1968* (London: Department of Employment and Productivity, 1971), 96 and Table 191, 392.
15. Brighton Education Committee, *Needs of Youth*, 10.
16. "*Living for Kicks*" was originally screened on ITV on 2 March 1960.
17. Robert Kerridge, "Making the Best of Brighton," *New Statesman* 58, no. 1497 (1959), 15.
18. Dick Hebdige, "Hiding in the Light: Youth Surveillance and Display," in *Hiding in the Light: On Images and Things*, ed. Dick Hebdige (London: Routledge, 1988), 19.
19. Geoffrey Pearson, "Falling Standards: A Short, Sharp History of Moral Decline," in *The Video Nasties: Freedom and Censorship in the Media*, ed. Martin Barker (London: Pluto, 1984), 88–103. See also Geoffrey Pearson, *Hooligan: A History of Respectable Fears* (London: Macmillan, 1983).
20. *Evening Argus*, 15 November 1954.
21. *Brighton and Hove Herald*, 14 July 1956.
22. *Evening Argus*, 29 August 1958.
23. *Brighton and Hove Herald*, 7 June 1958.
24. *Times*, 29 August 1962.
25. *Brighton and Hove Herald*, 1 September 1962.
26. *Evening Argus*, 21 March 1960.

27. Accounts of the rise of Mod style exist in a wealth of popular books. Evocative illustrated histories can be found in Richard Barnes, *Mods!* (London: Plexus, 1979) and Terry Rawlings, *Mod: A Very British Phenomenon* (London: Omnibus, 2000). Well-researched chronicles also exist in Paulo Hewitt (ed.), *The Sharper World: A Mod Anthology* (London: Helter Skelter, 1999) and Paolo Hewitt, *The Soul Stylists: Six Decades of Modernism—From Mods to Casuals* (Edinburgh: Mainstream, 2000). An expansive history of Mod style is also provided in Richard Weight, *Mod: A Very British Style* (London: Bodley Head, 2013). Many academic analyses also exist. One of the most astute is Christine Feldman, *We Are the Mods: A Transnational History of a Youth Subculture* (New York: Peter Lang, 2009).
28. Colin MacInnes, *Absolute Beginners* (London: MacGibbon and Kee, 1959).
29. Phil Cohen, "Subcultural Conflict and the Working Class Community," *Working Papers in Cultural Studies*, no. 2 (Birmingham: University of Birmingham, 1972), 23.
30. Dick Hebdige, "The Meaning of Mod," in *Resistance Through Rituals: Youth Subcultures in Post-War Britain*, eds Stuart Hall and Tony Jefferson (London: Hutchinson, 1976), 91.
31. Compared to the wealth of literature chronicling the Mod movement, material dealing with British Rocker style of the 1950s and 1960s is relatively sparse. That said, some excellent collections of photographs exist in Mike Clay, *Cafe Racers: Rockers, Rock 'n' Roll and the Coffee–Bar Cult* (London: Osprey, 1988), Johnny Stuart, *Rockers!* (London: Plexus, 1987) and Mick Walker, *Cafe Racers of the 1960s* (London: Windrow and Greene Automotive, 1994). Additionally, an account of the British biker scene in the mid-1960s can be found in the autobiography of Britain's first Hells Angels president, Jamie Mandelkau, *Buttons: The Making of a President* (London: Sphere, 1971). At a more academic level, ethnographic research conducted among Midlands bikers of the late 1960s is included in Paul Willis, *Profane Culture* (London: Routledge, 1978).
32. Paul Barker and Alan Little, "The Margate Offenders: A Survey," *New Society*, 30 July 1964, 6–10.
33. Hebdige, "Meaning of Mod," 88.
34. Stanley Cohen, *Folk Devils and Moral Panics: The Creation of the Mods and Rockers* (London: MacGibbon and Kee Ltd, 1972), 18–19.
35. Richard Grayson, "Mods, Rockers and Juvenile Delinquency in 1964: The Government Response," *Contemporary British History* 12, no. 1 (1998): 19–47.
36. Cohen, *Folk Devils*, 33.
37. *Daily Sketch*, 19 May 1964.
38. *Daily Mirror*, 19 May 1964.

39. *Evening Argus*, 18 May 1964.
40. *Evening Argus*, 19 May 1964; *Evening Argus*, 23 May 1964.
41. Paul Barker, "Brighton Battleground," *New Society*, 21 May 1964, 9.
42. Ibid.
43. Ibid.
44. *Evening Argus*, 18 May 1964.
45. *Evening Argus*, 19 May 1964.
46. Cohen, *Folk Devils*, 192.
47. Cohen, *Folk Devils*, 195.
48. Robert Freeman and Kathleen Halton, "Changing Faces," *Sunday Times Magazine*, 2 August 1964, 12–19.
49. John Clarke, "The Skinheads and the Magical Recovery of Community," in *Resistance Through Rituals: Youth Subcultures in Post-War Britain*, eds. Stuart Hall and Tony Jefferson (London: Hutchinson, 1976), 99.
50. *Evening Argus*, 18 May 1964.

Bibliography

Abrams, Mark. *The Teenage Consumer*. London: Press Exchange, 1959.
———. *Teenage Consumer Spending in 1959*. London: Press Exchange, 1961.
A Graduate of the University of London. *Brighton As It Is: Its Pleasures and Pastimes, With a Short Account of the Social and Inner Life of Its Inhabitants, Being a Complete Guide Book for Residents and Visitors*. Brighton: George Smart, 1860.
Barker, Paul. "Brighton Battleground," *New Society*, 21 May, 1964, 9–10.
Barker, Paul and Little, Alan. "The Margate Offenders: A Survey", *New Society*, 30 July, 1964, 6–10.
Barnes, Richard. *Mods!* London: Plexus, 1979.
Brighton Education Committee. *Report of the Commission of Enquiry into the Needs of Youth in Brighton*. Brighton: Brighton and Hove Council, 1959.
Clarke, John. "The Skinheads and the Magical Recovery of Community." In *Resistance Through Rituals: Youth Subcultures in Post-War Britain*, edited by Stuart Hall and Tony Jefferson, 99–102. London: Hutchinson, 1976.
Clay, Mike. *Cafe Racers: Rockers, Rock 'n' Roll and the Coffee–Bar Cult*. London: Osprey, 1988.
Cohen, Phil. "Subcultural Conflict and the Working Class Community," *Working Papers in Cultural Studies*, No. 2, Birmingham: University of Birmingham, 1972.
Cohen, Stanley. *Folk Devils and Moral Panics: The Creation of the Mods and Rockers*, London: MacGibbon and Kee Ltd, 1972.
Department of Employment and Productivity. *British Labour Statistics Historical Abstract, 1886–1968*. London: Department of Employment and Productivity, 1971.

The Economist. "Brighton on the Rocks," 26 August, 1961, 12–13.
Feldman, Christine. We *Are the Mods: A Transnational History of a Youth Subculture.* New York: Peter Lang, 2009.
Freeman, Robert and Halton, Kathleen. "Changing Faces."' *Sunday Times,* 2 August, 1964, 12–19.
Grayson, Richard. "Mods, Rockers and Juvenile Delinquency in 1964: The Government Response." *Contemporary British History* 12, no. 1 (1998), 19–47.
Greene, Graham. *Brighton Rock.* Harmondsworth: Penguin, 1938.
Jephcott, Pearl. *Time of One's Own: Leisure and Young People.* London: Oliver & Boyd, 1967.
Hebdige, Dick. "The Meaning of Mod." In *Resistance Through Rituals: Youth Subcultures in Post-War Britain*, edited by Stuart Hall and Tony Jefferson, 87–98. London: Hutchinson, 1976.
———. "Hiding in the Light: Youth Surveillance and Display." In *Hiding in the Light: On Images and Things*, edited by Dick Hebdige, 17–36. London: Routledge, 1988.
Hewitt, Paolo (ed.). *The Sharper World: A Mod Anthology.* London: Helter Skelter, 1999.
Hewitt, Paolo. *The Soul Stylists: Six Decades of Modernism - From Mods to Casuals.* Edinburgh: Mainstream, 2000.
Kerridge, Robert. "Making the Best of Brighton." *New Statesman* 58, no. 1497 (1959), 15–16.
MacInnes, Colin. *Absolute Beginners.* London, MacGibbon & Kee, 1959.
Mandelkau, Jamie. *Buttons: The Making of a President.* London: Sphere, 1971.
Pearson, Geoffrey. *Hooligan: A History of Respectable Fears.* London: Macmillan, 1983.
———. "Falling Standards: A Short, Sharp History of Moral Decline." In *The Video Nasties: Freedom and Censorship in the Media*, edited by Martin Barker, 88–103. London: Pluto, 1984, 88–103.
Rawlings, Terry. *Mod: A Very British Phenomenon.* London: Omnibus, 2000.
Smith, Cyril. *Young People at Leisure: A Report on Bury.* Manchester: University of Manchester, 1966.
Stuart, Johnny. *Rockers!* London: Plexus, 1987.
Todd, Selina and Hilary Young. "Baby-Boomers to 'Beanstalkers': Making the Modern Teenager in Post-War Britain." *Cultural and Social History* 9, no. 3 (2012), 451–467.
Walker, Mick. *Cafe Racers of the 1960s.* London: Windrow & Greene Automotive, 1994.
Weight, Richard. *Mod: A Very British Style.* London: Bodley Head, 2013.
Willis, Paul. *Profane Culture.* London: Routledge, 1978.

CHAPTER 3

"Who (the Fuck) Are You?": Out with the In-Crowd in *Quadrophenia*

Ben Winsworth

When *Quadrophenia* was released in the autumn of 1973 it was only about seven or eight years on from that transitional time when many Mods started to exchange amphetamines for marijuana and soul for psychedelia, but it was still far enough away from the world and culture it explored as to be something of an anomaly.[1] If the baroque grandeur of *Tommy* (1969) belonged to its time and the film version (1975) eventually slotted easily into the world of high glam, then on the surface of the early 1970s, Pete Townshend's second "rock opera" did not. But hold on a minute: David Cassidy was number one in the UK singles chart with a song called "Daydreamer," and Status Quo's *Hello* was just about to say "goodbye" by being knocked off the top of the album charts by David Bowie's *Pin Ups*, a retrospective album in its own right—one that contained a couple of old tracks by the Who—and one which found former Mod Ziggy digging deep into the back catalogue of the decade that had helped to create him.[2] The London Rock and Roll Show at Wembley Stadium the previous year stoked up a revival of interest in 1950s music and fashion, one that fused with contemporary "pop" culture as groups

B. Winsworth (✉)
University of Orléans, Orléans, France
e-mail: ben.winsworth@univ-orleans.fr

© The Author(s) 2018
P. Thurschwell (ed.), *Quadrophenia and Mod(ern) Culture*,
Palgrave Studies in the History of Subcultures and Popular Music,
https://doi.org/10.1007/978-3-319-64753-1_3

like the Glitter Band, Mud, and Showaddywaddy illustrated, and the success of films like *That'll Be the Day* (1973) testified.[3] The second coming of Mod, however—while undoubtedly kick-started by *Quadrophenia*—needed a film version (1979) before it was fully revived in the public consciousness towards the end of the decade. This was quite possibly due to the fact that while the concept is based upon Mod, the music itself is definitely not, and—unlike the artwork and the subject matter of the lyrics—anything but retrospective. Nonetheless, while the Who were continuing to transform themselves into one of the loudest stadium rock bands in the early to mid-1970s, *Quadrophenia* was Pete Townshend's own personal foray into the fairly recent past, one that consecrated Mod at the same time as it offered a model for the critical analysis of all youth subcultures: past, present, and still to come.

Even though back in the mid-1960s it was Pete Meaden's Mod re-styling of the Who that contributed to their early success, commentators like Eddie Piller have noted that Pete Townshend was the only "real" Mod in the band.[4] Richard Barnes has also spoken of the way in which Mod helped Townshend, who had always been something of a loner, to find a culture with which he could identify, but at the same time a culture to which he felt he could never fully belong.[5] This tension between the desire to be a part of the in-crowd, coupled with the inability to reconcile a nagging sense of personal alienation, is central to *Quadrophenia* and clearly Jimmy's sometimes ambivalent relationship with Mod reflects Townshend's own position. In his autobiography, *Who I Am* (2012), he recalls a memory experienced in January 1973 during a night of heavy rain at his cottage in Cleeve: a memory of walking on Brighton Beach with his then girlfriend after a concert at the Florida Rooms, Brighton Aquarium in 1964, one that coincided with the clashes between Mods and Rockers:

> As I thought back to that night, a sense of falling and vertigo came flooding back with the flooding river outside—I felt that same sense of depression and hopelessness. But I also felt again the remembered romantic warmth of nodding off on the milk-train home in the early hours, with Liz by my side. For a short time we had both felt like Mods. There was something wonderful in all that.[6]

It's a memory of not belonging and yet belonging, of individual anxiety being temporarily assuaged in the collective identity of Mod: a feeling intensified through the experience of falling in love, and paid back with interest in the act of recollection. But more than nostalgia, this moment of "epiphany"—as Townshend describes it—allowed him to sense something of the cultural and historical significance of the mid-1960s, and the Who's involvement with *that generation*, an apprehending of past experience that compelled him to write the short story of "Jimmy, a young Mod" (printed on the inner cover of the double album) that very same night.[7]

Townshend was already in retrospective mood before this, and *Quadrophenia* found its genesis in the aftermath of another setback in the unending and incomprehensible *Lifehouse* saga. Nik Cohn's *Rock is Dead, Long Live Rock* project encouraged Townshend to reflect on the past and seek inspiration there to carry the band into the future as a more solid unit: "My idea was to take the band back to our roots. We'd been different then; we'd been subsumed in the Mod gang, and we needed to do that again. At least I did."[8] The fact that the Who seemed to be falling apart prior to working on *Quadrophenia* encouraged Townshend to find a shared project that would heal the "anarchy of ego"[9] that threatened to pull them apart. For the most part recording the album was a "joyful experience,"[10] but also a serious and almost reverential business where "energetic musical rage would be used throughout. We didn't need throwaway tracks for light relief, we didn't need light and shade, irony or humour."[11]

In its celebration and exploration of Mod, *Quadrophenia* reflects upon a time when the Who seemed to have a place and purpose within the wider, vibrant youth culture that adopted them, and also—through looking back—attempts to come to terms with the past as a way of moving forward into a more creative and cohesive future. Even though *Tommy* in its various versions helped to carry the Who from the late 1960s into the early 1970s, a process completed with Ken Russell's film, the contemporary world must have felt like a "teenage wasteland" compared to those "crazy days" of 1964 and 1965.[12] At the same time, in his late twenties, Townshend might have started to feel that the Who were losing touch with the pulse of the changing environment around them, that their music was—like the Beatles and the Stones—a little *passé*.[13] Sentiments that encouraged a return to the past were equally an act of rejuvenation in allowing the Who to reject the teeny-bopper generation and the glitzy posturing of commercial pop. At the same time the Who resisted becoming atrophied by prog rock while the world, as Townshend has remarked in several interviews, was waiting for something more exciting to come along:

I kind of knew that punk was coming. I knew there was a musical revolution coming, but I obviously didn't know what shape it was. And in a sense what I wanted was to get the band back to - not only its roots - but also to kind of abandon - if you like - this move towards progressive rock. At the same time, I knew we had to make a progressive rock album because that's what the market was.[14]

In spite of the complexities of this "double bind," it was against an un(mod)ern modern world that *Quadrophenia* turned its back: the front cover showing Jimmy astride his GS scooter, tellingly facing away from the camera to reveal the name of the Who emblazoned on the back of his "wartime coat," a photograph creating/recreating an inseparable bond between the band and Mod, however much Townshend also hoped that the new album would be a cathartic experience freeing them from the weight of the past.[15, 16] Ambivalence prevails, for the iconography of Mod is so lovingly reproduced on the album cover and inner booklet that there is something of a "preservation society" aspect to the exercise. But this is no self-indulgent wallowing, for the various narratives in the original album package contain enough of a critique of Mod to check this temptation, and while "the past is calling" it is doing so to engage with the present. We might, quite literally, be travelling back through the mists of time swirling around Jimmy and his Vespa on the opening shot, but the four mirrored faces of the band belong to 1973, suggesting that while the Who are deeply embedded in Mod culture they have to a certain extent already moved on and can look back upon the past with both an affectionate and critical eye. Reflecting on the past, yet also reflected in Jimmy's chrome-framed mirrors, the Who of 1973 stare out at the viewer of the album cover, challenging him or her to reflect upon the seemingly vacuous nature of the contemporary popular cultural environment through taking a close look at an earlier youth movement that, for all its inevitable flaws, seemed to have a greater degree of existential authenticity than the apparent superficiality of the early 1970s.

Perhaps it is for this reason that the album artwork is in black and white, as stark a contrast with much of the pop/rock iconography of 1973 as the Beatles' "White Album" was with *Sgt. Pepper*, if not more so. *Quadrophenia* is setting itself apart, signalling retrospection and presenting a visual rejection of the garish technicolour of its own time.[17] Even if the rock and roll/Teddy Boy revival of the early 1970s may have been motivated by an equally serious desire to explore the origins of

British youth culture, this was all quickly subsumed into the commercial pop mainstream where its original energy was lost in rose-tinted nostalgia, as well as through its fluorescent hybridisation with glam.[18] In going back to re-explore Mod, Townshend offers a more realist view of the popular cultural past and even if that past is being reworked through a music (rock) that is very much a product of its own time (1973), there is no superficial dilution of the way of life it describes. Stephen Glynn, in his recent study of *Quadrophenia* (2014), observes that Townshend would have been interested in Stanley Cohen's *Folk Devils and Moral Panics* published in 1972, and its revisiting and rethinking of the role of the media in the Mod/Rocker confrontations and in the creation of various—often distorted—myths about the nature and purpose of these subcultural communities.[19] There is, of course, a sense in which Townshend is involved in the process of mythologising—*Quadrophenia* is a work of art after all, and not a sociology dissertation—but he can have had little idea of how both the album and the film version would achieve cult status, and in the case of the latter how it would exploit the sensationalism criticised by Stanley Cohen. Returning to think about the conception and creation of the original project of Mod and the Who in the early 1960s, there is a way in which Townshend is also attempting to set the record straight.

In so doing, *Quadrophenia* anticipates, illustrates and complements some of the key theoretical work on subcultures published in the 1970s. It explores—in both sound, text and image—the generational and class conflict first picked up by Phil (not Stanley) Cohen in his seminal paper from 1972, "Subcultural Conflict and Working Class Community," analysing subcultures and the destruction/relocation of East End communities: ideas later reworked and extended by Clarke, Hall, Tony Jefferson and Roberts in "Subcultures, Cultures and Class" (1975) to consider the relationship between the subcultural group and the wider "parental community."[20] The *Quadrophenia* booklet photograph of Jimmy in the cramped family kitchen, and tracks like "Cut My Hair" and "Sea and Sand" recreate something of this tension, and the complex, ambivalent nature of trying to negotiate one's own youth cultural identity both in historical and personal terms: Jimmy's old man may be "alright," but Jimmy has to be "different to them" if he is to find himself. To use the language of Clarke, Hall, Jefferson and Roberts, being part of the Mod community is a way for Jimmy to win his own cultural space, its distinctive style, collectivity of being, and shared "social rituals" a way of coping in the "theatre of struggle" and a form of resistance against traditional working class subordination.[21] However, as Clarke and his colleagues note, "membership of a subculture cannot protect them from the determining matrix of experiences and conditions which shape the life of their class as a whole."[22] This is something that Pete Townshend addresses throughout *Quadrophenia* in songs where Jimmy tastes the bitter reality of adult life, but being a Mod (already an act of defiance) he is able to reflect on what he sees with more of a critical eye than his straighter, conventional contemporaries.

"Dirty Jobs," for example, deals with hard manual work and the way in which it grinds people down into physical exhaustion and intellectual submission. Jimmy, however, may be "put down," "pushed round" and "beaten every day," but he is not prepared to take it anymore. He regrets that the older men who fought in the war seem to have given up and simply accept their tough working conditions, something that he is not willing to do even though the odds seem stacked against him. Having said this, Jimmy has the perspicacity to acknowledge that he has been "seeing only dreams" that he is "all mixed up," which is a fairly astute self-analysis suggesting that things may well be "changing" in his life to carry him beyond the drudgery and dead-end experience of the "Ace Face" narrated in "Bell Boy." At the same time, "I've Had Enough" entertains the idea that a straightforward progression through life is an illusion, that the "information" given by the system is "altered," false and untrustworthy, and that most people are sold a dream that is painfully eroded by experience, and no more so than when they are growing up. *Quadrophenia* looks at this difficult transition within a subcultural context and "I've Had Enough" provides another example of Jimmy's self-awareness and critical acumen. The difficult surrendering of youthful expectations may account for the preview of "Love Reign O'er Me" that appears almost as a grain of hope here: an optimistic anticipation of the way in which things can change/rearrange at a deeper level than simply trying to fit into the adult world and find one's place through acts of compromise. The end of the song with its suggestions of suicide—Jimmy howling that he has indeed "had enough of trying to love" as a train screams past—is (of course) the other, bleaker alternative that haunts the album.[23]

"Subcultures, Cultures and Class" makes the point, somewhat mistakenly in my opinion, that subcultures can offer no real resolution or solution to working-class oppression because they only exist on a symbolic level, and the space they inhabit is largely an imaginative one. As such, the resistance they offer is temporary and provisional. This is something suggested in *Quadrophenia* through the opposition between the positives and negatives of Jimmy's involvement with Mod, the almost fetishistic celebration of the style—the jackets, the parka, the scooter—balanced against disillusion with the dancehalls, the beach fights, the come downs. Clarke, Hall, Jefferson and Roberts observe that there can be no long-term career as a subculturist—something that Jimmy finds difficult to accept—but *Quadrophenia* is not suggesting that subcultures serve no valuable purpose in the formation of the individual or in the way in which they function as a critique of straight society. Jimmy finds it difficult to be a Mod, to "move with the fashions" ("Cut My Hair"), but is insistent on the fact that "you'll all see, I'm one," and even if his clothes are "ill fitting" ("I'm One") he dreams of slim, checked jackets or "maybe a touch of seersucker," riding his GS scooter with a neat haircut, and wearing his parka in "the wind and sleet" ("I've Had Enough," reprised in "Sea and Sand"). Throughout these songs, Townshend is also presenting Mod as a subculture that operates on a symbolic level of resistance, but one that leads to a reanimation of the self, able to resist in the real world those forces that threaten to subjugate it. Even though Jimmy's struggle to reconcile the real and imaginary makes for a difficult rite of passage, one that contains its fair share of pain, anguish and frustration, the experience is—as I shall be arguing shortly—ultimately positive.

It is Jimmy's association with the above mentioned objects and activities—an association amplified in the short story and photo-narrative—that establishes the portrayal of Mod in *Quadrophenia* as a "spectacular subculture," a term first used by Dick Hebdige in *Subculture: The Meaning of Style*, published six years after the album in 1979. According to Hebdige, spectacular subcultures "represent 'noise' as opposed to sound," they create "interference" in their disruption of the semantic order, in their resistance to the efforts of the media to understand and appropriate them, especially in their early and unfamiliar incarnations.[24] As such, they are forces of anarchy and disorder within the dominant culture/parental community, and yet paradoxically the style of these subcultures is highly codified and homogenous, and is anything but thrown together. Through acts of bricolage and subversion in which subcultures appropriate and give new meaning to objects, symbols and items of clothing that are taken out of their "normal" contexts, they mark themselves out as being in a state of opposition towards the mainstream.

With this in mind, the photographs in *Quadrophenia* read almost as a style guide to Mod, and offer themselves as a visual companion to—and anticipation of—subcultural theory. It is interesting to note that Townshend refers to Ethan Russell's contribution as a "photo-document," stressing the importance of "an approach that was photographic, truly authentic in detail" to the project.[25] The booklet is not a passive illustrative accompaniment to the music, but—like the short story—a vital and dynamic part of the whole. The customised Vespa, the smart suits, neat haircuts, the parka, the boating blazers, the cycling tops, Levi's, desert boots, trainers, and target tee shirts all reveal Mod to be a subculture held together as a highly organised form of resistance. If Mod is about attention to detail, then the photo-narrative respects this dictum, and in visual terms it offers Townshend's own interpretation of the meaning of the Mod style as an art form/subculture based on intelligent choices and careful selection in an ongoing struggle against more conventional ways of dressing, behaving, thinking. Through a process of cultural recycling, the appropriation and transformation of raw material normally associated with more conservative and affluent modes of being, Mod rejected traditional working-class lifestyle (and subordination), and drew attention to everything that was wrong and yet everything that could be right with post-war British society. As such, it became a much needed thorn in the side of hegemony.[26] *Quadrophenia* shows how subcultures like Mod can become catalysts for change, how they can break down barriers and encourage creative ways of thinking about oneself and the social world one inhabits. Jimmy has some difficult lessons to learn, but the collective nature of his experiences is educational and encourages him to think more critically about himself, about life, even about the highs and lows of being a Mod. In the short story Jimmy writes, "I never thought I'd feel let down by being a mod," but he needs to go through the pain of disillusion with the subculture if he is to fully integrate the positive effect that it has had upon him.

The biggest problem facing Jimmy is how to accept the inevitability of this "let down," which eventually results in evasive action that finds him "pilled up" and catching the "5:15" to Brighton. This journey to "my land of dreams," as Brighton is referred to in the album's short story, is a step back into the purely imaginative, an escape from the pressing demands of reality. Townshend's songs warn against the dangers of such regression, signalling the importance of maintaining an interplay between fantasy and reality, between the subculture and the wider community that it transforms, resists and rearranges. At the same time, *Quadrophenia* accepts the temporal nature of subcultural involvement and yet suggests that it can continue to contribute in positive ways to one's sense of self as an adult. From an autobiographical perspective, "Love Reign O'er Me" testifies to Townshend's own growing away from Mod into a more transcendental perception of the world, but it is possible to argue that he would not have reached this position without having gone through the whole Mod experience. While the lyrics quite possibly reflect the influence of Meher Baba on Townshend's life in their surrender to an almost divine and universal love, he writes in *Quadrophenia, The Director's Cut* of how the song was composed to "demonstrate the most extreme and miserable pathos of the soul ridiculed and abandoned by everyone and everything."[27] Ultimately, it is a song about the teenage angst that brings Jimmy to "consider suicide," a decision over which Townshend felt he had no real power: "As a jaded rock star without any rights to the travails of youth in the 70s and as an always nostalgic ex-Mod, I had a duty to let Jimmy decide for himself."[28]

With respect to Townshend's decision, and to embrace something of its speculative nature, it is possible to argue that perhaps what really dies on the rock is Jimmy's identity as a Mod. Even though Townshend comments that Jimmy hears no "benign and guiding voice," and "all that happens is that he gets wet," the fact that he has "lost everything that meant anything to him" is—paradoxically—a significant enough place from which to re-begin and reconstruct.[29] Meher Baba's philosophy of renunciation and the creation of a "New Life" seems present at this point in the narrative, even if Jimmy is looking for something less spiritually profound than the path chosen by Baba and his followers.[30] "Love Reign O'er Me" may be about the reality of teenage pain and angst, as well as an unanswered call for "divine love," but it is also a prayer of mourning for the death of Jimmy the Mod, as well as a moment of epiphany in which Jimmy casts off his former self and expresses his desire for a new and potentially more fulfilling existence.[31] Looking back on his experiences from the rock—the point of departure for the whole narrative—Jimmy's return to Brighton can be viewed as a working through towards a deeper understanding of himself, of his involvement with Mod, and the way in which it points towards the creation of a better future in which he can find a measure of reconciliation. A similar idea is present in "Drowned," a song written two years before the *Quadrophenia* project crystallised, but like "Love Reign O'er Me" an expression of "Jimmy's longing for some spiritual sublimation he could hardly articulate."[32] Jimmy hints at this unconscious aspect to his experience in the short story when he tells us, "I didn't know then what I was up to, but I know now," which also suggests that the alternative ending of suicide that Townshend played with (and still plays with) is rejected by his hero. This idea of "redemption"—a word that continually surfaces in Townshend's musings on *Quadrophenia*—seems to be the overriding feeling: looking back on the album in 2011 Townshend reflected that it was the perfect medium to recount the story of "a young Mod living through a crash and moving on to a hopeless, dangerous but ultimately freeing apotheosis."[33, 34]

Clearly, the process of writing and recording *Quadrophenia* provided a similar function for Pete Townshend himself, enabling him to go back and yet move on and carry something from the past into the present through both the physical, material creation of the album itself, and in terms of the way in which it allowed him to repay a debt to Mod in his development as an artist and an individual. Furthermore, there is a way in which *Quadrophenia* offers an antidote to what many theorists in the 1970s understood as a pre-punk, popular cultural malaise. In *Subculture: The Meaning of Style*, Dick Hebdige grudgingly acknowledges that David Bowie was at the higher end of the glam spectrum, but none the less understands him to have been motivated by "a deliberate avoidance of the 'real' world" and escapism into a "fantasy past or a science fiction future."[35] He quotes Taylor and Wall's comment that Bowie helped to create:

> passive teenage consumers in the purchase of leisure prior to the assumption of "adulthood" rather than being a youth culture of persons who question (from whatever class or cultural perspective) the value and meaning of adolescence and the transition to the adult world of work.[36]

Similarly, while Hebdige seems aware that Bowie and other glam artists were working to encourage young people to experiment in more creative and polymorphous ways with sexual and gender identity, such a revolutionary challenge to convention is regarded as being less serious or potent than more obvious forms of political reaction and resistance. Bowie himself is described as being a celebrant of "disguise and dandyism," an ambivalent rather than "genuine" presence in youth reaction(s) against the conservative mainstream.[37]

It seems obvious now that Hebdige is not giving Bowie (or glam) enough credit here, possibly because the "glitter boys" are sandwiched chronologically between Mod and punk—two subcultures that Hebdige is clearly more excited about as more obvious, and more masculine examples of subversion. Even though there are elements of truth in his observations about the more commercial aspects of pop consumerism in the early 1970s, it is important to note that Townshend *and* Bowie, who both grew out of the original Mod subculture in the 1960s, reacted to the new decade in different ways that were ultimately related in terms of trying to re-energize youth culture through popular music and its packaging. *Quadrophenia* recreates the past in a gritty, black-and-white starkness that flies in the face of all the colour and glitz of the early 1970s, and in so doing invites serious consideration of subcultural practices both "then and now." Bowie, on the other hand, in an album like *The Rise and Fall of Ziggy Stardust and the Spiders from Mars*, is looking in glorious technicolor to the future (both real and imagined) as a means of encouraging reflection(s) on the ways in which music and style can be used as creative explorations and projections of the self in the contemporary world.[38] As such, his influence is more palpable than Hebdige admits. To a certain extent *Pin Ups*, released after Ziggy's transatlantic adventures in *Aladdin Sane*, finds Bowie falling to Earth and following a similar trajectory to the Who.[39, 40] In this album of cover versions, Bowie shows through his musical re-workings—as well as through an album cover that is equally retrospective and of its own time—just how the past shapes and (in)forms us in the present.[41] In a sense, *Ziggy*, *Aladdin Sane* and *Pin Ups* build the kind of bridge between the mid-1960s and early 1970s that the Who are seeking to construct in *Quadrophenia*, albeit in a less colourful way.

Quadrophenia intervenes as a counterweight to the kind of sociopolitical passivity and decadent indifference that Hebdige observes in his slightly blurred analysis of the wider cultural environment, where "the subversive influence was shifted away from class and youth," rather than against the interest in "sexuality and gender typing" that replaced it.[42] Lyrics on the album such as "He-man drag in the glittering ballroom/

Grayly outrageous in my high heel shoes," ("5:15") suggest that these were areas that Townshend was starting to acknowledge and/or think about, if only in a fairly casual and peripheral manner at this point in time.[43, 44] This creates another interesting link between Pete and David. However, in exploring his own youth in *Quadrophenia*, Townshend is more concerned with other important questions apparently being ignored by the more overtly hedonistic and superficial adherents of the early 1970s music scene.[45] In "Helpless Dancer," a song that turns its attention more to the present in offering a catalogue of the economic and social problems caused by a growing recession, Townshend writes that "something in us is going wrong" and the brief extract from "The Kids are Alright" that follows the climactic despair of "…you stop dancing" looks back to a vibrancy that he feels has been lost. As such, it seems as if *Quadrophenia* is trying to offer a lesson in "subcultural seriousness." On one level the album can be read as a marker of the social changes taking place in the early to mid-1960s through the wider empowerment of post-war youth, but it is not only a snapshot of history.

Like Hebdige, Townshend is aware of the ways in which spectacular subcultures are eventually appropriated by the mainstream and so lose their original dynamism and difference. Mod is no exception, but in releasing *Quadrophenia* when he did Townshend is resurrecting something of its power and commitment into the popular cultural mix of 1973 as a way of shaking up the present generation of teenagers, many of whom were struggling to find their own autonomy and direction. They may, as Bowie writes in "All the Young Dudes" have left their brothers at home with their Beatles and their Stones and failed to get off "on all that revolution stuff," but which direction to take now? Commenting on this period and the "*dis*-illusion that follows a revolutionary sequence," Simon Critchley remarks:

> For us this was the fucked up, disappointed solidarity of the early 1970s most powerfully expressed in "All the Young Dudes," written by Bowie for Mott the Hoople. This song was like Kerouac's *On the Road* for a beaten generation who knew they were going absolutely nowhere.[46]

Interestingly enough, towards the end of "All the Young Dudes," Ian Hunter calls out to this "beaten generation" demanding "I wanna hear you, I wanna see you, I wanna relate to you." *Quadrophenia* is also attempting to communicate with a younger generation of potential rebels. However, unlike Bowie who was teaching a way forward through lessons in "the deceptive nature of illusion and its irresistible power," *Quadrophenia* points towards this by serving up a realistic reconstruction of the past which, to quote from a later Who track, challenges the listener as powerfully as the fade out to "All the Young Dudes": "who the fuck are you?" As such, it can be understood in part as Pete Townshend's own wake-up call to the nation and while it helped to carry the news about Mod to a new generation—one that revived it towards the end of the 1970s with the additional help of the film version and new soundtrack—it also anticipated punk in its anger and energy, in its attempt to engage with social and political injustice, and in its demonstration of the ways in which youth subcultures can have a dynamic and wide-ranging influence on society and the individuals who are engaged within them.[47]

NOTES

1. 26 October 1973.
2. Terry Rawlings notes that along with *Quadrophenia*, *Pin Ups* was one of the albums from the early 1970s that helped to ignite the Mod revival. Terry Rawlings, *Mod A Very British Phenomenon* (London: Omnibus Press, 2000), 171.
3. The Kinks' album *Preservation Act One*, released only a few weeks after *Quadrophenia*, contains a song called "Where are They Now?" in which Ray Davies offers both an ironic and nostalgic reflection on past subcultures from the Teds to the hippies, at one point expressing his hope that the Rockers and Mods all have steady jobs now!
4. Lindsell, Alec, dir. *The Who, The Mods and The Quadrophenia Connection* (Sexy Intellectual 2009) DVD.
5. Ibid.
6. Pete Townshend, *Who I Am* (London: Harper Collins, 2012), 245.
7. Ibid., 246.
8. Ibid., 236.
9. www.youtube.com/watch?v=RDQ6TEDFPEk.
10. Townshend, *Who I Am*, 248.
11. Ibid.
12. Simon Wells refers to the landscape of the early 1970s as "moribund" as an "unforgiving environment" in which "culture and fashion had become complacent and *lazziez faire* (sic)" and where "rock music and its attendant cultures had lost their collective mojos," *Quadrophenia: A*

Way of Life (Inside the Making of Britain's Greatest Youth Film) (London: Countdown Books, 2014), 33.
13. In 1972, Townshend was irritated by his part-time secretary's descriptions of Bowie's "brilliant make up as Ziggy Stardust," but responded by suggesting that *Tommy* was Bowie's original inspiration. While this points to an interesting link between the Who and Bowie, it is also possible to detect Townshend's concerns about the continuing relevance of his own work, *Who I Am*, 231.
14. Interview with Pete Townshend, www.youtube.com/watch?v=RDQ6TEDFPEk.
15. Ibid.
16. In *The Who, The Mods and The Quadrophenia Connection*, Richard Barnes recalls Townshend telling him that "in celebrating the Mod thing we're going to free ourselves from our legend and we can go in new directions."
17. *Aladdin Sane* and *Goodbye Yellow Brick Road* are good examples.
18. Barney Hoskyns makes some interesting comments on the glam/rock 'n' roll hybrid artists that were making their presence felt in the UK charts in 1973, *Glam! Bowie, Bolan and the Glitter Rock Revolution* (London: Faber, 1998), 84–85.
19. Stephen Glynn, *Quadrophenia* (New York: Columbia University Press, 2014), 17.
20. Stuart Hall and Tony Jefferson, *Resistance Through Rituals: Youth Subcultures in Post-War Britain* (London: Hutchinson, 1976), 9–74.
21. Ibid., 44–47.
22. Ibid., 15.
23. Either way, Jimmy is shown to be contradicting what Dick Hebdige refers to as the "myth of consensus," *Subculture: The Meaning of Style* (London: Metheun, 1979), 18.
24. Ibid., 90.
25. Pete Townshend, *Quadrophenia: Director's Cut* (Polydor, 2011), 13.
26. See Hebdige, *Subculture: The Meaning of Style*, 15–16.
27. Townshend, *Quadrophenia: Director's Cut*, 35.
28. Ibid.
29. Ibid., 89.
30. See Purdom, *The God-Man: The Life, Journeys & Work of Meher Baba with an Interpretation of His Silence and Spiritual Teaching* (London: George Allen and Unwin, 1964), 187.
31. Townshend, *Quadrophenia: Director's Cut*, 89.
32. Ibid., 25.
33. Townshend, *Who I Am*, 246.
34. Townshend, *Quadrophenia: Director's Cut*, 13.
35. *Subculture: The Meaning of Style*, 61.

36. Ibid., 61.
37. Ibid., 62.
38. 6 June 1972.
39. 19 October 1973.
40. 13 April 1973.
41. *Aladdin Sane* sets in motion this particular retrospective process with "Drive in Saturday" exploring 1950s American youth culture within a post-apocalyptic context, while the cover version of "Let's Spend the Night Together" reflects both transatlantic and transgenerational influences in popular music.
42. Townshend, *Quadrophenia: Director's Cut*, 61–62.
43. Surely I can't be the only listener to have thought that Roger Daltrey was really singing "gaily outrageous" before checking out the lyrics?
44. On a demo track for *Quadrophenia*, "You Came Back," Townshend sings: "That girl with the umbrella he used to be a fella, he used to be my very good friend."
45. Simon Critchley comments that "this whole trope of androgyny and floating boy/girl identity became completely vulgarised in the horrors of British glam rock, with bands like Sweet, Gary Glitter and the execrable Mud", *On Bowie* (London: Serpents Tail, 2016), 54.
46. Ibid., 91.
47. Ibid., 91.

BIBLIOGRAPHY

Cohen, Phil. 'Subcultural Conflict and Working Class Community'. In *The Subcultures Reader*, 90–99. Edited by Ken Gelder and Sarah Thornton. London: Routledge, 1997.

Cohen, Stanley. *Folk Devils and Moral Panics: The Creation of the Mods and Rockers*. London: Routledge, 1972.

Critchley, Simon. *On Bowie*. London: Serpents Tail, 2016.

Glynn, Stephen. *Quadrophenia*. New York: Columbia University Press, 2014.

Hall, Stuart and Jefferson, Tony. *Resistance Through Rituals: Youth Subcultures in Post-War Britain*. London: Hutchinson, 1976.

Hebdige, Dick. *Subculture: The Meaning of Style*. London: Metheun, 1979.

Hoskyns, Barney. *Glam! Bowie, Bolan and the Glitter Rock Revolution*. London: Faber, 1998.

Lindsell, Alec, dir. *The Who, The Mods and The Quadrophenia Connection*. Sexy Intellectual, 2009. DVD.

Purdom, Charles B. *The God-Man: The Life, Journeys and Work of Meher Baba with an Interpretation of His Silence and Spiritual Teaching*. London: George Allen and Unwin, 1964.

Rawlings, Terry. *Mod A Very British Phenomenon*. London: Omnibus Press, 2000.

Townshend, Pete. *Quadrophenia: Director's Cut*. 'Super-deluxe' limited edition box set. Polydor, 2011. CD.

———. *Who I Am*. London: Harper Collins, 2012.

Wells, Simon. *Quadrophenia: A Way of Life (Inside the Making of Britain's Greatest Youth Film)*. London: Countdown Books, 2014.

CHAPTER 4

Discovering the Who's Mod Past: The American Reception of *Quadrophenia*

Christine Feldman-Barrett

Between 2003 and 2008, I interviewed scores of Mods past and present as well as self-proclaimed 1960s enthusiasts to better understand both how and why they were attracted to Mod style and various aspects of the original subculture. During the course of this ethnographic research, which was conducted for my Ph.D. examining Mod's history in Britain, Germany, the United States, and Japan between 1964 and the early 2000s, and which served as the basis for my 2009 book *"We are the Mods": A Transnational History of a Youth Subculture*, it soon became clear how important the Who's 1979 film *Quadrophenia* was in terms of attracting Generation X youths to mod culture. As I listened to my interviewees recall their first encounters with the film, I could not help but reflect on my own.

While *Quadrophenia* debuted in the United States in early November 1979, it continued being shown at art-house and university-affiliated movie theatres throughout the early 1980s.[1] Though I do not remember if I saw it in 1981 or 1982, I vividly recall my then-teenaged sister taking me to see a double feature of Jeff Stein's Who documentary *The*

C. Feldman-Barrett (✉)
Griffith University, Gold Coast, Australia
e-mail: c.barrett@griffith.edu.au

Kids are Alright (also released in 1979) and *Quadrophenia* at a theatre in Evanston, Illinois. Only ten years old at the time, but already aware of 1960s-era "British Invasion" bands thanks to my sister and her record collection, *Quadrophenia* nonetheless managed to confuse me. Watching the film, I asked myself: *"Who were these unattractive, besuited guys on their 'motorbikes'?" "Why did everything look so drab? Weren't the 1960s colourful?" "Where are the Who?".* While the Stein documentary, with its compiled footage of the Who's career, confirmed familiar sounds and images I had of the band, both in their earlier and more recent incarnations, *Quadrophenia* was something unrecognizable. Instead of the band appearing in the film, I was confronted with Jimmy the Mod and his mob of unruly friends. Unlike the many people I interviewed twenty-five or so years later, who were fascinated and inspired by the film's narrative and style, I was not impressed with what I saw.

This said, given that I was only ten and not a teenager, it mattered little if I was impressed with the film; I was not part of the intended demographic. For this next generation of American, teenage fans, my sister included, the Who symbolized both the increasingly canonized rock music culture of the 1960s and, ostensibly more so than the Rolling Stones (who were also still together and touring), a sense of "outsider" sensibilities and adolescent rebellion. This second aspect, as will be discussed further, was especially palpable in *Quadrophenia*.[2] Interestingly, my sister was as keen to listen to the Who's 1965 Mod standard "My Generation" as she was to the band's 1982 arena rock anthem "Athena" when either came on the radio. And, while she also started listening to 2 Tone artists like the Specials at the time she took me to see *Quadrophenia*, I do not remember her mentioning anything about "Mod culture" per se.[3] In this respect, my sister's interest in the Who at this time was typical of the Gen X's fan experience in 1980s America: there was some knowledge of the Who's history, but their specifically Mod past was a less immediate focal point for this cohort.

In reflecting on my own inaugural *Quadrophenia* memory, and in light of the subsequent ethnographic research I conducted on Mod years later, I contend that it is difficult to understand *Quadrophenia*'s American reception more fully without first acknowledging the Who's longstanding "special relationship" with the United States and their American fans. As rightly noted by British journalist John Diamond, the lingering association American audiences had with the Who at this time was their hugely successful 1969 rock opera *Tommy*.[4] Their Mod past was likely only familiar to either their oldest or most historically attuned fans. Instead, for most Americans who came of age in the 1970s and early 1980s, the Who was on par with similar "arena rock" bands like Led Zeppelin.[5]

Though the *Quadrophenia* album had been released in the United States in 1973, with accompanying tour dates as well, it was not until the 1979 stateside premiere of the film that these second-generation, American fans really discovered the band's Mod past. The film's songs, taken directly from the album, and which offered more familiar and contemporary rock sounds to American youth, was countered by the film's seemingly "foreign" and past-tense narrative of Jimmy the Mod, the former London Mod scene itself, and, importantly, the 1964 Brighton riot between Mods and Rockers. Direct Franc Roddam's cinematic recreation and reinterpretation of the original Mod subculture presented an unfamiliar history to a wide swathe of the Who's contemporary US fan base. Parallel to this, another cohort of young people, those who were not necessarily Who fans and who generally loathed the excesses of stadium rock, found themselves drawn to the film's Mod theme. Thus, this chapter tries to understand the American reception of *Quadrophenia* in the context of late 1970s and early 1980s youth culture and how both second-generation Who fans and other young Americans reacted to the most quintessentially "English" media release the band had shared with the US market since their 1965 debut as a second-wave "British Invasion" band.

THE WHO IN AMERICA, 1965–1979

The US release of *Quadrophenia* in November 1979 occurred during a time when young, American fans associated the Who primarily with sold-out, deafeningly loud stadium concerts and anthems like 1971's "Baba O'Riley" and its famous summoning of an iconic 1970's "teenage wasteland." If any aspects of the British band's earlier career were familiar to these second-generation fans, it was likely the on-stage destruction of guitars and drums as well as the group's continuously relevant 1965 hit "My Generation." Such connotations of the Who could be read as indicative of changing youth culture tastes from the 1960s to the 1970s, but it also underscores what I see as the Who's own "special relationship" with the United States and the country's fans. For the Who, the United States was the place to play in front of massive crowds and where much money could be made. For American fans, the Who's narrative was one primarily of theatricality, and noise.

It is fitting that American Who fan and filmmaker Jeff Stein would open his 1979 documentary of the band, *The Kids are Alright*, with the group's 1967 television appearance on the *Smothers Brothers Comedy Hour*. The US show, which was popular with young audiences due to Tommy and Dick Smothers' irreverent and topically relevant humour, proved a perfect fit for the equally irreverent Who. While this performance of "My Generation" is best known for the huge explosion at the end of the song, causing Pete Townshend's hair to catch fire and triggering hearing loss, it is also notable for being when most Americans first caught glimpse of the Who.[6] Alongside witty banter between Tommy Smothers and each band member prior to the performance (Keith Moon: *"My friends call me Keith, you can call me John"*), the Who appear resplendent in the psychedelic, Rococo-inspired outfits. Except for John Entwistle, who sports a dapper, mod-style suit, Roger Daltrey, Pete Townshend, and Keith Moon look as if they just have arrived from Baroque Vienna rather than Swinging London. This, one of the first mass-circulated media image of the Who, helped set the tone for their reputation and reception in the United States.[7]

Stein soon follows this clip with an earlier one from 1965 that was also broadcast on a popular American TV show. The black and white clip, recorded in the United Kingdom, but appearing on the teen music show *Shindig!*, presents the band in more traditional Mod attire. Unlike other British Invasion bands such as the Beatles, the Rolling Stones, and the Kinks, the Who were overtly "marketed" as a Mod group in their home country. Although I have discussed in *"We are the Mods"* that these bands also were considered Mod at one time or another both in and outside the United Kingdom, the Who is the only one of these groups to be promoted to British audiences as a specifically Mod band. This was due to efforts made by both their early publicist Pete Meaden, who was a Mod himself, and their original managers Kit Lambert and Chris Stamp.[8] It is also likely that the first wave of American Who fans circa 1965 would have been aware of this association, too. While a popular misconception is that Mod culture was unknown to Americans in the mid-1960s, primary sources tell another story. Notably, between 1964 and 1996, many American teen and fashion magazines used the term "Mod" to describe the youth culture style emanating from the United Kingdom at this time.[9] While having shed most of its specifically subcultural connotations, the term nonetheless spoke to the music and fashions that British bands like the Who brought to their American audiences. Moreover, manufactured as their Mod image was, the Who still was the only band to provide a glimpse of the subculture's harder edge. As American academic and 1960s-era Who fan John Dougan remembers,

> The handful of teen magazine photographs I saw [of the Who] suggested…[that] these were clearly not eager-to-please pretty boys, but rather West London hooligans who, even when not trying, hinted that their rock aesthetic was fueled by a shared understanding of the expressive power of conflict and violence.[10]

If the suit-wearing Beatles circa 1964 were representative of Mod's diffusion into commercial sensibilities, then the Who's sharp, angular energy suggested the freneticism of the original subculture. American fans like Dougan may not have heard of clashing "Mods and Rockers," but this riotous aspect of the Mod subculture was nonetheless palpable in the Who's self-presentation and repertoire.

Despite initially less media attention given the Who as compared to "first wave" British Invasion bands like the Beatles and the Rolling Stones, the development of the Who's American fan base began in earnest during 1967's "Summer of Love." This was when the Mod-dominated years of the decade, which had been ushered into the United States via the British Invasion, gave way to American-born hippie sensibilities.[11] In 1967, alongside their memorable (and explosive!) appearance on the *Smothers Brothers Comedy Hour*, the Who embarked on their first US tour and, in similarly "smashing" style, dazzled audiences at the Monterey Pop Festival outside San Francisco. The festival, captured in D.A. Pennebaker's 1968 film, can be seen as a turning point for both 1960s youth culture and the Who. It not only shifted young people's attention back from Britain to what was happening in the United States, with San Francisco replacing London as the most popular youth-centric hub, but it also paved the way for both the "festivalization" of rock music and the "arena rock" ethos of the 1970s—two things the Who came to symbolize.[12] This aspect of the Who's career and reputation in America was cemented by the band's 1969 performance at the Woodstock Festival. In particular, the image of Roger Daltrey, wildly swinging his microphone around and clad in a fringed, suede vest, seems both iconic and symbolic in marking the Who's final transformation from Mods to edgy hippies. Moreover, performing their then newly released "rock opera" *Tommy*, the band would become known to subsequent American audiences as a hard-rocking group that sold-out stadiums across the United States.[13]

The peace-and-love music festivals of the 1960s, which already had pointed to the importance of mass audiences in the development of rock music culture, gave way to large, stadium concerts of the 1970s. The Who both enjoyed and profited from this arena rock culture during the run of the decade, touring the United States seven times between 1970 and 1979. By 1975, the Who would shatter concert attendance records at the Metropolitan Stadium in Pontiac, Michigan with 78,000 fans present. The same show earned them more than $600,000 and was the first rock concert to feature closed-circuit video screens for those concert-goers whose seats were far from the stage.[14] The spectacle that the Who had initiated via smashed guitars, drums, and small, on-stage explosives during the late 1960s had taken on a new level of bombastic grandeur. It seemed that crowd size and increasingly loud volume began to define "Who Culture" even more than Townshend's trail of wrecked guitars. It is fitting, then, that in 1976, after a thunderous London show, the *Guinness Book of World Records* hailed the Who as the loudest band in the world.[15] Importantly, though, it was in the United States where the precedent for stadium rock had been set. In embracing and helping shape the decade's new norm for the rock music experience, the Who, alongside other British "supergroups" like Led Zeppelin, forged a distinct relationship with their American fans. This relationship had nothing to do with a youth subculture like Mod, which was one that had sought something outside the mainstream of popular culture.

Alongside the power of the arena concerts, FM radio also proved a defining element in the way in which the Who's American fan base was galvanized during this period. Susan J. Douglas charts the way in which FM radio, by the late 1960s, had become not only youth-oriented but a highly experimental and countercultural medium.[16] A particular aspect of this experimentation, which became standard (and mainstream) by the mid-1970s, was the album-oriented rock (AOR) format, which allowed DJs to potentially play whole sides of LPs rather than just the singles or "hits." This proved a boon for bands like the Who, whose rock opera *Tommy*, for instance, fit such formatting to a tee.[17] Thus, American teenagers of the 1970s and early 1980s were exposed to the Who as masterful composers of complicated, "progressive" hard rock that warranted such airtime—more Beethoven than British Invasion. By becoming kings of "arena rock" and assisted by heavy rotation on AOR-formatted FM radio, both the Who and their US audience helped define and celebrate the commerciality and excess that would dominate the rock-oriented youth culture of the 1970s.

"Teenage Wasteland?": Youth Culture and Music in 1970s America

Quadrophenia, debuting when it did in late 1979, entered the American teenage imagination in the context of the Who as an established rock band that attracted throngs of fans to stadium shows and a group that was also an FM radio favourite. This reputation came to define the band for their second-wave, US fans. This conceptualization of the Who is succinctly portrayed in the American TV series *Freaks and Geeks* (1999–2000). The show, which only lasted one season but similar to *Quadrophenia* has achieved cult status, takes a nostalgic look at American high school culture circa 1980 in the fictionalized Detroit suburb of Chippewa, Michigan. The "freaks" of the program's title, whom protagonist and "good girl" Lindsay Weir befriends in the pilot episode, refers to the rock-loving and pot-smoking teenagers at high school; those whom sociologist Donna Gaines would later document and describe as "burnouts."[18] In the episode "Dead Dogs and Gym Teachers," Lindsay tries convincing her father to let her attend the upcoming Who concert with her new "freak" friends. Throughout the episode, which features two songs from *Quadrophenia* ("I am One" and "Love Reign o'er Me"), the Who is discussed in ways that would have been familiar to many Americans growing up at that time. In the opening scene, Lindsay's younger brother, in trying to sabotage her bid to go to their concert, mentions that the band "smash their guitars" and are "the loudest band on Earth," while Lindsay tries making the group sound more respectable to her parents by countering that "the Who wrote a rock opera."[19]

In another scene, as Lindsay's "burnout" friends Nick, Ken, and Daniel discuss the show, Nick evokes the Who's arena rock prowess by saying "No disrespect of Zeppelin, but I saw the Who two weeks ago at Indianapolis and it blew my mind. It was crazy." The band's reputation for loudness is mentioned again, this time by Ken, who says, "I can't wait 'till they hit Detroit. I hope my ears start bleeding." Daniel, in referencing the 1970 Who hit "Magic Bus," says he will borrow his cousin's old school bus for pre-concert tailgating outside the stadium. The fact that the Who, and not another rock band, is featured in an episode of this period-perfect TV drama is significant. Based on his own memories of suburban, high school life in 1970s and 1980s America, the show's creator and primary writer Paul Feig succinctly captures the way the Who is inextricably linked to a distinct teenage cohort of this era.[20] Significantly, while the show is set in the 1980–1981 school year, the "freak" characters often reference bands and styles associated with 1970s culture. Just as historian Arthur Marwick posits that the "long sixties" lasted until 1974, I argue that the some sensibilities of 1970s culture still made their mark on American teenagers throughout the early 1980s.[21]

Unlike the 1960s, though, with its easily identifiable music-driven youth culture (whether in the United Kingdom or the United States), the 1970s has proved a little trickier to define. Despite retrospective media texts that have tried to do so such as the films *Dazed and Confused* (1993), *Velvet Goldmine* (1998), *Last Days of Disco* (1998), and *Almost Famous* (2000) as well as the American TV program *That '70s Show* (1998–2006), scholarship about young people and their culture during this time, especially as regards American youth, remains minimal.[22] Perhaps this is because 1960s youth culture, on both sides of the Atlantic, can be more easily divided into two main categories and time periods: Mod (1963–1967) and hippie (1967–1969).

The 1970s, however, is more fragmented and, in most cases, varies more so between the United States and the United Kingdom than during the previous decade.[23] For example, the 1970s produced the already discussed arena rock phenomenon, which was more pronounced in the United States than in Britain given that there were generally more such venues in the United States. The 1970s also offered young audiences glam rock, which, though popular in the United States, was more influential on youth culture per se in the United Kingdom.[24] Similarly, while the mid-1970s produced American and British punk almost simultaneously, it remained unknown in most parts of the United States until the early to mid-1980s. This differed from the British experience, where more of the population was familiar with the phenomenon by the late 1970s due to punk's presence in mainstream media. Finally, disco music was American-born and, certainly, was the decade's other dominant, popular music genre in the United States alongside arena rock.[25]

The 1977 disco-themed film *Saturday Night Fever* was one of the highest grossing films of the decade and was a huge sensation with teenagers. Disco's success prompted the era's biggest "turf war": one between American youth loyal to rock (who were mostly white, male, and suburban), versus a more multicultural, cross-gender and urbane cohort that embraced the disco craze.[26] In reflection, 1970s youth culture, driven by such diverse musical forces, was an incredibly heterogeneous one. American scholars Breeden and Carroll (2002), both of whom attended high school in the 1970s, speak to this quality of the 1970s via a "my decade/your decade" debate as to how each remember those years differently. They write, "We spent our teens in the same decade, yet when we discuss the past, we discover our perceptions appear quite divergent, indeed at some points unrecognizable." Carroll's memories of high school in Central Texas, in particular, are reminiscent of those presented in Paul Feig's *Freaks and Geeks*, where teenagers established disparate-yet-parallel enclaves inclusive of the hard-rock-loving, burnout "heads."[27]

Trying to understand the youth culture nuances of the decade in light of the Who's *Quadrophenia* is even more interesting in the context of British punk and the Mod revival scenes, both of which helped populate the latter half of the 1970s there. Unlike in the United States, both subcultural groups were active prior to production of the film itself.[28] While large segments of English youth were undoubtedly still listening to mainstream, arena rock bands like Emerson, Lake and Palmer, and probably followed the Who as well, their American counterparts—especially those living beyond cosmopolitan cities like New York or Los Angeles—were arguably more likely to follow the mainstream trends than opt for underground and harder-to-source alternatives. Thus, *Quadrophenia* entered American youth culture in 1979 with most young people (whether they were Who fans or not) largely unfamiliar with Mod or the band's former associations with it.

Quadrophenia and (Re-?)Discovering the Who's Mod Past

The year of *Quadrophenia*'s cinematic release was a pivotal one for both the Who and their fans. Though drummer Keith Moon's death in September 1978 surely marked the band's ultimate low point, 1979 proved a complex one in its blend of success and adversity. Both *The Kids are Alright* documentary and the film version of *Quadrophenia* were released that year and the Who decided to embark on a US tour with former Small Faces drummer Kenney Jones. Horrifically, and just a month after *Quadrophenia* hit American movie theatres, the US stadium circuit that had provided the band with both fortune and fame throughout the decade suddenly bore deadly consequences on December 3, 1979. Eleven fans were asphyxiated and/or crushed to death while awaiting entrance into a Who concert at Cincinnati's Riverside Coliseum. This was the same tour that Who management, notably Bill Curbishley, hoped would also further promote *Quadrophenia* by sharing clips of the film in lieu of an opening band.[29] Both the Who and their US fans were seriously shaken up by this devastating event. As the band struggled to stay positive in light of Moon's recent death and the Cincinnati tragedy, the band's two film releases proved to be high points of this challenging year.

The nostalgic project of *Quadrophenia*, both the 1973 album and 1979 film, was meant to act a vehicle documenting the band's—and more specifically Townshend's—relationship with Mod culture. The storyline of Jimmy's search for identity and belonging served as a reflection of these cultural roots. At the time of the album's release, cultural critics and rock journalists on both sides of the Atlantic, and especially those in the United States, offered readers and fans rich analysis of *Quadrophenia* that also included summaries of the Who's Mod past.[30] Including such information suggests that the young, American readers of music magazines like *Rolling Stone* or *Creem* would have needed a "briefing" on the cultural meaning and British backstory to the album's narrative. Similarly, before and after the film's release, press surrounding *Quadrophenia*, whether articles in music- or youth-oriented publications or in widely read newspapers and magazines, made sure to describe what Mod was and why the Who would create a story about such a phenomenon. For instance, an article from the *National Review* describes Mods as "sharp-dressing, motorscooter-riding fans of bands like the Who, Small Faces, and the Kinks [who] were popularizers of skinny ties, miniskirts, and indiscriminate use of amphetamines."[31] While young, American Who fans of the early 1970s may have been old enough to have had some knowledge about the band's ties to Britain's Mod subculture, press surrounding the film imply that a newer generation of fans would have been mostly unaware of the band's close association with this originally, London-based youth scene.

There is little doubt that at the time of *Quadrophenia*'s debut, the Who, alongside bands like Pink Floyd and Led Zeppelin, continued to appeal to American teenagers who followed "hard rock" and listened to album-oriented radio stations. While such youths often were seen as outliers at most suburban high schools across America, unlike the cliques of (mainstream) jocks and preppies who tended to dominate during this era, the so-called freaks or "burnouts" were still more ubiquitous than punks or "new wavers." Because of this, *Quadrophenia* had another surprising effect in the United States. Unlike in the United Kingdom, where Mods already existed prior to the release of the film, *Quadrophenia* served as a catalyst for Mod scenes to emerge in the United States.[32] In this sense, the film created an entirely new audience for the Who because this group of teenagers was drawn to how Mod was portrayed in *Quadrophenia*. I have not uncovered evidence that suggests that the original hard-rocking Who fans, those who would have attended their stadium concerts in 1979 or before, became Mods or changed their assessment of the Who as a band. It is possible that some of them did, but such narratives remain undocumented.

Primary sources do show, however, that American youth who were interested in finding an "alternative" to the bloated, mainstream and commercial aesthetic that bands like the Who came to represent, found something new and inviting when they realized the Who's former links to something called "Mod culture" via *Quadrophenia*.[33] This means that *Quadrophenia*, as Pete Townshend's meditation on the Who's past, provided the band with another avenue of influence in terms of the Who's effect on US youth culture. Though the American youths who had grown up with the Who as the ultimate, iconic rock band during the 1970s likely would continue to see the group as one associated with the rock opera *Tommy*, intense decibel levels, and sold-out arena shows, a new cohort of those who had been born around the time of the release of "My Generation", saw the Who in new light. This outcome of *Quadrophenia* was a powerful one in terms of its ramifications for American youth culture the following decade—one where Mod culture would become more commonplace and recognizable. Though *Quadrophenia*'s narrative was meant to serve as a testament to the Who's Mod past, it unexpectedly created a new youth culture phenomenon in America at the dawn of the 1980s.

NOTES

1. Sheila Benson, "'*Quadrophenia*:' A Welcome Return," *Los Angeles Times*, July 21, 1980, H3; Deborah Caulfield and Jade Garner, "'Fringe' Teens versus Mainstream Flicks," *Los Angeles Times*, May 24, 1981, L22.
2. Jeff Stein mentions this younger cohort of fans in an interview about his documentary. See Ira Robbins, "The Who Movie," *Trouser Press*, April 1979, accessed April 13, 2016, www.rocksbackpages.com/Library/Article/the-who-movie.
3. When consulting with my sister on this, she says that she did actually consider herself both "new wave" and "Mod" her second year of high school (1981–1982), though she was never a purist in terms of youth culture affiliations. That said, I still do not remember her mentioning this or my picking up on her interest in Mod per se.
4. Cited in Kevin Davey, *English Imaginaries: Six Studies in Anglo-British Modernity* (London: Lawrence & Wishart, 1999), 93.
5. Michael Ethen, "A Spatial History of Arena Rock 1964–1979" (PhD diss., McGill University, 2011).
6. Kory Grow, "Flashback: Watch the Who Blow Up 'Smothers Brothers' in Prime Time, *Rolling Stone*, March 4, 2016, accessed January 9, 2017, www.rollingstone.com/music/news/flashback-the-who-blow-up-smothers-brothers-in-primetime-20160304.
7. *The Kids are Alright*, DVD, directed by Jeff Stein (1979; Long Beach, CA: Pioneer, 2003).
8. *Amazing Journey: The Story of the Who*, DVD, directed by Murray Lerner (Universal City, CA: Universal Pictures, 2007); "Undiscovered British Groups: They're Part of the New Wave in Raves!" *Boyfriend*, August 8, 1964, 17.
9. Christine Jacqueline Feldman, *"We are the Mods": A Transnational History of a Youth Subculture* (New York: Peter Lang, 2009), 121–122.
10. John Dougan, *The Who Sell Out* (New York: Continuum, 2006), 10–11.
11. As to the start of the "Summer of Love," see Derek Taylor, *It Was Twenty Years Ago Today: An Anniversary Celebration of 1967* (New York: Fireside, 1987), 13.
12. The term "festivalization" comes from Andy Bennett, Jodie Taylor and Ian Woodward. See their book *The Festivalization of Culture* (New York: Routledge, 2014). For "arena rock" as a phenomenon of the 1970s, see Ethen, "A Spatial History."
13. Simon Wells, *Quadrophenia—A Way of Life (Inside the Making of Britain's Greatest Youth Film)* (London: Countdown Books, 2014), 23.
14. Andy Neill and Matt Kent, *Anyway Anyhow Anywhere: The Complete Chronicle of the Who, 1958–1978* (London: Virgin Books), 267.

15. Dave Marsh, *Before I Get Old: The Story of the Who* (London: Plexus, 1983), 477.
16. Susan J. Douglas, Listening In: Radio and the American Imagination (Minneapolis: University of Minnesota Press, 2004), 219–255; 258–259.
17. Larry Starr and Christopher Waterman, *American Popular Music: The Rock Years* (Cary, US: Oxford University Press, 2005), 184.
18. Donna Gaines, *Teenage Wasteland: Suburbia's Dead End Kids* (Chicago: University of Chicago Press, 1998), 9. A specific link between these kinds of suburban teenagers and the Who is made in Casey Harison, *Feedback: The Who and Their Generation* (London: Rowman & Littlefield, 2015), 135.
19. "Dead Dogs and Gym Teachers," *Freaks and Geeks*, NBC, Oct. 10, 2000.
20. Jan Jagodzinski, *Television and Youth Culture: Televised Paranoia* (New York, Palgrave Macmillan, 2008), 77.
21. Arthur Marwick, *The Sixties: Revolution in Britain, France, Italy and the United States, c.1958–c.1974* (Oxford: Oxford University Press, 1998), 7.
22. The general lack of attention to 1970s' youth in scholarship as compared to both the 1960s and 1980s is emphasized in Barbara Jane Brickman, *New American Teenagers: The Lost Generation of Youth in 1970s Film* (New York: Bloomsbury, 2012), 1–2. One book that does attempt to examine the changes in youth culture during the 1970s is Gary Schwartz, *Beyond Conformity or Rebellion: Youth and Authority in America* (Chicago: University of Chicago Press, 1987).
23. Andy Bennett, "The Forgotten Decade: Rethinking the Popular Music of the 1970s," *Popular Music History* 2:1 (2007): 5–24.
24. Phillip Auslander, *Performing Glam Rock: Gender and Theatricality in Popular Music* (Ann Arbor: University of Michigan Press, 2006), 49.
25. Matthew Worley, "Shot By Both Sides: Punk, Politics and the End of 'Consensus," *Contemporary British History* 26:3 (2012): 335; David Breeden and Jami Carroll, "Punk, Pot and Promiscuity: Nostalgia and the Re-Creation of the 1970s," *Journal of American and Comparative Cultures* 25:1–2 (2002): 100.
26. Paula Massood, "1977: Movies and a Nation in Transformation," in *American Cinema of the 1970s: Themes and Variations*, ed. Lester D. Freedman (New Brunswick, NJ: Rutgers University Press, 2007), 196–199; Gillian G. Gaar, "Disco Demolition Marks 35th Anniversary," *Goldmine* 40:10 (2014): 10.
27. Breeden and Carroll, "Punk, Pot and Promiscuity," 100, 103.
28. Feldman, *"We are the Mods,"* 43–46.
29. Bill Curbishley, introduction to *Quadrophenia—A Way of Life (Inside the Making of Britain's Greatest Youth Film)*, by Simon Wells (London: Countdown Books, 2014), 4; Chet Flippo, "Rock & Roll Tragedy:

Why 11 Died at the Who's Cincinnati Concert," *Rolling Stone*, Jan. 24, 1980, accessed April 13, 2016, www.rollingstone.com/music/news/rock-and-roll-tragedy-why-eleven-died-at-the-whos-cincinnati-concert-19800124?page=7.
30. Lenny Kaye, "The Who: *Quadrophenia*," *Rolling Stone*, December 20, 1973, accessed April 13, 2016, www.rocksbackpages.com/Library/Article/the-Who–quadrophenia; Dave Marsh, "The Who: *Quadrophenia* Reconsidered," *Creem*, March 1974, accessed April 13, 2016, www.rocksbackpages.com/Library/Article/the-who-iquadropheniai-reconsidered; Charles Shaar Murray, "The Who: Quadrophenia," *New Musical Express*, January 21, 1978, accessed April 13, 2016, http://www.rocksbackpages.com/Library/Article/the-who-iquadrophenia; Greg Shaw, "The Who's Mod Generation: *Quadrophenia* Through the Years," *Phonograph Record*, December 1973, accessed April 13, 2016, www.rocksbackpages.com/Library/Article/the-whos-mod-generation-quadrophenia-through-the-years.
31. John Buckley, "Who's Generation," *National Review*, March 21, 1980, 365. For other descriptions of mod culture via *Quadrophenia* reviews, see Janet Maslin, "Screen: Rock Drama from a Who Album—Mods and Rockers," *New York Times*, November 2, 1979; Richard Grenter, "The '60s in Soft Focus," *Commentary*, March 1980, 70.
32. Feldman, *"We are the Mods,"* 134–135.
33. Terry Atkinson, "Mods Revealed By Secret Affair," *Los Angeles Times*, August 15, 1980; G5.Thomas K. Arnold, "Lifestyle: Mod Music, Clothes Make Comeback with San Diego Teen-Agers, *Los Angeles Times* [San Diego Edition], October 18, 1982, SD_B1; Ann Japenga, "Kids Say, 'Excuse Me.' Mods: Stylish Code Makes a Movement," *Los Angeles Times*, September 20, 1982, G1.

Bibliography

Amazing Journey: The Story of the Who. DVD. Directed by Murray Lerner. 2007; Universal City, CA: Universal Pictures, 2007.

Arnold, Thomas K. "Lifestyle: Mod Music, Clothes Make Comeback with San Diego Teenagers." *Los Angeles Times* [San Diego Edition], October 18, 1982.

Atkinson, Terry. "Mods Revealed by Secret Affair." *Los Angeles Times*, August 15, 1980.

Auslander, Phillip. *Performing Glam Rock: Gender and Theatricality in Popular Music*. Ann Arbor, MI: University of Michigan Press, 2006.

Bennett, Andy, Taylor, Jodie, and Ian Woodward. *The Festivalization of Culture*. New York: Routledge, 2014.

Bennett, Andy. "The Forgotten Decade: Rethinking the Popular Music of the 1970s." *Popular Music History* 2:1 (2007): 5–24.

Benson, Sheila. "'Quadrophenia': A Welcome Return." *Los Angeles Times*, July 21, 1980.
Breeden, David and Jami Carroll. "Punk, Pot, and Promiscuity: Nostalgia and the Re-Creation of the 1970s." *Journal of American and Comparative Cultures* 25:1–2 (2002): 100–104.
Brickman, Barbara Jane. *New American Teenagers: The Lost Generation of Youth in 1970s Film*. New York: Bloomsbury, 2012.
Buckley, John. "Who's Generation." *National Review*, March 21, 1980.
Caulfield, Deborah, and Jade Garner. "'Fringe' Teen Films Versus Mainstream Flicks." *Los Angeles Times*, May 24, 1981.
Curbishley, Bill. Introduction to *Quadrophenia—A Way of Life (Inside the Making of Britain's Greatest Youth Film)*, by Simon Wells, 3–4. London: Countdown Books, 2014.
Davey, Kevin. *English Imaginaries: Six Studies in Anglo-British Modernity*. London: Lawrence & Wishart, 1999.
Dougan, John. *The Who Sell Out*. New York: Continuum, 2006.
Douglas, Susan J. *Listening In: Radio and the American Imagination*. Minneapolis: University of Minnesota Press, 2004.
Ethen, Michael. "A Spatial History of Arena Rock 1964–1979." PhD diss., McGill University, 2011.
Feldman, Christine Jacqueline. *"We are the Mods": A Transnational History of a Youth Subculture*. New York: Peter Lang, 2009.
Flippo, Chet. "Rock & Roll Tragedy: Why 11 Died at the Who's Cincinnati Concert." *Rolling Stone*, January 24. Accessed April 13, 2016. http://www.rollingstone.com/music/news/rock-and-roll-tragedy-why-eleven-died-at-the-whos-cincinnati-concert-19800124?page=7.
Freaks. NBC "Episode 17: Dead Dogs and Gym Teachers." October 10, 2000.
Gaines, Donna. *Teenage Wasteland: Suburbia's Dead End Kids*. Chicago: University of Chicago Press, 1998.
Grenter, Richard. "The '60s in Soft Focus." *Commentary*, March 1980.
Grow, Kory. "Flashback: Watch the Who Blow Up 'Smothers Brothers' in Prime Time." *Rolling Stone*, March 4, 2016. Accessed January 9, 2017. http://www.rollingstone.com/music/news/flashback-the-who-blow-up-smothers-brothers-in-primetime-20160304.
Harison, Casey. *Feedback: The Who and Their Generation*. London: Rowman & Littlefield, 2015.
Jagodzinksi, Jan. *Television and Youth Culture: Televised Paranoia*. New York: Palgrave Macmillan, 2008.
Japenga, Ann. "Kids Say, 'Excuse Me.' Mods: Stylish Code Makes a Movement." *Los Angeles Times*, September 20, 1982.
Kaye, Lenny. "Who, The: Quadrophenia." *Rolling Stone*, December 20, 1973. Accessed April 13, 2016. http://www.rocksbackpages.com/Library/Article/the-who-quadrophenia.

The Kids are Alright (Special Edition). DVD. Directed by Jeff Stein. 1979; Long Beach, CA: Pioneer Entertainment, 2003.

Marsh, Dave. *Before I Get Old: The Story of the Who*. London: Plexus, 1983.

———. "Who, The: Quadrophenia Reconsidered." Creem, March 1974. Accessed April 13, 2016. http://www.rocksbackpages.com/Library/Article/the-who-iquadrophenia-reconsidered.

Marwick, Arthur. *The Sixties: Revolution in Britain, France, Italy and the United States, c.1958–1974*. Oxford: Oxford University Press, 1998.

Maslin, Janet. "Screen: Rock Drama from Who Album—Mods and Rockers." *New York Times*, November 2, 1979.

Massood, Paula. "1977: Movies and a Nation in Transformation." In *American Cinema of the 1970s: Themes and Variations*, edited by Lester D. Freedman, 182–204. New Brunswick, NJ: Rutgers University Press, 2007.

Murray, Charles Shaar. "Who, The: Quadrophenia." *New Musical Express*, January 21, 1978. Accessed April 13, 2016. http://www.rocksbackpages.com/Library/Article/the-who-quadropheniai.

Neill, Andy and Matt Kent. *Anyway Anyhow Anywhere: The Complete Chronicle of the Who, 1958–1978*. London: Virgin Books, 2002.

Robbins, Ira. "The Who Movie." *Trouser Press*, April 1979. Accessed April 13, 2016. http://www.rocksbackpages.com/Library/Article/the-who-movie.

Schwartz, Gary. *Beyond Conformity or Rebellion: Youth and Authority in America*, Chicago: University of Chicago Press, 1987.

Shaw, Greg. "The Who's Mod Generation: Quadrophenia Through the Years." *Phonograph Record*, December 1973. Accessed April 13, 2016. http://www.rocksbackpages.com/Library/Article/the-whos-mod-generation-quadrophenia-through-the-years.

Starr, Larry and Christopher Waterman. *American Popular Music: The Rock Years*. Cary, US: Oxford University Press, 2005.

Taylor, Derek. *It Was Twenty Years Ago Today: An Anniversary Celebration of 1967*. New York: Fireside, 1987.

"Undiscovered British Groups: They're Part of the New Wave in Raves!" *Boyfriend*, August 8, 1964.

Wells, Simon. *Quadrophenia—A Way of Life (Inside the Making of Britain's Greatest Youth Film)*. London: Countdown Books, 2014.

Worley, Matthew. "Shot By Both Side: Punk, Politics and the End of 'Consensus.'" *Contemporary British History* 26:3 (2012): 333–354.

CHAPTER 5

Heatwave: Mod, Cultural Studies, and the Counterculture

Sam Cooper

In July 1966, a mimeographed pamphlet titled *Heatwave* began to circulate around London's counterculture. Its title was taken from a track released by Martha and the Vandellas three years previously and recently covered by the Who on their album *A Quick One*. The pamphlet looked like a fanzine, with cartoonish hand-drawn fonts and a playful DIY aesthetic. Its contents page even read like an album's tracklisting, or perhaps a concert bill: "The Great Accident of England," "The Seeds of Social Destruction," "The Shapes of Things." But the pamphlet hardly discussed music at all.

Instead, *Heatwave* served as a primer to what it called "the youth revolt." Its articles identified and analysed—here with sociological detachment, there with gonzo immersion—a selection of the many international iterations of this youth revolt. Each was more outlandishly named than the last: in Britain, the Teddy Boys, the Ban the Bombers, the Ravers; in the States, the Resurgence Youth Movement and the Wobblies; in Holland, the Provos; in France, the Blousons Noirs; in Russia, the Stilyagi. The pamphlet's variously anonymous or

---

S. Cooper (✉)
London, UK
e-mail: sam.martin.cooper@gmail.com

pseudonymous authors took clear delight in the fashions, slang, and idiosyncrasies of each of these tribes, but insisted nonetheless that these rebellious youths needed to be recognised as legitimate political subjects. "We believe the time is ripe," the editorial announces, "for an explosion of revolutionary energy which would alter the face of the Earth."[1]

Heatwave was out to convince its readers that the first sparks of that world-transforming revolutionary energy could be located in youth culture. And it was not alone in that contention. Other radical groups within and beyond the British counterculture were also beginning to understand youth culture as an expression, however faltering, of a growing dissatisfaction with the postwar status quo. One of the clearest articulations of youth culture's antinomian instincts was provided by the Mod movement, with its working-class authenticity and the factional drama of its rivalry with the Rockers.

At the same mid-1960s moment, the discipline of Cultural Studies had started to appear within British universities. It argued that the study of mass culture might provide a unique access point to broader questions about contemporary society and politics. Cultural Studies researchers believed that politics happened on the dancefloor, in the café, and in front of the television—that is, how people behaved in their everyday lives reflected and responded to a complex set of political conditions. For those researchers, Mod served as a prime example of how questions of class, race, and gender could be addressed through fashion, music, and consumption. This particular approach to quotidian habits and activities, comprehended now as demotic indices of contemporary politics, became known as "the cultural turn."[2]

I want to propose in this chapter that the cultural turn as it was experienced in Britain in the postwar period—specifically the turn to everyday life as an object of political study and an arena of political combat—was facilitated and perhaps even catalysed by Mod youth culture. Within a broad vista of youth movements, Mod was particularly significant because it was perceived to be both vernacular and cosmopolitan; more than that, it was modern. As the "original Mod" Steve Sparks remembers:

> Mod has been much misunderstood. Mod is always seen as this working class, scooter-riding precursor of skinheads, and that's a false point of view. Mod before it was commercialised was essentially an extension of the beatniks. It comes from 'modernist,' it has to do with modern jazz and Sartre. It was to do with existentialism, the working class reaction to existentialism.[3]

Mod, perhaps more than any other movement within the youth revolt of the 1960s, was a product of its historical conditions and simultaneously a critique of those conditions. This chapter will tell the history of Mod's reception by two different activist traditions in Britain in the 1960s: the counterculture and Cultural Studies. Both recognised that Mod, for however brief a moment, was able to make clear the contradictions faced by its contemporary working class. That Mod was subsequently co-opted and commercialised is perhaps evidence that it had got something right.

**

Heatwave can be traced to a young man moving within the anarchist milieu of the British anti-nuclear movement of the 1960s. This was Charles Radcliffe, an activist who also wrote about jazz and blues for a variety of underground magazines. Towards the end of summer 1965, Radcliffe made contact with a small group based in Chicago that published a magazine titled *Rebel Worker*. The group shared Radcliffe's interests in anarchism and what they called "Black American" music. Another of *Rebel Worker*'s interests was Surrealism, and the Americans' enthusiastic essays introduced Radcliffe not only to the work of André Breton and his group in Paris, but also to their ancestors, not least the Marquis de Sade, the utopian socialist Charles Fourier, the young Karl Marx, and the poet Lautréamont.

Rebel Worker was expressly proud of the eclectic scope of its interests. Its authors insisted on the direct connections between free jazz and proletarian consciousness, between Bugs Bunny and ludic emancipation, between black humour and revolution. But they were also aware that this irreverent approach would not be easily received by their readership. While the *Rebel Worker* group positioned itself in opposition to bourgeois society and its values, it also opposed the institutional left.[4] In his article "Mods, Rockers and the Revolution," *Rebel Worker*'s editor Franklin Rosemont claimed that rock 'n' roll music is "the only mass protest music today," far superior to the folk revival then endorsed and fostered by the unions and institutions of the traditional left. The folk revival had resolutely failed to attract the attention of working-class kids, who preferred louder, angrier rock music. "We must recognize," Rosemont implored, "that the rock 'n' rollers, despite the hesitations of 'socialist' politicians, are our friends and fellow workers."[5]

"True revolutionaries," Rosemont continued, must pay attention to "'superstructural' anthropological factors" like the youth revolt because such things represented efforts to "live some sort of decent life against all the obstacles presented by a society divided into classes."[6] Pete Meaden, the first manager of the Who and quintessential "face" in the Mod scene, would later make a similar claim for Mod. "Modism, mod living is an aphorism," he said (launching a similar assault on highfalutin language to Rosemont's scare-quoting of Marxian jargon), "for clean living under difficult circumstances."[7] The difficult circumstances were those experienced by young working-class people in the changing economic and cultural landscape of postwar Britain. The clean living was their emphasis on a sharp personal appearance facilitated by suits, scooters, and films from France and Italy, and a "hip" attitude learned from the West Indian communities newly arrived in London.

This talk of "decent" and "clean" living might come as a surprise, given the Mods' hedonistic reputation. Indeed, Mod cleanliness was aesthetic, but also moral—or, perhaps, existential. They didn't want to live the compromised, bad faith lives of their parents and bosses; they wanted instead to be true to themselves. However, that vexed cleanliness anticipates a contradiction within Mod's sense of its own socio-historical place, which I'll discuss in more detail later in this chapter. Briefly, Mod was about escaping from a grubby background (a form of "embourgeoisement"), but experiencing that escape in the form of transgressive misbehaviour (drugs, fighting, itinerancy). Not only does this misbehaviour itself connote uncleanness, but when those transgressions are eventually punished—as they are in most Mod narratives—the individual Mod is pushed back further into the subordinate role they originally rebelled against.

Nonetheless, if we are willing to think of Mod as a radical protest movement, Meaden's account soon converges with Rosemont's—that is, Mod quickly takes shape as a manifestation of the subversive impulses of young people as disaffected with traditional forms of political contestation as they were with postwar capitalist society itself. In *Absolute Beginners*, Colin MacInnes's proto-Mod novel of 1959, the unnamed 18-year-old protagonist weaves his way through London in search of good times, trying to brush off the influence of his staid, repressed, and ambitionless family. An outburst against his 25-year-old (ancient!) half-brother confirms his rejection of traditional class politics:

> "You poor old prehistoric monster," I exclaimed. "I do not reject the working classes, and I do not belong to the upper classes, for one and the same reason, namely, that neither of them interest me in the slightest,

never have done, never will do. Do try to understand that, clobbo! I'm just not interested in the whole class crap that seems to needle you and all the other tax-payers …"⁸

The protagonist, for most of the novel, is more interested in the emergence of youth as a dynamic social group, and his place therein, than in political ideologies. He and his friends are able to traverse many of the lines of class, race, gender, and sexuality maintained by the older generations.

**

Franklin and his partner Penelope Rosemont came to visit Radcliffe in London in April 1966. Collectively, they produced a special issue of *Rebel Worker*, to which Radcliffe contributed an essay about the Who. Its title, "Crime Against the Bourgeoisie," was taken from Pete Townshend's own description of what his band represented. Radcliffe explained that "the whole effect of the Who on stage is action, noise, rebellion and destruction—a storm of sexuality and youthful menace."⁹ What differentiated the Who from the many other Mod R&B groups on the "hip" scene was their violence. They wanted, Radcliffe wrote,

> to generate in the audience an echo of their own anger. If their insistence on Pop Art, now dying a little, is reactionary—for of all art, pop art most completely accepts the values of consumer society—there is still their insistence on destruction, the final ridicule of the Spectacular commodity economy.¹⁰

In this analysis, Radcliffe makes two important observations about the Who, which are worth considering in some detail.

First, he recognises that the group bore some relation to avant-garde artistic traditions, and specifically to the Dadaist practice of anti-art. This association, today, might be quite surprising, not least because of Mod's retrospective reconstruction as a nationalist phenomenon, all draped in Union flags, and because of the Who's eventual status as quintessential rock dinosaurs. Nonetheless, Radcliffe describes the Who's music as "auto-destructive Pop," an allusion to the influence on Townshend of his former teacher Gustav Metzger, the pioneer of auto-destructive art. The most famous example of Metzger's auto-destructive art was acid action painting, for which the artist flung acid rather than paint at the canvas, which would then rapidly dissolve as the audience looked on.

Auto-destructive art was a critique of consumerist values and a metaphor for destructive Cold War politics.

More significantly, Radcliffe uses the term "Spectacular commodity economy" to describe consumer society. He would likely have read this term not long before writing his piece, in a pamphlet issued by the Situationist International, the ultra-left avant-garde group based in Paris. The Situationist International presented itself as the culmination of the Dada and Surrealist lineage, though in 1966 it was almost unheard-of in Britain. Before the Rosemonts had arrived in London to meet Radcliffe, they had visited Paris to seek out their hero André Breton. There, they were introduced to Guy Debord, central impresario of the Situationist International. Although the meeting was not a harmonious one, the Americans took 300 copies of a pamphlet titled "Decline and Fall of the Spectacle-Commodity Economy" to distribute in London and Chicago. This was an important moment in the dissemination of Situationist ideas in the English-speaking world. That Radcliffe borrowed the pamphlet's vocabulary so soon after receiving a copy from the Rosemonts is evidence of its powerful impact on his thinking. He would soon become one of the four members of the Situationist International's English Section, though the latter was short-lived.

The "Decline and Fall of the Spectacle-Commodity Economy" pamphlet, one of the Situationist International's few English-language texts, argues provocatively that the 1965 Watts riots in Los Angeles were not race riots, nor even class riots as such. Neither the institutional left nor figures like Martin Luther King had recognised the full extent of the protestors' radical disaffection. Instead, the Situationists claim, the riots were "a rebellion against the commodity, against the world of the commodity in which worker-consumers are hierarchically subordinated to commodity standards."[11]

For the Watts protestors—and, in Radcliffe's reading, for the Who—riotous destruction was an active affront to capitalist values and an affirmation of other ways of living. This was a common argument throughout the Situationists' work. An earlier incarnation of the group, the Lettrist International, had named its journal *Potlatch* after the gift-giving ceremonies held by the indigenous people of the Pacific Northwest, in which exuberant and excessive gift giving—that is, giving away more than the community can actually afford to give away—was a sign of social status (rather than, for example, hoarding material possessions). Via Marcel Mauss's anthropological take on potlatch in *The Gift*

(1925) and Georges Bataille's economic reworking in *The Accursed Share* (1949), the Lettrists had begun to conceptualise the potlatch ceremony as a type of carnival, a celebration of essentially anti-capitalist values, the abolition rather than the creation of surplus.

The second significant observation that Radcliffe makes about the Who in his article for *Rebel Worker* is that, at the same time as he insists that they are political, their politics are limited. Townshend's views, Radcliffe writes, are expressed "freely and frequently" but are "weirdly confused." The Who are "symptomatic of discontent," but their fury might consume them—before, one assumes, "true revolutionaries" like he and the Rosemonts can win them onside.[12] In retrospect, the emphasis in *Rebel Worker* on the youthfulness of the Who and other Mods might have been shortsighted: youthful discontent is necessarily limited, because youth passes. But, importantly, Mod was always aware of its limited tenure, of its need to die before it got old.

When the Rosemonts returned to Chicago, Radcliffe launched *Heatwave*, which lasted only two issues, both published in 1966. The first issue demonstrated a clear inheritance from *Rebel Worker*. Like its American forebear, *Heatwave* sought to introduce its readership to avant-garde traditions and political movements from continental Europe, and to search for any sign of similar revolutionary practices in homegrown youth cultures.

In the first issue's main article, "The Seeds of Social Destruction," Radcliffe restates his interest in "the emergence, one after the other, of groupings of disaffected youth." These "exist wherever modern, highly bureaucratised consumer societies exist." They "have little immediately in common but their implicit rejection of the positions allocated to them in society."[13] Radcliffe again borrows vocabulary and ideas from the Situationists, but the pamphlet's overall tone is hyperbolic and alarmist. It parodies the infamous tabloid stories and courthouse reports that were elsewhere making folk devils of the Mods.[14]

As Radcliffe continues, he surveys the panorama of British youth movements. He describes Rockers as "the entrenched traditionalists of teenage fashion." Mods, on the other hand, are "perhaps more experimental than any other group." Radcliffe recognises that in their sartorial sensibilities and their slang, Mods were mimicking European avant-garde artists as well as the fashions and behaviours of the West Indians who had arrived in London to fill the postwar labour gap. Nonetheless, he restates his concern that the Mods' destructiveness was turning inward rather than outward: while the "furious consumption programme of the mods" was once a "grotesque parody of the aspirations of [their] parents," by 1966 it had become an end in itself. Mod culture was beginning to be reduced to a spectacle. Mod–Rocker skirmishes served only "to keep blimpish magistrates busy [...] in those quiet seaside towns where the bourgeois go to living-die like happy squires."[15]

Mod culture occurred at a moment of plenitude and loss when, on the one hand, a British youth culture was most directly informed by radical political and cultural currents from abroad, but also, on the other hand, when the "spectacular-commodity economy" had developed to the point at which it was able to co-opt whatever radical potential was sparked by those meetings. As such, Mod was transformed into teenage rite of passage, consumer identity, mere fashion.

Even if Mod as a protest movement had self-imploded or had been co-opted, Radcliffe remained hopeful. His *Heatwave* article ends:

> What is important about the youth revolt at this stage is not so much what it is, but that it is; that in some ways and however hesitantly, however unsurely, youth recognises its exploiters and is, if only temporarily, prepared to pay them off in a currency they can understand.[16]

Qualifiers and concessions overweigh the passage: "if only temporarily" is troublesome. But Radcliffe did not simply project this anxious temporality onto Mod culture. An awareness that Mod would soon fizzle out or be transformed into something unrecognisable was always already present in Mod culture. This anxious temporality—Mod's desire to die before it got old—is best demonstrated by *Quadrophenia*, both the Who's 1973 concept album that looks back on the Mod days, and Franc Roddam's 1979 film version that looks back over an even greater distance. The protagonist of both, Jimmy the Mod, doesn't want to grow up. He doesn't want to become his parents; he doesn't identify with "adult" aspirations; he finds no satisfaction in steady, gainful employment. He wants to stay young and cool and carefree for as long as possible. He tries to defer his future through shirking his responsibilities, burning bright but briefly, and pouring scorn on those whom he considers to have sold out.

The anxieties borne of Mod culture's sense of its own impermanence may be discounted as simple teenage angst. But, if we turn to the assessment made within Cultural Studies's founding discussions, we can understand Mod's anxious temporality as a sign of its consciousness that it sat on a historical juncture into which it could easily disappear.

*

The cultural historian Jon Savage writes that in "The Seeds of Social Destruction," Radcliffe "laid the foundations for the next 20 years of sub-cultural theory."[17] Because of its samizdat circulation, it remains difficult to gauge *Heatwave*'s readership and reach, but its treatment of Mod certainly anticipated that of British Cultural Studies, a much more widely known body of work.

In "The Seeds of Social Destruction," Radcliffe identifies the Ton-Up Kids as antecedents of the Rockers. Named for riding their motorbikes at 100mph, the Ton-Up Kids represented an early stage in the Americanisation of British youth culture. Radcliffe indulges in their mythology. He describes these "Coffee Bar Cowboys" as wilful outcasts from straight society, rebels without causes. Richard Hoggart, in his pivotal study of postwar working-class culture, *The Uses of Literacy* (1957), takes aim at a similar demographic. Of the "Juke Box Boys," with their milkshakes and pinball, Hoggart can trace only "a sort of spiritual dry rot amid the odour of boiled milk." The Juke Box Boys live "in a myth-world compounded of a few simple elements which they take to be those of American life."[18] They were, for Hoggart, symptomatic of the loss of traditional English working-class culture through the top-down imposition of spectacular, American mass culture.

Clearly, Hoggart's response to this youth culture was antithetical to Radcliffe's: the former entirely dismissive, the latter cautiously celebratory. Nonetheless, they shared a more fundamental belief that culture and "superstructural" phenomena are indeed places were politics happen, and as such are worthy of serious political investigation. This is hardly news to us now, but—as we saw in *Rebel Worker*—these types of cultural politics had to be defended from the left as well as the right when they first appeared. In Britain, the Centre for Contemporary Cultural Studies (CCCS) that Hoggart founded at the University of Birmingham in 1964 was crucial to this cultural turn and to the development of Cultural Studies as an academic discipline. As Stuart Hall, who became the Centre's director in 1968, explains, Hoggart viewed culture as "the practices of making sense," which "was very far removed indeed from 'culture' as the ideal court of judgement, whose touchstone was 'the best that has been thought and said,' which animated the tradition from Arnold to Eliot and Leavis."[19]

Of what, then, did the Mods make sense? How did Mod, over and above any other tribe within the youth revolt, contribute to this epistemological shift? Like Radcliffe, researchers within the CCCS recognised that Mod culture contained within itself an anxious temporality, an uneasy sense of its own impermanence. Mods implicitly understood their structural, socio-economic position, but they also understood that the socio-economic structure itself was changing. Hall emphasises the importance of "affluence" as a concept within the CCCS's thinking. In the 1950s, the British working class had been increasingly drawn into consumption, rather than just production; it had become increasingly affluent. Alongside the emergence of the welfare state and changing forms of employment, traditional working-class identities had been destabilised—hence Hoggart's hostility towards American mass culture, which had come to supplant established British working-class identity.

These changes were not met without resistance, however, and the CCCS sought to develop an account of how youth cultures were responding to the shift from traditional working-class values to those of a new mass culture. In a paper titled "Working Class Youth Cultures," for example, John Clarke and Tony Jefferson constructed a complex diagram to demonstrate and explain how Mod culture straddled a division that ran right through working-class culture. Mod identity, Clarke and Jefferson proposed, was split between "embourgeoisement" and "ghettoisation": the former represented the changes to working-class identity that had resulted from the new availability of disposable commodities; the latter represented the dogged maintenance of a static conception of working-class identity within the new "classless" and "mobile" society.[20] Rockers and Greasers, in contrast, were mere traditionalists, a "new lumpen" thoroughly entrenched in the ghettoised working class.

In the first instance, this division manifested itself as a contradiction evident in Mod's uneasy introduction of signifiers of cosmopolitan cool into musty, shabby locales like the dance halls, office blocks, and terraced houses that are the settings of its texts like *Absolute Beginners* and *Quadrophenia*. Pete Townshend captured the Continental–British contrast in the following lyric from "Sea and Sand": "I ride a GS scooter with my hair cut neat / I wear my wartime coat in the wind and sleet ."

Clarke and Jefferson offered a more specific example. Mod performed a contradiction in working-class identity through, on the one hand, its embrace of "plastic" culture (suits, mopeds, records) and, on the other hand, its retention of what Clarke and Jefferson call the "parental argot," or vernacular speech patterns.[21] As Jimmy the Mod puts it in the film of Quadrophenia, "Look, I don't wanna be the same as everyone else. That's why I'm a Mod, see?"

In a 1974 CCCS occasional paper titled "The Style of the Mods," Dick Hebdige also tried to isolate the qualities of this particular youth revolt that gave it such resonance. Hebdige's paper would inform his landmark 1979 book *Subculture: The Meaning of Style*. He argued that Mod at its peak was "pure, unadulterated style." It appropriated the commodities of mass culture and performed a "semantic rearrangement" of them: sleek Vespas in grey council estates, French cigarettes in fish 'n' chip shops, expensive suits on minimal salaries. Mod style was a parody of the dominant, consumerist culture: superficially similar, but also incomprehensible to the adult world. Its excessive consumption—of commodities and of speed, both types—was, like the potlatch, a carnival of destruction.

Hebdige also followed Radcliffe in emphasising the Mods' avant-garde inspiration:

> Like the Surrealists and Dadaists, the mods relied principally on the dissonance between object and context to evince the desired disturbed response from the dominant parent culture, and learned to make their criticisms obliquely, having learned by experience (at school and work) to avoid direct confrontation where age, experience, and civil power would, inevitably, have told against them.[22]

Still following Radcliffe, Hebdige lamented how rapidly Mod had become addicted to the consumption that it once subverted. It was too willing to perform, to become a spectacle, a part of the thing it once rallied against. Hebdige points out that the area of Brighton Beach where the Mods and Rockers fought, famously recreated in *Quadrophenia*, is even structured like an amphitheatre: a central performance space, watched over by two piers and a raised promenade.

It is difficult not to be disappointed, when reading the many oral and popular histories of Mod culture, by the various reports of how strictly hierarchical and socially coded the movement became. Hard distinctions were made between the "faces" on the scene and the wannabes; those with the right clothes and those with the wrong ones. Not only did Mod become addicted to what it once subverted, it ended up reproducing the social structures from which it once fled. Hebdige took solace in the knowledge that while Mod failed to exacerbate the contradictions of capitalism, "it did at least beat against the bars of its own prison."[23]

**

What the activists of the counterculture and the researchers of the CCCS saw in Mod was a youth culture that was more than simply symptomatic of its age. Back in *Absolute Beginners*, as he turns the grand old age of 19, the narrator–protagonist finds himself disillusioned with the London life that had previously captivated him. In particular, he cannot understand white Londoners' growing racism towards the West Indians whose company he enjoys so much. He shows signs of softening ("it's all very well sneering at universities, and students with those awful scarves and flat-heeled shoes, but really and truly, it would be wonderful to have a bit of kosher education") but he remains unconvinced by class-based analyses.[24] In particular, he doubts the historical materialist credentials of the Marxists, who are "in history, yes," but "outside it, also […] living in the Marxist future."[25]

The narrative ends as he contemplates leaving London and Britain altogether, his determination swayed only by the sight of the happiness of new arrivals from Africa. Most Mod narratives culminate in a similar moment of crisis for their young protagonists (usually white men, which shows the limits of this chapter's claims about Mod's cosmopolitanism). *Quadrophenia* ends with Jimmy the Mod symbolically adrift, alone on a rock out at sea in the Who's version, and propelling a scooter over a cliff in the film.

Mod, or at least the version of Mod constructed in the writings of figures like Radcliffe and Hebdige, was self-aware and historically conscious. Its anxieties were borne not, or not only, from the hormonal alienation of its teenage subjects. Those anxieties were a result of an intense-because-firsthand knowledge of the difficult circumstances faced by its contemporary working class. For all of its attention to the most minute of details in its appearance and conspicuous consumption, Mod's real focus was on the epistemic shifts in class and social relations in the postwar period. As a result, contemporary observers like Radcliffe and Rosemont, Hall and Hebdige were able to argue that the field of political contestation had expanded into the practices of everyday life, which is to say that British culture had finally begun to digest the lessons of the European avant-gardes of the earlier twentieth century.

NOTES

1. "First Statement," *Heatwave* 1 (1966). Articles from *Heatwave* have been reproduced in Tom Vague (ed.), *King Mob Echo: English Section of the Situationist International* (London: Dark Star 2000) and Franklin Rosemont and Charles Radcliffe (eds.) *Dancin' in the Streets! Anarchists, IWWs, Surrealists and Provos in the 1960s as recorded in the pages of The Rebel Worker and Heatwave* (Chicago: Charles H. Kerr 2005).
2. John Akomfrah's documentary *The Stuart Hall Project* (BFI 2013) provides an excellent introduction to the work of Stuart Hall and the Centre for Contemporary Cultural Studies.
3. Steve Sparks in Jonathon Green (ed.), *Days in the Life: Voices from the English Underground 1961–1971* (London: William Heinemann Ltd. 1998), quoted in Paolo Hewitt (ed.), *The Sharper Word: A Mod Anthology* (London: Helter Skelter 2009), 65.
4. *Rebel Worker* was instead keen to revive the International Workers of the World, or the Wobblies, the "One Big Union" whose presence in the United States in the 1960s was much smaller than in its pre-war heyday, a consequence of sustained government repression.
5. Franklin Rosemont, "Mods, Rockers and the Revolution," *Rebel Worker* 3 (1965), in Rosemont and Radcliffe (eds.), *Dancin' in the Streets!*, 127–131.
6. Ibid., 127.
7. Steve Turner, "The Ace Face's Forgotten Story: An Interview with Pete Meaden," *New Musical Express* (17 November 1979), reprinted in Hewitt (ed.), *The Sharper Word*, 198.
8. Colin MacInnes, *Absolute Beginners* (London: Alison and Busby 1980), 38.
9. Charles Radcliffe, "Crimes Against the Bourgeoisie," *Rebel Worker* 6 (1966), in Vague (ed.) *King Mob Echo*, 14.
10. Ibid., 15.
11. Situationist International, "Decline and Fall of the Spectacle-Commodity Economy" (1965), in Ken Knabb (ed. and trans.), *Situationist International Anthology* (Berkeley: Bureau of Public Secrets 2006), 197.
12. Radcliffe, "Crimes Against the Bourgeoisie," 15.
13. Charles Radcliffe, "The Seeds of Social Destruction," *Heatwave* 1 (1966), in Vague (ed.), *King Mob Echo*, 27.
14. Stanley Cohen, *Folk Devils: The Creation of the Mods and the Rockers* (London: MacGibbon and Kee Ltd. 1972).
15. Radcliffe, "The Seeds of Social Destruction," 30–31.
16. Ibid., 31.

17. Jon Savage, *England's Dreaming: Sex Pistols and Punk Rock* (London: Faber and Faber 1991), 32.
18. Richard Hoggart, *The Uses of Literacy* (London: Penguin 1960), 204.
19. Stuart Hall, "Richard Hoggart, *The Uses of Literacy* and the Cultural Turn," *International Journal of Cultural Studies* 10: 39 (2007): 43.
20. John Clarke and Tony Jefferson, "Working Class Youth Cultures," Stencilled Occasional Papers of the Centre for Contemporary Cultural Studies, University of Birmingham (November 1973), 11. Available at: www.birmingham.ac.uk/Documents/college-artslaw/history/cccs/stencilled-occasional-papers/1to8and11to24and38to48/SOP18.pdf. (Accessed 6 June 2016).
21. Ibid.
22. Dick Hebdige, "The Style of the Mods," Stencilled Occasional Papers of the Centre for Contemporary Cultural Studies, University of Birmingham (Spring 1974), 9.
23. Ibid., 8.
24. MacInnes, *Absolute Beginners*, 143.
25. Ibid., 127.

Bibliography

Akomfrah, John. *The Stuart Hall Project*. BFI, 2013.
Clarke, John and Tony Jefferson. "Working Class Youth Cultures," Stencilled Occasional Papers of the Centre for Contemporary Cultural Studies, University of Birmingham (November 1973), 11. Available at: http://www.birmingham.ac.uk/Documents/college-artslaw/history/cccs/stencilled-occasional-papers/1to8and11to24and38to48/SOP18.pdf (accessed 6 June 2016).
Cohen, Stanley. *Folk Devils: The Creation of the Mods and the Rockers*. London: MacGibbon and Kee Ltd. 1972.
"First Statement," *Heatwave* 1 (1966) in Tom Vague (ed.), *King Mob Echo: English Section of the Situationist International* (London: Dark Star 2000): 20.
Green, Jonathon (ed.). *Days in the Life: Voices from the English Underground 1961–1971*. London: William Heinemann Ltd., 1998.
Hall, Stuart. "Richard Hoggart, *The Uses of Literacy* and the Cultural Turn," *International Journal of Cultural Studies* 10: 39 (2007): 39–49.
Hebdige, Dick. "The Style of the Mods," Stencilled Occasional Papers of the Centre for Contemporary Cultural Studies, University of Birmingham (Spring 1974).
Hewitt, Paolo (ed.). *The Sharper Word: A Mod Anthology*. London: Helter Skelter, 2009.

Hoggart, Richard. *The Uses of Literacy*. London: Penguin 1960.
MacInnes, Colin. *Absolute Beginners*. London: Alison and Busby, 1980.
Radcliffe, Charles. "Crimes Against the Bourgeoisie," *Rebel Worker* 6 (1966), in Vague (ed.) *King Mob Echo*, 14–15.
Radcliffe, Charles. "The Seeds of Social Destruction," *Heatwave* 1 (1966), in Vague (ed.), *King Mob Echo*, 27–32.
Rosemont, Franklin and Charles Radcliffe (eds). *Dancin' in the Streets! Anarchists, IWWs, Surrealists and Provos in the 1960s as recorded in the pages of The Rebel Worker and Heatwave*. Chicago: Charles H. Kerr, 2005.
Rosemont, Franklin. "Mods, Rockers and the Revolution," *Rebel Worker* 3 (1965), in Rosemont and Radcliffe (eds), *Dancin' in the Streets!*, 127–131.
Savage, Jon. *England's Dreaming: Sex Pistols and Punk Rock*. London: Faber and Faber 1991.
Situationist International, "Decline and Fall of the Spectacle-Commodity Economy" (1965), in Ken Knabb (ed. and trans.), *Situationist International Anthology* (Berkeley: Bureau of Public Secrets 2006), 194–203.
Turner, Steve. "The Ace Face's Forgotten Story: An Interview with Pete Meaden," *New Musical Express* (17th November 1979), reprinted in Hewitt (ed.), *The Sharper Word*, 191–209.
Vague, Tom (ed.). *King Mob Echo: English Section of the Situationist International*. London: Dark Star 2000.

PART II

The Mobility of Mod: Class, Culture, and Identity

CHAPTER 6

Class, Youth, and Dirty Jobs: The Working-Class and Post-War Britain in Pete Townshend's *Quadrophenia*

Keith Gildart

This chapter examines Pete Townshend's *Quadrophenia* (1973) and the way in which it depicts continuity and change in the lives of the British working class in the period that the album documents (1964/1965), the political milieu in which it was written (1972/1973), and the legacy of the concept that was depicted in the screen version directed by Franc Roddam (1978/1979).[1] *Quadrophenia* was recorded and released in a fraught period of industrial militancy in Britain that had not been witnessed since the general strike of 1926.[2] The album can be "read" as both a social history of an element of youth culture in the mid-1960s, but also a reflection on contemporary anxieties relating to youth, class, race, and national identity in the period 1972/1973.[3] Similarly, the cinematic version of *Quadrophenia* was conceived and directed in 1978/1979 in the months prior to and after Margaret Thatcher was swept to power, ushering in a long period of Conservative politics that economically, socially, and culturally reshaped British society.[4]

K. Gildart (✉)
University of Wolverhampton, Wolverhampton, UK
e-mail: Keith.Gildart@wlv.ac.uk

Quadrophenia is a significant historical source for "reading" these pivotal years and providing a sense of how musicians and writers were both reflecting and dramatizing a sense of "crisis," "continuity," and "change" in working-class Britain.[5]

Along with the novels and films of the English "new wave" and contemporary sociological examinations of working-class communities and youth culture, *Quadrophenia* represents a classic slice of "social realism," social history, and political commentary. It is a useful companion piece to Alan Sillitoe's *Saturday Night and Sunday Morning* (1958), which similarly centres on an anti-hero in the shape of Arthur Seaton who is alienated from the working-class world into which he was born. *Quadropenia*'s Jimmy was similarly conflicted regarding the cultural norms of the working-class family, the deference articulated by the post-war generation in the workplace, and the particular forms of politics that underpinned the post-war consensus.[6] In substance and tone it offers a similarly nuanced view of youth culture and experiences that was first articulated by the director Karel Reisz in his ground-breaking documentary *We Are The Lambeth Boys* (1959).[7]

Quadrophenia also provides similar insights to the ground-breaking sociological research deployed in Young and Willmott's *Family and Kinship in East London* (1957).[8] The politics of the album share the critiques of British society expressed by Anthony Sampson in his *The Anatomy of Britain* (1962) particularly in relation to the rigidity of the class structure and the continuing dominance of social elites.[9] The images that adorn the accompanying photo-essay by American photographer Ethan Russell complement Nell Dunn's ethnography of working-class Battersea and the East End in novels such as *Up the Junction* (1963) and *Poor Cow* (1967).[10] Battersea had a long tradition of labour politics, trade unionism, and attendant working-class cultures that remained a significant feature of the district in the 1960s and 1970s, which can be seen and experienced in some of the tracks included on *Quadrophenia*, in the album's sleeve notes, and in the overall imagery of the package. Aware of its roots in working-class localities across London and beyond, Townshend dedicated the finished album in 1973 to the teenagers from "the Goldhawk Road … Stevenage New Town and to the kids from the East End."[11]

Quadrophenia and the Mod culture it depicts has often quite erroneously been compared to the presentation of affluence, social mobility, and mould-breaking youth cultures that are central to Colin MacInnes's much mythologised novel *Absolute Beginners* (1959).[12] Yet in contrast to the conventional images of modernity, affluence, colour, and the mythology of the "swinging sixties," Townshend's *Quadrophenia* and *his* British 1960s is a "black and white world" of domestic drudgery, egg and chip breakfasts, dirty jobs, vandalism, cheap pornography, racism, the faded grandeur of seaside resorts, political alienation, class divisions, and social deference. As such, Townshend's role as musician, writer, performer, and commentator was more nuanced than some of his musical contemporaries and he shared with Ray Davies of the Kinks an acute sense of social observation and knowledge of working-class history and culture.[13] Here was an attempt not to just capture the popular zeitgeist of 1964/1965 and 1972/1973, but a sophisticated attempt to understand the complexity of the British working-class and the place of youth, fashion, and popular music in its "everyday life."

Popular Music, the Working-Class, and the World of Pete Townshend[14]

Townshend was a writer and performer who was not content crafting pop songs, but also wanted to provide narratives and analyses of youth culture and how it posed a challenge to the social conventions of British society.[15] Doggett argues that Townshend was different from other performers of the 1960s in that he saw his "role not to provide false hope, but to reflect the negativity felt by 'the kids'."[16] For Townshend, "popular music had a serious purpose" and that was "to defy post-war depression."[17] Like many of his musical contemporaries, he was aware of the British class structure and his position within it that defined him as middle-class. He expressed his feelings to the *New Musical Express* in 1983 stressing that "class, the attributes and consciousness … has always been something that has evaded me."[18] Yet like John Lennon, he was connected to the working-class through friendship, popular music, geographical proximity, and a fascination with its youth culture.[19] As a songwriter, he felt "that the best pop songs always offered a space in the middle for the listener to inhabit."[20] This goes some way to explaining the "cult status" of *Quadrophenia* and its lasting legacy. The narrative and the music spoke to working-class youths of the 1970s and reflected their anxieties, aspirations, and complexities.

Townshend's parents were musicians and his father traversed the country as a member of the popular dance band the Squadronaires.[21] As a child in the mid-1950s, Townshend visited provincial theatres and holiday camps where a pre-war working-class culture now mixed with the contemporary sounds of rock 'n' roll. It was on the Isle of Man in 1957 where he attended a screening of *Rock Around the Clock* (1956) and "nothing would ever be quite the same."[22] He followed what would become a fairly typical route into a music career and shared with his contemporaries the transformative experience of American rhythm and blues music.[23] He was a member of a skiffle band before establishing a successful recording and performing career as a member of the Who along with Roger Daltrey, John Entwistle, and Keith Moon.[24] Through his involvement in art school, the music industry, and the cosmopolitan culture of London, Townshend would connect with a variety of characters that epitomised the British class system.[25] According to Davey, Townshend was a member of the Campaign for Nuclear Disarmament and the Young Communist League and had played banjo as part of one of the Aldermaston marches against nuclear weapons.[26] Denselow claims that Townshend had also discussed politics with veteran leftists who were on the trad-jazz scene.[27] Yet ultimately, he was more interested in youth culture as a political form of expression that operated outside *of* and could not be defined *by* particular ideological and organisational structures. This appears most starkly through the experiences of Jimmy in *Quadrophenia*. Jimmy struggles with the conventional expressions of working-class identity such as trade unions and the strictures of the street and the broader community.

Townshend wanted to articulate the feelings and emotions of working-class youth through song and performance and as a result, his work with the Who was far more ambitious than the Beatles and the Rolling Stones in attempting to make sense of post-war Britain. According to Denselow, "Townshend believed in his audiences, believed it was they and not the performers who were the real sixties idealists."[28] Songs such as "I Can't Explain," "Anyway, Anyhow, Anywhere," and "My Generation," which charted in 1965 became Mod anthems providing a soundtrack for a working-class youth who expressed an inarticulate but keenly felt sense of liberation and transgression in the coffee bar, dance hall, provincial theatre, and coastal resort.[29] For Townshend, the Who "… married their audience, they reflected them."[30] Mods present a particular image of Britain where some things changed and others remained the same. Yet within this image we see challenges to the boundaries of class, social convention. and numerous examples of "historic encounters" between white working-class youth, West Indian migrants, and the sounds and struggles of black America.[31] *Quadrophenia* goes beyond the inarticulateness of the three key Who singles noted above and attempts to convey a more detailed depiction of class as a lived experience that is punctuated by popular music, subcultural identity, and social change.

The connection between Who fans and the band is expressed through testimony of Mods from the 1960s. Jack Lyons witnessed the spectacle of the High Numbers during their residency at the Railway Hotel in Harrow and felt that here was a group that seemed to be speaking directly to him and his working-class friends.[32] Mim Scala remembers it "as a madhouse with hundreds of Vespa scooters outside."[33] Their manager Pete Meaden also got the group a residency at the Scene Club, which was a working-class Mod hangout.[34] Through *Quadrophenia*, Townshend was to accurately capture the Mod phenomenon and the ways in which it reflected aspects of British society in 1964/1965. To Marsh, *Quadrophenia* "is a marvellous piece of social criticism, trying to place the public and private history of the 1960s into a context from which something more productive can be built."[35] To Davey, it "is an audit of the successes and failure of the 1960s, the illusions of its youth cultures, and the failure of political projects to connect with popular aspirations" and "provided a bleaker but more telling account of the sixties than cultural studies would soon produce."[36] Townshend himself claimed that in preparation for *Quadrophenia* he "needed to look at the people I was writing about. This was almost Socialist writing for me."[37]

The accompanying photo-essay setting out the visual narrative of *Quadrophenia* captured the working-class aspects of Mod subculture.[38] Many of the youths used for the images were from the working-class council estates of Battersea, where the Who recorded the album.[39] Photographer Ethan Russell recalled that "nothing much subtler than the Industrial Revolution really changes the face of England, and mod was something that lived and thrived in the same back streets of row houses … to be found in Battersea in 1973."[40] A precursor to this social realist approach is evident in the artwork that accompanied the release of the compilation album of Who singles in the form of *Meaty Beaty Big and Bouncy* (1971). The front cover features a section of slum housing with working-class kids hanging on the front steps of one of the dwellings with members of the band looking down at them through a broken window. This insight into working-class street kids is taken much further in the imagery and narrative of *Quadrophenia*. This was not really a swinging Britain, but a one that was bumping and grinding against poverty, inequality, and a rigid class structure. As such, the album is relevant for unmasking the reality of the "everyday life" of the working-class in 1964/1965 and 1972/1973.

Class, Politics, and Mod Culture (1964–1965)

Writers on youth culture have tended to view Mod as either apolitical or fundamentally conservative.[41] Yet it can be argued that the Mod subculture to which Townshend attempted to become a spokesman was political in the sense that it posed a challenge to particular social boundaries that were a feature of 1960s Britain. Moreover, Mod was an identity, subculture, and movement that seemingly aimed to transcend class but in many ways was an expression of its resilience.[42] The network of clubs, performers, and consumers that created Mod exhibited a sense of style and hedonism that had been a feature of pre-war working-class culture and had produced a particular critique of authority and convention expressed through fashion, music, and subcultural identity.[43] Strands of such a pre-war working-class culture remain in *Quadrophenia* and mesh sometimes uneasily with the affluence, consumerism, and modernity of the 1960s.

Townshend's history of Mod contained on *Quadrophenia* was based on events surrounding a concert by the Who at Brighton Aquarium on 29 March 1964, where he had witnessed the energy, excitement, and violence of working-class youths who had embraced the culture as a source of individual and collective identity.[44] The narrative documents the frustrations of a working-class youth, his connection and distance from the social milieu in which he was raised, and ultimately his attempt to transcend the conventions of his home, workplace, and locality through becoming a Mod. Songs making up the seventeen tracks on the album such as "Cut My Hair" (track 4), "The Punk and the Godfather" (track 5), "I'm One" (track 6), "The Dirty Jobs" (track 7), "Helpless Dancer" (track 8), and "I've Had Enough" (track 10), provide examples of the limitations of social, organisational, and subcultural identities and how a working-class teenager simultaneously feels a sense of both "belonging" and "distance". Such experiences are contextualised in a period in which Britain is still recovering from the impact of the Second

World War and significant social ruptures are transforming inner-city working-class communities.

Townshend aimed to create a "working-class hero" that the fans of the Who could identify with.[45] This would be somebody who reflected their desires, multiple identities, and imperfections. Aspects of working-class Britain are to the fore in Townshend's short essay that is printed on the album sleeve, the specially commissioned photographs that are used to convey a sense of period, in the lyrics, and the soundscapes located in the gaps between the conventional tracks. Townshend's rough and final drafts of the essay firmly locate Jimmy in a domestic and public working-class milieu. He lives on a diet of "chops, chips and fish fingers" and spends Saturday watching Brentford Football Club, who in the 1963/1964 season finished sixteenth in the third division of the English Football League. Jimmy's father would be drunk every night, refuelling on the "quintessentially cockney" pie and mash and his mother had a penchant for bottles of Guinness.[46] Townshend had explored similar themes in a much more superficial way on the Who single "Dogs" (1968). Lyrically this song highlighted Townshend's awareness of the resilience of a pre-war working-class culture. There are references to greyhound racing, gambling, heavy drinking, and the consumption of meat pies. There is a clear nod here to Hoggart's working-class community and the way in which particular cultures and identities underpinned the everyday life of labour, leisure, and domestic relationships. Similarly, one of the photographs in the *Quadrophenia* photo-essay contains its own image of a Hoggartian coffee bar adorned with pinball machines, Americana, and Pepsi-Colas. Yet it remains quintessentially British with its basic bare furnishings and lacking the colour and vibrancy of an American diner.[47]

Quadrophenia charts Jimmy's experiences in the home, workplace, club, and coffee bar, but it is also a comment on the experiences and problems that youth faced more generally in the post-war Britain of the mid-1960s and the period 1972/1974. Jimmy's father is a "socialist" and "war veteran" who espoused the pragmatism of Attlee's post-war policies that by the 1960s were being challenged by a new generation of activists in the party and the wider trade union movement who were critical of the limitations of established labour leaders.[48] Leaving school at fifteen, Jimmy is later employed by the local authority as a dustman and like Arthur Seaton in *Saturday Night and Sunday Morning* (1958) sees work as a means to an end in fuelling his hedonism. His attitude reflects the declining deference that was a feature of the trade union movement and labour politics more generally in the 1960s. In the essay, Townshend notes that Jimmy felt that the workers saw the local council as "a sort of church," and "the mayor as the Pope."[49] This was a characterisation of pragmatic Morrisonian socialism that had delivered much to the post-war working class.[50] Yet to Jimmy's generation this had almost anaesthetised the working-class of the 1960s to the point in which "they sit and stew while whole the world gets worse and worse."[51] The conflict between the socialism of Jimmy's father and the youths of the 1960s is further expressed in the track "Is It Me" that was not included on the original release, but later appeared on Townshend's director's cut in 2011.[52] Here we are introduced to a conversation between two fathers as they extoll the virtues of the British working-class, and the decency and dignity gained from Attlee's post-war socialism of public ownership and the creation of the welfare state. The patriarchs are perplexed by the fact that their "chosen path" had led to such a generational fracture in working-class families. The father of "Ace" (Bell Boy) another central character in *Quadrophenia* was a friend of Jimmy's father and they "were old-school working-class socialists" both disdainful of the fact that their Mod sons were immune to the solidarities and communalities of pragmatic post-war British socialism.[53]

Quadrophenia's Jimmy sees only conservatism and conformity in his parents' generation, but he also feels the pull and push of the London working-class from which he emerged. Through self-reflection he questions his own critique of his father's "chosen path" which is articulated in "Is It In My Head" (track 9). This process was also noted by Hoggart in his characterisation of the "grammar school" boy in *The Uses of Literacy* (1957). Yet unlike Hoggart's youths, Townshend's Jimmy is not the "depressing" "juke-box boy" and "passive consumer" of popular music. He represents a section of working-class youth who in the mid-1960s were using song, sound, and lyrics as a source of expression to make sense of their lives and their role in wider British society. The promise and futility of this is most clearly expressed in *Quadropenia*'s, "The Punk and the Godfather" (track 5). A key event in the 3-day chronology of the album's narrative is Jimmy's sense of betrayal at the distance created between Townshend, The Who, and the Mod fan base that they had attracted. Townshend's "Godfather" is one of many characters created in the 1960s and early 1970s symbolising the messianic potential of the rock star; see also Steven Shorter in Peter Watkins' film *Privilege*

(1967), Johnny Angelo in Nik Cohn's novel *I Am Still The Greatest Says Johnny Angelo* (1967), and Ziggy Stardust in David Bowie's album *The Rise and Fall of Ziggy Stardust and the Spiders from Mars* (1972).[54] The potency of rock music and its contribution to new forms of politics and struggles is also explored in Tony Palmer's documentary *All My Loving* (1968).[55] In all of these examples there is a clear sense that popular music and the rock star are offering something new to working-class youth that might to some seem to be ambiguous, shallow, corrupting, ultimately futile, but is nonetheless potent and transformative. The promise and betrayal of popular music that is encapsulated in "The Punk and the Godfather" is also a reflection on the limitations of the counter-culture that Townshend had first explored in "Won't Get Fooled Again" (1971) as part of the aborted Lifehouse project.[56]

Jimmy's engagement with the Mod subculture is conditioned by his inability to truly belong. In "Cut My Hair" (track 4), he is self-critical of the perceived unwritten rules and codes of the Mod subculture and acknowledges that his father is "really alright." The track spans the domestic sphere and the more open/public terrain of fashion, violence, and public transport. The historical focus of the album on 1964/1965 reveals much about the period and the continuities and ruptures in the working-class world of work, home, and street. A similarly un-swinging 1960s is also uncovered in Geoffrey Moorhouse' *The Other England* (1964).[57] The domestic images in *Quadrophenia*'s accompanying photographic essay bear similarities to Ken Loach's drama *Cathy Home* (1966) and the "kitchen sink politics" of the working-class home.[58] Domestic roles are clearly defined and Jimmy's interventions both strengthen and subvert the functioning of the nuclear family. Such reinforcement comes from Jimmy's embrace and promotion of gender identities and contemporary conceptions of masculinity and femininity. His bedroom is plastered with the low-grade and gritty pornography indicative of the English 1960s as opposed to the high-end eroticism and "swinging imagery" of the period's mythology. A scene similar to the one Townshend had earlier evoked on the hit single "Pictures of Lily" (1967) (Fig. 6.1).

Yet Jimmy's apparent alienation from the post-war norms and attitudes of the working-class also forms a critique of such culture. The images in *Quadrophenia* and the attitudes evoked contrast with the mythologies of "swinging London" and the narratives and images of the Wilson Government's new society built on the "white heat of

Fig. 6.1 Jimmy's bedroom. Photograph by Ethan Russell. Copyright © Ethan Russell. All rights reserved

technology." Wilson was elected in October 1964 after the seaside clashes of the Mods and Rockers that had taken place between March and August. His rhetoric and the liberalising reforms of his administrations between 1964/1966 and 1966/1970 have been used by some historians to highlight the ruptures in society and the creation of a "new Britain."[59] Yet contemporary observers such as Townshend and Ray Davies of the Kinks were already critiquing the claims being made for the changing lives of the working-class in this period. The workers featured in *Quadrophenia* are clearly an industrial and traditional proletariat and their teenage children are grappling with the legacy, meaning, and tensions of such experience and identity in the domestic and public sphere. Jimmy's frustrations and keenly felt in "I'm One" (track 6) and the repetitive nature of a proletarian world underpinned by the rigidity of work and the monotony of physical labour. The temporary release provided by being a Mod remains ultimately unfulfilling in the search for identity. Similar experiences are depicted in Sidney J. Furie's film of the pulp novel *The Leather Boys* (1964).[60] As in *Quadrophenia*, working-class youths soon become aware of the limitations of youth culture in being able to transcend social status, conventions, and economic inequalities.

The themes, images, sounds, and experiences that are contained in *Quadrophenia* highlight the continuities in working-class class culture in the post-war period. Sea, sand, sex, hedonism, deference, and rebellion all feature in the lyrical content, sonic components, and accompanying text and photographs. Rain, water, waves, and sand complement the key themes/personalities/soundscapes of the opening track "I Am The Sea" (track 1). The sea remains a source of escape and reflection, the sand represents the collective memory of annual holidays and collective forms of leisure. The seaside is a space for the hedonism of drink, dance, and sex. The rebellion is illustrated by the rampaging Mods and Rockers. In contrast to Ray Davies' nostalgic colourful presentation of Blackpool in "Autumn Almanac" (1967), Townshend's and Jimmy's Brighton is both a scene of transgression and liberation, but also one of conservatism, conformity, and class rigidities.[61] It is also an image of a darker Britain beyond the bright lights and candy floss. The photos depict a weather-beaten resort of empty beaches, brown seas, windswept promenades, down-at-heel cafes, and creaking piers.

Brighton dominates two sides of the album and is featured most prominently in "Sea and Sand" (track 12), "Drowned" (track 13), and "Bell Boy" (track 14). The seaside here being both a traditional working-class one of collective hedonism, but also in Jimmy's case providing a geography of expulsion, self-discovery, and ultimate failure. The personal journey here moves from his eviction from the family home to the bright lights and pulsating music of the "ballroom", through to the self-doubt and painful discovery that the Mod subculture cannot provide any answers to his inner longings and confusions. In "Drowned" (track 13), Jimmy places hope and the possibility of release/escape in the tides of the ocean; this being a reflection of the working-class culture and collective memories of Brighton, Margate, Southend, and Clacton. Contemporaries of Townshend, including John Lennon, Georgie Fame, and Van Morrison also recalled the importance of the British resorts such as Blackpool, Douglas, and Bangor as having similarly mythical qualities.[62] In "Bell Boy," Jimmy is exposed to both the liberating aspects of Brighton and its place as the site of the betrayal of the Mod subculture.

Jimmy's return to Brighton depicts a faded resort beyond the bright lights, hedonism, and escape of the seaside. The greasy spoon café, deserted pier, and grey/black sky, providing an image more attuned to the reality of the working-class holiday than to the colour, warmth, and levity of the mythical British postcard.[63]

The death of Winston Churchill in January 1965 and the election of Ted Heath as Conservative Party leader in the following July might have signalled a new politics, but the re-election of Wilson in 1966 and the subsequent fall of Labour in 1970 again exposed the rigidity of the class system and the limitations of British socialism. *Quadrophenia* captures the complexity and personal experience of this process. After 1966, the Mods might have grown up, fragmented, or moved into other examples of subcultural activity such as skinhead and northern soul, but music and fashion remained a source of identity, escape, and protest. The writing, recording, and release of *Quadrophenia* in 1972/1973 provides a further insight into a Britain that was beset by economic problems, political extremism, nationalist tensions, and the cultural politics of class.

CRISIS, CONFLICT, AND THE POST-WAR CONSENSUS (1972–1973)

Quadrophenia was written and recorded in the "two stormy summers" between 1972 and 1973.[64] The soundscapes between the seventeen tracks on the album are markers of a collective working-class experience of work, home, and leisure that was both contemporary and historical. Some of the tracks reflected the economic, cultural, and social contexts of British life in the early 1970s. In 1973, the recording sessions for *Quadrophenia* could have been hampered by the energy shortages that occurred as a result of the miners' overtime ban and the Who's Ramport Studios in Battersea were supplied with a generator to minimise any disruption.[65] The recording of the album had already been completed before the 3-day week to conserve energy came into effect in 1974. Nonetheless, the blackouts of 1972 engendered by the first national miners' strike since 1926 and the announcement by the Conservative Prime Minister Ted Heath that the country was now in "a state of emergency" did much to instil a sense of "crisis." In the same year, unemployment had risen to the highest levels since the depression of the 1930s.[66] The everyday life of the working-class in this period was punctuated by rising food prices, fuel shortages, and violence on the streets with the bombs of the Provisional Irish Republican Army (IRA) and agitation by the extreme right and left in the form of the National Front and the International Socialists. Youth culture was inhabited by a number of subcultures, tribes, and styles including glam Rockers, teddy boys, skinheads, suedeheads, hell's angels, and Northern Soul.[67] Unlike much of the counter-culture of the late 1960s, all of these identities/movements were firmly rooted in working-class communities.[68]

Townshend's Mods in general and Jimmy in particular are not the sophisticated, metropolitan mould-breakers of MacInnes' *Absolute Beginners* (1959) or the "dandies" of the 1960s. The Jimmy of *Quadrophenia* is a young working-class "dustman" who is disdainful of the way in which older trade unionists have been moderated by a particular form of Labour socialism that promised so much in the 1960s. The trials, tribulations, and political dislocation of Jimmy are of relevance to both 1964/1965 and 1972/1973. Generational conflict in the workplace and in the trade union movement had been highlighted by the Donovan Commission in 1968, which had noted declining deference between leaders and members and the growing power of shop stewards on the shop floor.[69] The Labour Government's attempt to tackle particular industrial relations problems in 1969's "In Place of Strife proposals" created divisions in the wider movement and ended in failure. The election of the Conservatives under Ted Heath in 1970 symbolised a rightward shift in the party, but his attempts to enforce the principles of his industrial relations policies in 1971 led to a mass campaign by the trade union movement, which effectively rendered the legislation powerless and it was repealed in 1974.[70]

There is no doubt that when writing *Quadrophenia*, Townshend was writing about the past, but with one eye on the contemporary events of 1972/1973. The Mods' relationship with aspects of working-class politics, identity, and experiences is explored most directly in "The Dirty Jobs," where Jimmy confronts his fellow workers by critiquing their industrial and political moderation. The song was recorded in the summer of 1972 during a year of a national miners' strike that had seen the effective use of mass picketing and a younger more militant strand of trade unionists challenging the diktats of their moderate leaders.[71] Sonically, the song was also able to "evoke the sense of men at painful work, being used like machines rather than human beings with feelings."[72] The track also contains sound samples/effects that sound like they are from a trade union demonstration and or picket line chanting.[73] Recorded in July it echoes working-class militancy and strike action that reached its most dramatic stage in the miner's dispute that lasted from 9 January to 28 February of that year. The moderate president of the National Union of Mineworkers (NUM), Joe Gormley, was unable curtail the mood of his members who had been suffering from falling wages, rising prices, and colliery closures in the previous six years.[74]

Jimmy's short exposure to the political moderation of his co-workers leads him to question their masculinity and to "remember how they used to fight." The title of the track is a direct reference to the "dirty jobs" dispute that erupted in October 1970 and led to the "dust men" going on strike amid scenes of uncollected rubbish and the increase of pollution in London.[75] Gormley himself was critical of the way in which "dust men" were now overtaking miners in terms of income levels. He told the NUM conference in 1971 that he was "not going to be a miners' leader if I cannot claim a bigger minimum wage for the lads who go underground than the lads carting the dustbins around London."[76] Townshend references the coal industry and the 1972 miners' strike in the lyrics of "The Dirty Jobs," which also features a bus driver (in some live presentations the driver appears as Jimmy's uncle) who transports the "miners to pits" that were presumably closed because of strike action. Interestingly, in 1972 the closest coal mines to London were Betteshanger, Snowdown, and Tilmanstone located in the Kent coalfield around 80 miles away but one which was steeped in trade union militancy.[77] Yet such was the country's dependence on coal that no locality was immune to impact of disputes in the industry. The National Coal Board (NCB) remained a huge concern in 1972 employing more than 260,000 and the NUM membership standing at well over 200,000 miners.[78] The closure of the Saltley fuel depot in Birmingham in February 1972 marked a symbolic victory for the miners and organised labour. In the period in which *Quadrophenia* was written, recorded, and released, the coal industry was regularly headline news. The picket line chanting that precedes "Helpless Dancer" (track 8) reflected the activism, collective voice, and power of the trade union movement.

In "Helpless Dancer," Townshend exposes the inequality, racism, and poverty that remained a feature of British society in 1972/1973. He later claimed "the song is about the last vestiges of a real Red Flag inspired worker's revolution through flash miners' strikes in the United Kingdom in 1972 that were sparked by mining disasters and poor working conditions from 1963 all the way to the recording."[79] Townshend had no doubt heard reports in March and July 1973 of the disasters at Lofthouse Colliery in Yorkshire and Markham in Derbyshire, which left 25 miners dead and many others injured. The sample of a brass band that precedes the track is also evocative of a pre-war Hoggartian working-class culture that was fragmenting, but still remained a crucial feature of coalfield communities.[80] Townshend also understood the ideological battles that were being fought in the British labour movement and the "mood of disgruntled British workers in unions being forced to consider Marxism over socialism."[81] Jimmy himself expresses "rage at both the oppressed worker's impotence and those who oppressed them."[82] Similar ground is covered by Ray Davies in the ambiguous critique of trade union leadership "Get Back In Line" (1970).[83] The power of organised labour ultimately found its apotheosis in the Strawbs hit single "Part of the Union" (1973) released in the same year as *Quadrophenia*.

Townshend's awareness of the limitations of the counter-culture of the 1960s and the continuing extent of inequality that is articulated in "Helpless Dancer" was also being given more serious and analytical treatment in social investigations such as Ken Coates and Alan Silburn's, *Poverty: the Forgotten Englishmen* (1970).[84] The track also references violent attacks on homosexuals and ethnic minorities that were a significant feature of urban and rural localities in 1972/1973.[85] On 1 July 1972, the first Gay Pride March had traversed the familiar route of mass protest from Trafalgar Square to Hyde Park.[86] A year later, studies exposed the level of endemic racism in the police force.[87] In "Helpless Dancer," Britain is a country that remains desperately divided by class and ethnicity. Here again we see Townshend's and Jimmy's frustration with the limitations of the post-war consensus. The track also contains a darkness that conveys the city as a place of immorality and urban danger where "if you complain you disappear."[88] In the early 1970s the metropolis was being investigated by reporters and concerned politicians who aimed to expose its endemic social problems. For runaway teenagers the bright lights of the city invited opportunity and transgression, but also a reality of poverty, violence, and sexual abuse.[89] To Blackwell and Seabrook, "the better world that that had been constructed on the ruins of the Victorian manufacturing towns was already beginning to show signs of disrepair. Not only had the factory-constructed blocks begun to leak and subside and graffiti and litter disfigure the landscaped surroundings, but also many of the structures of common life itself seemed to be breaking under the strain."[90]

A further microcosm of the British class structure and struggle is encapsulated in the photograph in the album that is placed to underpin the narrative that complements Jimmy's return to Brighton on "5:15" (track 11). Unlike the Kinks "Last of the Steam Powered Trains" (1968), which is an elegiac and nostalgic lament for a lost Britain and individual identity, Townshend's train remains a site of social contempt and class struggle.[91] In the "first class" compartment of the London to Brighton train, Jimmy attempts to subvert the generational and class divide of post-war Britain. Seated "magically bored" between the bowler-hatted city gents, his demeanour and deportment suggesting a sneering but ultimately futile critique of the class structure that Labour's post-war socialism had failed to dismantle. The heavily unionised British Rail was both a conduit for industrial militancy, and a symbol of the pragmatism of the post-war consensus. The "Beeching cuts" that led to the closure of branch lines and stations (peaking in 1964) and the replacement of steam by diesel failed to diminish the role of the railways in British national identity and in the collective psyche of the post-war working class. By 1972/1973, trains were transporting armies of young people to football matches where terrace violence was becoming endemic, and to the traditional seaside resorts for drink, music, sex, and summer violence.[92]

The characters depicted in *Quadrophenia*'s photo-essay were mostly drawn from the working-class youth who lived in the Thessaly Road area of Battersea and the Patmore council estate. A formal politics remains absent from the images, but when viewed in conjunction with listening to the sonic narrative, the everyday life of Battersea's working-class becomes apparent. The shot of the terraced housing, Queenstown Road with Battersea Power Station in the background, the greasy breakfast, and the piles of rubbish, create a scene largely untouched by the affluence and consumerism of the 1960s. Politically, Battersea remained solidly Labour from 1964 to 1979 in voting patterns and in the broader cultural pursuits of its working-class. The constituency had been represented by the socialist pioneer John Burns from 1892 to 1918. In 1922, Battersea North had been won by the Communist Sharpurji Saklatvala. From 1964 to 1979 the two seats (Battersea North and South) were held by Ernie Parry and Douglas Jay. The neighbouring Vauxhall seat was also strongly Labour and was represented by George Strauss.[93]

Fig. 6.2 Jimmy's Battersea is largely untouched by post-war affluence. Photograph by Ethan Russell. Copyright © Ethan Russell. All rights reserved

The Mods of the 1960s in this area and the then contemporary youth of 1972/1973 of Battersea were not the upwardly mobile affluent consumers of 1960s mythology, but industrial workers steeped in traditional working-class culture that was yet to be swept away by the forces of deindustrialisation and the later politics of Thatcherism (Fig. 6.2).

The spiritual dimension of *Quadrophenia* and Jimmy's quest for some kind of enlightenment also reflects the then contemporary working-class interest in the esoteric, the supernatural, and the fantastic. Jimmy's Catholic background no doubt shaped his quest for some kind of religious confirmation. The legendary record producer Joe Meek and Dave Davies of the Kinks also made incursions into alternative forms of knowledge and belief systems in the 1960s.[94] John Entwistle, the Who's bassist, was a practising freemason with a fascination with the macabre. Keith Moon, the drummer, was an avid viewer of British horror films.

Townshend himself had become a devotee of the Indian spiritual master Meher Baba.[95] In "Drowned," his characterisation of Jimmy's engagement with the sea is a quest for enlightenment. The 1970s ushered in a "golden age" of supernatural television and film and what were perceived to be the "real" hauntings of working-class domesticity. This culture reached its most sensational peak in 1977 with the Enfield poltergeist case, one of many working-class ghosts of the 1970s.[96] With its thunder, rain, and crashing waves *Quadrophenia* evoked a similar darkness. The last five pictures of the photo-essay depict a dark, gothic image of the sea, sand, and doom-laden sky. The economic and cultural crisis of the years 1972 to 1979 no doubt added to the sense of foreboding that gained popular currency in the media and the rhetoric of politicians of both left and right. Yet it was also indicative of the continuities in aspects of working-class culture that had been immune to affluence and new forms of consumerism and technology.

In cultural terms, *Quadrophenia* was both a historical perspective on the 1960s, and a contemporary critique of British society in 1972/1973. It shared particular themes and tropes with two key films that were released in the same year: Claude Whatham's *That'll Be The Day* (1973), and Lindsay Anderson's *O Lucky Man!* (1973); and to a lesser extent, Stanley Kubrick's *A Clockwork Orange* (1971) that was on general release a year later.[97] These films bear similarities to *Quadrophenia* in terms of period and subject matter, and offer particular versions of the numerous "state of the nation" polemics and interventions that were a feature of the decade. Whatham's *That'll Be The Day* (1973) based on a screenplay by the journalist Ray Connolly explores the impact of American rock 'n' roll on British society and is very loosely based on the career trajectories of the seminal working-class British pop/rock stars of the 1950s and 1960s.[98] Its release also chimed with a Teddy Boy revival that was symbolised by the "Rock 'n' Roll Festival" at London"s Wembley Stadium in August 1972. Anderson's *O Lucky Man!* (1973) follows the trials and tribulations of Mick Travis through a country beset by local government corruption, rigid class hierarchies, and decaying urban environments. And finally, Alex in *A Clockwork Orange* (1971) is the anti-hero of a dystopian society beset by juvenile delinquency and gang violence.[99]

Given the contemporary context, Jimmy was as much a character of 1972/1973 as he was of 1964/1965. The violent aspect of youth culture was also exploited in 1970–1974 through cult novels by Richard Allen, particularly *Skinhead* (1970), *Skinhead Escapes* (1972), and *Trouble for Skinhead* (1973).[100] The visual style of the album artwork shares similarities with the cinematic depiction of "suedeheads" in Barney Platts Mills' *Bronco Bullfrog* (1969), which also features a more nuanced and darker vision of late 1960s London.[101] In the months following the release of *Quadrophenia*, the vermin carrying the dreams of children referenced in "Helpless Dancer" rampage through London's urban landscape in James Herbert's hugely successful horror novel *The Rats* (1974).[102] The filth, greyness, and detritus of London's streets had been amply depicted on pages 9, 10, and 11 of the album's photo-essay. Four year later, the screen version of *Quadrophenia* was developed and directed in a further period of economic crisis and litter-strewn streets, leading to impending political transformation.

Quadrophenia Redux, Thatcherism, and the Fragmentation of Britain (1978–1979)

The salience and longevity of *Quadrophenia* was confirmed by the cinematic treatment that the album received at the end of the decade. The film was directed in 1978/1979 by Franc Roddam who himself had aimed to explore the character of Jimmy in the broader social and cultural context of post-war Britain.[103] He came to the film with little knowledge of the album, but an acute awareness of the importance that popular music had played in the construction of teenage working-class identities in the 1960s. Influenced by the generation of film and documentary makers of the British "new-wave" he was less concerned with the "spiritual aspects" of the narrative and more interested in making a youth film that was rooted in the realities, lives and experiences of the 1960s and 1970s.[104] Yet the attempt to "centre" class in the overall scope and feel of the film is only partly successful. The politics of the "everyday lives" of the working-class that are a solid feature of the films of British directors such as Ken Loach and to a lesser extent Mike Leigh are marginalised in favour of documenting familiar and mythologised aspects of the popular culture of the 1960s. Roddam aimed to capture the detail of the period and the visible impact that social changes were having on urban working-class youth and in this respect the film is largely convincing. The cinematic version complements the album in a number of ways, but ultimately the cultural and industrial politics of class that featured on the record is largely absent.[105]

The film has been the subject of some excellent critical analysis and it has found a place in the pantheon of British cult classics.[106] Yet most scholars and critics have failed to examine the differences between the album and its cinematic treatment and the ways in which the making of the film corresponded with the final assault on the post-war consensus, industrial miltancy, and the advent of the politics of Thatcherism. Roddam's attempt at social realism in his endeavours to capture the "reality" of the Mod culture of 1964/1965 was mostly successful, but the film is lighter in colour and tone than the original album narrative and accompanying photo-essay. The first photograph in the album's booklet features the grey-terraced housing of Battersea (a scene that owes much to stock images of the streets of the northern working-class that appeared on television and film in the 1960s and 1970s) is replaced by Jimmy riding his scooter down a vibrant road containing the pulsating features of the affluent British High Street. In many ways, the film signposts aspects of youth culture and the dilution of working-class identity in its individual and collective form that would become a feature of Britain in the 1980s.

Production started in the summer of 1978 with filming beginning in September and general release in August 1979. As with the "two stormy summers" of the making of the original album, the shooting of the film coincided with seismic shifts in Britain's economy, politics and popular culture. The economic instability that had rocked the country in 1976–1977 had been temporarily halted by Jim Callaghan's Labour Government. The trade unions had been placated by the "social contract," but by 1978, the fragile unity between the party and the movement began to fragment. In the month that *Quadrophenia* began filming, Callaghan refused to call an expected general election. The events that followed would transform British politics and the Labour Party would remain out of power until 1997. The "Winter of Discontent," which centred on low-paid workers in the public sector in 1978–1979, once again exposed the fault lines in British society that remained divided by class, ethnicity, and region.[107] The dramas of "The Dirty Jobs" and "Helpless Dancer" were played out over kitchen tables, clubs, pubs, bingo halls, and party committee rooms. Miners continued to die in the mines evidenced by the Golbourne explosion in 1978, and trade union solidarity was expressed in the mass pickets of the Grunwick dispute of 1976–1978. Yet this period was to witness the defeat of the organised working-class in a most systematic way through electoral politics, government legislation, and the forces of the British state. The minorities of "Helpless Dancer" continued to face daily racism and exploitation. Attempts to fight back, such as in Southall in 1979, led to violence and the death of Blair Peach, and campaigns against persecution by an institutionally racist Metropolitan Police, were exposing significant fault lines in British society.[108]

The election of Margaret Thatcher in May 1979 and subsequent victory of the Conservatives in 1983 reversed many of the advances that the organised working-class had made in the years 1964–1974. The labour institutions that had shaped the political and cultural consciousness of Jimmy's father, and to a lesser extent Jimmy himself, were systematically dismantled through significant pieces of legislation that eroded the rights of employees in the workplace. The failure of the strike in the steel industry in 1980 was followed by the calamitous defeat of the coal miners in 1984/1985, and the printers a year later.[109] The "chosen path" of Jimmy's father's generation was destroyed by deindustrialisation, privatisation, and the economics of globalisation and neoliberalism. The working-class of Shepherd's Bush and Battersea largely continued to vote for the Labour Party, but the broader zeitgeist suggested that the Labour socialism that had been constructed by Attlee in the post-war period was in retreat. This aspect of *Quadrophenia* continued to inform the Who's vision of the piece in the subsequent concert tour of 2012–2013 with accompanying film presenting a montage of the post-war consensus that included the welfare state, the National Health Service (NHS), and the NCB.[110]

The filming of *Quadrophenia* was bookended by two waves of youth subculture that once again given rise to vibrancy, violence, and a working-class incursion into the music industry and the politics of the street. Some of the Mods and skinheads who had been contemporaries of the album had found a home in the pulsating working-class Northern Soul scene of the industrial English Midlands, Lancashire/Yorkshire, and North Wales. Elements of the original rhythm and blues and soul sounds that the Mods had absorbed in 1964–1965 were now being devoured in draughty provincial halls and the faded grandeur of the Wigan Casino.[111] From late 1976 to 1978, punk rock had made records, anti-heroes, and headlines. The energy and experiences of punk are clearly there in the origins, personnel, and filming of *Quadrophenia*, but the politics is largely absent.[112] When the film was completed, a full-scale Mod revival that had germinated prior to the film's initial production schedule in 1978 was underway, and by the time of its release a year later it was a national phenomenon.[113] Roddam's film was strengthened by the contributions of original Mods and Who fans such as Pete Meaden, Alan Fletcher, and Jack Lyons.[114]

The film treatment lacks the gritty realism of the album and in many ways articulates many of the stock mythologies of the 1960s. The fact that it was shot in colour is a significant departure from the feel and tone of the album. On one level, it depicts the "swinging London" of MacInnes's Soho rather than the coffee bars and jukebox boys of Hoggart's working-class. Jimmy in this version is not a "dust-man" but a runner for an adverting agency. His father on screen is constructed here as rather "one dimensional" as opposed to the veteran socialist and trade unionist that Townshend had in the mind for the original concept. The dirt, grime, and monotony of everyday life and the working-class politics of "The Dirty Jobs" and "Helpless Dancer" is also notably absent. Both tracks are omitted from the accompanying soundtrack album.[115] Some of the original pieces from the 1973 album are also given polish through orchestration. The inclusion of an assortment of rhythm and blues tracks from the 1960s also gives the soundtrack an overt sense of nostalgia and plasticity.

The individualism and autonomy of the Mods on screen is perhaps a pointer to the politics of the 1980s where solidarity, communality, and the remnants of a working-class culture that had been preserved by the post-war consensus would be almost destroyed through deindustrialisation, a rapid collapse in the number of trade unionists, and the neutralisation of the political left. However, the reception, consumption, and use of the film and the soundtrack suggest a greater complexity. The Mod revival that accompanied the production and release of the film was predominantly working-class.[116] Once again, thousands of teenagers were defining themselves through a subcultural identity and activity that formed one response to the economic and social context of 1978–1980. Mods appeared in schools, youth clubs, factories, coalmines, and the service sector of the economy. Violence was reported at seaside resorts and the incoming Conservative government constructed sections of working-class youth as a contemporary social problem. The success of the film and subsequent live tours, theatrical productions, and even an academic conference gave Townshend's *Quadrophenia* greater salience in the twenty-first century.[117] The music of the Who and the place of the Mods remain symbolic as markers of the explosion and impact of popular culture on working-class youth in post-war Britain.

In conclusion, the work of Pete Townshend in general and *Quadrophenia* in particular has been overlooked by historians when charting the ways in which popular music was providing a critical commentary on the continuities and changes that were a feature of British working-class life in the 1960s and 1970s. *Quadrophenia* presents a more nuanced and sophisticated analysis of Mod and "swinging London" than exists in some of the more popular and academic narratives of the period. The album is a compelling slice of social history that should be "read" alongside the sociological and historical explorations of youth in post-war Britain. Moreover, it offers an insight into the world of London's working-class in Shepherd's Bush and Battersea in 1964/1965 and 1973/1974 that would never quite be the same again after the impact of Thatcherism, de-industrialisation, and the neutralisation of particular forms of labour politics. The promise of the post-war consensus in these years had its limitations, but offered much to Jimmy's generation in terms of affluence, economic democracy, and equality. Yet, this proved to be brittle. From the vantage point of the twenty-first century, we can now see that "things ain't quite that simple."

Notes

1. The album was recorded and released under the name of the Who, but the concept, lyrics, and music were credited to Townshend. In the sleeve notes to the album the credits list "Quadrophenia" in its entirety by Pete Townshend. The Who, *Quadrophenia* (Track Records, 1973) LP.
2. For details of strikes in this period see Dave Lyddon, "Glorious Summer, 1972", in John McIlroy, Nina Fishman and Alan Campbell (eds), *The High Tide of British Trade Unionism: Trade Unions and Industrial Politics, 1964–1979* (Monmouth, 2007), pp. 326–352.
3. Roger Daltrey of the Who made a significant contribution to anchoring the narrative of *Quadrophenia* in the broader context of post-war politics, deindustrialisation and the plight of the British working-class in later incarnations of the piece for live performances in 1996/1997 and 2012/2013. For details see audio commentary on the Who, *Tommy and Quadrophenia Live* (Rhino, 2005) DVD.

4. *Quadrophenia* in particular and Townshend's work more generally has been neglected by historians of the post-war period. The album does not merit a reference in three highly regarded books on the history of the 1970s: Dominic Sandbrook, *State of Emergency: The Way We Were, 1970–1974* (London: Allen Lane, 2010); Andy Beckett, *When the Lights Went Out: Britain in the Seventies* (London: Faber and Faber, 2009); and Alwyn W. Turner, *Crisis? What Crisis? Britain in the 1970s* (London: Aurum Press, 2008).
5. For a similar use of popular music as a significant historical source see Keith Gildart, *Images of England Through Popular Music: Class, Youth and Rock 'n' Roll, 1955–1976* (Basingstoke: Palgrave Macmillan, 2013).
6. Alan Sillitoe, *Saturday Night and Sunday Morning* (London: W. H. Allen, 1958).
7. Karel Reisz, *We Are The Lambeth Boys* (1959) (Duke Video, 2009) DVD.
8. Michael Young and Peter Willmott, *Family and Kinship in East London* (Harmondsworth: Penguin, 1957).
9. Anthony Sampson, *The Anatomy of Britain* (London: Hodder and Stoughton, 1962).
10. Nell Dunn, *Up The Junction* (London: Macgibbon and Kee, 1963) and *Poor Cow* (London: Macgibbon and Kee, 1967).
11. Pete Townshend, *Quadrophenia: The Director's Cut* (UMC, 2011) CD.
12. Colin MacInnes, *Absolute Beginners* (London: Macgibbon and Kee, 1959). The link between Mod, affluence, and the "new" working-class of post war-Britain is also reiterated in the two significant critical studies of the film: Stephen Glynn, *Quadrophenia* (London: Wallflower Press, 2014) and Simon Wells, *Quadrophenia A Way of Life- Inside The Making of Britain's Greatest Youth Film* (London: Countdown Books, 2014).
13. For the Kinks and the working-class see Keith Gildart, "From Dead End Streets to Shangri Las: Negotiating Social Class and Post-War Politics with Ray Davies and the Kinks," *Contemporary British History* 26: 3 (2012): 273–298.
14. Some of the material in this section also appears in Gildart, *Images of England*, Chapter 4.
15. For autobiographical/biographical details see Pete Townshend, *Who I Am* (London: Harper Collins, 2012); Geoffrey Gialiano, *Behind Blue Eyes. A Life of Pete Townshend* (London: Hodder and Stoughton, 1996) and Mark Wilkerson, *Who Are You. The Life of Pete Townshend. A Biography* (London: Omnibus Press, 2009). There is also some useful information in the early chapters of Dave Marsh, *Before I Get Old: The Story of the Who* (London: Plexus, 1985).

16. Pete Doggett, *There's A Riot Going On: Revolutionaries, Rock Stars and the rise and fall of the 60s Counter Culture* (Edinburgh: Canongate, 2007).
17. Townshend, *Who I Am*, p. 4.
18. *New Musical Express*, 12 March 1983.
19. Along with John Lennon, Ray Davies and John Lydon, Townshend was arguably one of the four most significant "organic intellectuals" in the post-war popular music industry who through their work explored and critiqued aspects of British society. For further discussion of musicians as "organic intellectuals" see Gildart, *Images of England*, introduction.
20. Pete Townshend, "Two Stormy Summers," in *Quadrophenia: The Director's Cut*, p. 16.
21. In the 1930s, Townshend's father had briefly been a member of the British Union of Fascists. See Townshend, *Who I Am*, p. 8.
22. Townshend, *Who I Am*, p. 35.
23. Townshend, *Who I Am*, p. 33.
24. For the roots of the Who and the various permutations that led to their formation see the early chapters of Marsh, *Before I Get Old*.
25. See Townshend, *Who I Am*, p. 56. For the culture of art schools and their connection to the popular music scene of the 1960s see Simon Frith and Howard Horne, *Art into Pop* (London: Methuen, 1987), Chapter 3.
26. Kevin Davey, *English Imaginaries: Six Studies in Anglo-British Modernity* (London: Lawrence and Wishart, 1999), p. 81. Townshend does not shed light on whether he was a member of these organisations in his autobiography.
27. Robin Denselow, *When The Music's Over: The Story of Political Pop* (London: Faber and Faber, 1989), 93.
28. Denselow, *When The Music's Over*, p. 95.
29. Townshend claims that the title came from *Generations* a collection of plays by the socialist playwright David Mercer. Townshend, *Who I Am*, p. 83.
30. Townshend, "Two Stormy Summers," p. 20.
31. For the place of Mods in this process see Paul Gilroy, *There Ain't No Black in the Union Jack* (London: Routledge, 1987), p. 215.
32. For recollections see Mark Sargeant, "Looking back with Irish Jack," *Scootering*, 163, September 1999. "Irish Jack" Lyons was one of a number of Mods who Townshend drew on in creating the Jimmy character for the *Quadrophenia* album in 1972–1973.
33. Mim Scala, *Diary of a Teddy Boy: A Memoir of the Long Sixties* (London: Headline, 2000), 80.

34. Joe McMichael and Jack Lyons, *The Who Concert File* (London: Omnibus, 1977), 14.
35. Marsh, *Before I Get Old*, p. 423.
36. Davey, *English Imaginaries*, p. 100, 102.
37. *Uncut*, June 2009.
38. The photographs were taken by Ethan Russell. For background and his work on popular music, see Ethan Russell, *Dear Mr Fantasy. Diary of A Decade: Our Time and Rock 'n' Roll* (London: Houghton Mifflin, 1985).
39. See Ritchie Unterberger, *Won't Get Fooled Again: The Who from Lifehouse to Quadrophenia* (London: Jawbone Press, 2011), 241.
40. Russell, *Dear Mr Fantasy*, p. 210.
41. Such assumptions have been largely drawn from the interviews in the seminal article on Mods that appeared in *Town* magazine in September 1962.
42. The working-class aspect of Mod has often been downplayed by commentators and historians. For discussion see Richard Weight, *Mod: A Very British Style* (London: The Bodley Head, 2013) Chapter 2.
43. For inter-war working-class consumption see David Fowler, "Teenage Consumers? Young wage-earners and leisure in Manchester, 1919–1939", in Andrew Davies and Steven Fielding (eds.), *Workers' Worlds: Cultures and Communities in Manchester and Salford, 1880–1939* (Manchester: Manchester University Press, 1992), 133–155.
44. For a short insightful critical analysis of *Quadrophenia* see James Wood, "The Kids Are Alright," *The Guardian*, 30 May 2009. Another source has claimed that it was a show a year later in Brighton on 17 April 1965 that was the impetus for *Quadrophenia*. See McMichael and Lyons, *The Who Concert File*, p. 29. In the hand-written notes to Townshend's *Quadrophenia; The Director's Cut* (2011) he dates it as the summer 1964 but dedicated to the fans of 1966. Yet he has more recently reiterated that 1964 was the year. See Townshend, *Who I Am*, p. 245.
45. Townshend, "Two Stormy Summers," p. 15.
46. Pete Townshend, draft essay included in *Quadrophenia: The Director's Cut*.
47. The coffee bar in *Quadrophenia* is far less glamorous and sophisticated than those in Soho depicted by the Rank Organisation's short film on the subject in the *Look at Life* series made in 1959.
48. For a critical appraisal of party in this period see James Hinton, *Labour and Socialism: A History of the British Labour Movement 1867–1974* (London: Wheatsheaf Books, 1983) Chapter 11. For the shifting politics of the trade unions see essays in John McIlroy, Nina Fishman and Alan Campbell (eds.), *The High Tide of British Trade Unionism: Trade*

Unions and Industrial Politics, 1964–1979 (Monmouth: Merlin Press, 2007).
49. The Who, *Quadrophenia* (Track, 1973) LP.
50. Herbert Morrison was a Labour MP, Cabinet Minister, and London County Councillor who provided the blueprint for the party's programme of nationalisation in the post-war period. For biography, see Bernard Donoghue and George Jones, *Herbert Morrison—Portrait of a Politician* (London: Littlehampton Book Services, 1973).
51. The Who, *Quadrophenia* (Track, 1973) LP.
52. Pete Townshend, *Quadrophenia: The Director's Cut*.
53. Townshend, "Two Stormy Summers," p. 88.
54. Peter Watkins *Privilege* (1967) (BFI, 2011) DVD; Nik Cohn, *I Am Still the Greatest Says Johnny Angelo* (London, 1967); David Bowie, *The Rise and Fall of Ziggy Stardust and the Spiders from Mars* (RCA, 1972) LP.
55. Tony Palmer, *All My Loving* (1968) (Plastic Head, 2007) DVD.
56. For an extended critical analysis of the Lifehouse project, see Unterberger, *Won't Get Fooled Again*.
57. Geoffrey Moorhouse, *Britain in the Sixties: The Other England* (Harmondsworth: Penguin, 1964).
58. For discussion of *Cathy Come Home* see John Hill, *Ken Loach: The Politics of Film and Television* (London: Palgrave Macmillan, 2011), Chapter 3.
59. For example, see Arthur Marwick, *The Sixties: Cultural Revolution in Britain, France, Italy and the United States* (Oxford: Oxford University Press, 1998).
60. Gillian Freeman, *The Leather Boys* (London, 1969).
61. In Blackpool on 23 September, the High Numbers supported the Beatles and the Kinks at the Opera House; the only time that three of the key-groups of the 1960s would share a stage together and influence for lyric in "5:15" referring to "Eau-de-cologning."
62. See Gildart, *Images of England*, Chapter 1.
63. A similar scene is created later by Morrissey in his single "Everyday Is Like Sunday" (HMV, 1988) Single.
64. For chronology and recording process, see Townshend, "Two Stormy Summers."
65. For the development of Ramport, see interviews in the television documentary *Quadrophenia: Can You See The Real Me?* (BBC, 2012).
66. For the best insightful narrative of the period see Beckett, *When the Lights Went Out: Britain in the Seventies* (London: Faber and Faber, 2009).

67. For a recent reappraisal of glam rock see Simon Reynolds, *Shock and Awe: Glam Rock and its Legacy* (London: Faber and Faber, 2016). See also Gildart, *Images of England*, Chapter 7.
68. This period also ushered in a "golden age" of academic studies of youth and popular music epitomised by the Birmingham Centre for Contemporary Cultural Studies. For summary and critique, see Gildart, *Images of England*, pp. 3–5.
69. For a survey of trade union politics in this period see John McIlroy and Alan Campbell, "The High Tide of Trade Unionism: Mapping Industrial Politics, 1964–1979," in McIlroy, Fishman and Campbell, *The High Tide of British Trade Unionism*, pp. 93–130.
70. The industrial militancy of the period 1970–1974 is in need of serious historical reappraisal. A brief but flawed survey can be found in Dave Lyddon, *Glorious Summer: Class Struggle in Britain 1972* (London: Bookmarks, 2001).
71. A militant miner's perspective of these events can be found in Malcolm Pitt, *The World on Our Backs: the Kent Miners and the 1972 Miners' Strike* (London: Lawrence and Wishart, 1979).
72. Townshend, "Two Stormy Summers," p. 83. The track also echoes Daltrey's experiences when he was employed for five years as a sheet-metal worker in a local factory.
73. The author of this chapter was also responsive to the industrial elements of *Quadrophenia* reciting tracks from the album to get through the monotony of working seven-hour shifts underground in a North Wales coal mine.
74. For an insightful account of pit closures and their impact on the politics of mining trade unionism, see Vic Allen, *The Militancy of British Miners* (Shipley: The Moor Press, 1981) Chapter 7.
75. For a contemporary account of the politics of labour in this period, see Tony Benn, *Office Without Power: Diaries 1968–1972* (London: Hutchison, 1988).
76. David Powell, *The Power Game: The Struggle for Coal* (London: Duckworth, 1993), 187.
77. For the Kent coalfield in this period see Pitt, *The World On Our Backs*.
78. For the union in this period, see Andrew Taylor, *The NUM and British Politics Volume 2: 1969–1995* (Aldershot: Ashgate, 2005), Chapter 2.
79. Townshend, "Two Stormy Summers," pp. 32–34.
80. The Who's bass player John Entwistle was also a fan of brass bands and the music that had emerged from the mining communities of England, Scotland, and Wales.
81. Townshend, "Two Stormy Summers," p. 85.
82. Townshend, "Two Stormy Summers," p. 85.

83. For a discussion of "Get Back In Line," see Gildart, *Images of England*, p. 143.
84. Ken Coates and Alan Silburn, *Poverty: The Forgotten Englishman* (Harmondsworth: Penguin, 1970).
85. This period was also the high point of corruption in the Metropolitan Police. For details, see Barry Cox, John Shirley and Martin Short, *The Fall of Scotland Yard* (Harmondsworth: Penguin, 1977).
86. For the role of gay liberation in the wider politics of the left see Lucy Robinson, *Gay Men and the Left in Post-war Britain: How the Personal got Political* (Manchester: Manchester University Press, 2011).
87. Maureen Cain, *Society and the Policeman's Role* (London: Routledge, 1973).
88. The violence of sections of working-class youth that remained a feature of London's council estates in 1973 is explored in David Robbins and Philip Cohen, *Knuckle Sandwich: Growing up in the Working-class City* (Harmondsworth: Penguin, 1978) part two.
89. For example, see Michael Deakin and John Wills, *Johnny Go Home* (London: Futura, 1976).
90. Trevor Blackwell and Jeremy Seabrook, *A World Still To Win: The Reconstruction of the Post-War Working Class* (London: Faber and Faber, 1985), 137.
91. For a discussion of the Kinks music and social class in the 1960s/1970s, see Gildart, *Images of England*, Chapter 6.
92. For a social history of the railways in this period, see Simon Bradley, *The Railways: Nation, Network and People* (London: Profile Books, 2015).
93. For the economic and social context of the Battersea constituencies between the general elections of 1964 and 1974, see Robert J. Waller, *The Almanac of British Politics* (London: Routledge, 1983).
94. See John Repsch, *The Legendary Joe Meek: The Telstar Man* (London: Cherry Red Books, 1989) and Dave Davies, *Kink: An Autobiography* (London: Boxtree, 1996) especially Chapter 15.
95. For Townshend's devotion to Baba, see sections in Townshend, *Who I Am*.
96. See Guy Lyon Playfair, *This House Is Haunted: The True Story of the Enfield Poltergeist* (London: White Crow Books, 2011).
97. For a critical reading of the development of the British pop music film, see Stephen Glynn, *The British Pop Music Film: The Beatles and Beyond* (Basingstoke: Palgrave Macmillan, 2013).
98. Ray Connolly, *That'll Be The Day* (Glasgow: Harper Collins, 1973).
99. For British cinema in this period, see Sue Harper and Justin Smith, *British Film Culture in the 1970s: The Boundaries of Pleasure* (Edinburgh: Edinburgh University Press, 2012) particularly Chapter 8.

100. For a critical appraisal of Allen's novels, see Bill Osgerby, "Bovver Books of the 1970s: Subcultures, Crisis and 'Youth-Sploitation' Novels," *Contemporary British History*, 26: 3 (2012): 299–331.
101. For links between *Quadrophenia and Bronco Bullfrog* see Unterberger, *Won't Get Fooled Again*, p. 240.
102. James Herbert, *The Rats* (London: New English Library, 1974).
103. For a detailed account of the making of the film, see Wells, *Quadrophenia A Way of Life*.
104. For a critical assessment of the "new wave" and its impact on working-class cinema, see John Hill, *Sex, Class and Realism: British Cinema 1956–1963* (London: British Film Institute, 1986).
105. For minutiae relating to the film, see Gary Wharton, *Chasing the Wind: A Quadrophenia Anthology* (Somerset: Lushington Publishing, 2002).
106. For example, see Stephen Glynn, *Quadrophenia*.
107. For a recent narrative of events, see John Shepherd, *Crisis? What Crisis? The Callaghan Government and the British Winter of Discontent* (Manchester: Manchester University Press, 2013).
108. For the cultural response to racism, see Gilroy, *There Ain't No Black in the Union Jack*.
109. For the most recent detailed account of the miners' strike, see Francis Beckett and David Hencke, *Marching to the Fault Line: The 1984 Miners' Strike and the Death of Industrial Britain* (London: Constable, 2009).
110. See *The Who: Quadrophenia Live in London* (UMC, 2014) DVD.
111. For an autobiographical insight into the history of Northern Soul, see Stuart Cosgrove, *Young Soul Rebels: A Personal History of Northern Soul* (London: Polygon, 2016).
112. The best book on the social and political context of punk remains Jon Savage, *England's Dreaming: Sex Pistols and Punk Rock* (London: Faber and Faber, 1991).
113. For the Mods of 1979, see Gary Bushell, *Time For Action: The Mod Revival 1978–1981* (London: Bertrams, 2012).
114. For a recent biography of Meaden, see Pete Wilky and John Hellier, *I'm the Face: Pete Meaden* (London: Griffith Books, 2016).
115. "Helpless Dancer" is included on the film soundtrack, but is a truncated twenty-two-second version that contains no lyrics. See *Music from the soundtrack of The Who film Quadrophenia* (Polydor, 1979) LP.
116. See Bushell, *Time For Action*.
117. The conference that led to the publication of this book: Here By The Sea And Sand: A Symposium on *Quadrophenia*, University of Sussex, 10–11 July 2014.

BIBLIOGRAPHY

Sources

A Clockwork Orange, directed by Stanley Kubrick, Hawk Films, 1971.
All My Loving, directed by Tony Palmer, BBC, 1968.
Allen, Richard. *Skinhead*. London: New English Library, 1970.
Allen, Richard. *Skinhead Escapes*. London: New English Library, 1972.
Allen, Richard. *Trouble for Skinhead*. London: New English Library, 1973.
Allen, Vic. *The Militancy of British Miners*. Shipley: The Moor Press, 1981.
Beckett, Andy. *When the Lights Went Out: Britain in the Seventies*. London: Faber and Faber, 2009.
Beckett, Francis and Hencke, David. *Marching to the Fault Line: The 1984 Miners" Strike and the Death of Industrial Britain*. London: Constable, 2009.
Benn, Tony. *Office Without Power: Diaries 1968-72*. London: Hutchinson, 1988.
Blackwell, Trevor and Seabrook, Jeremy. *A World Still to Win: The Reconstruction of the Post-War Working Class*. London: Faber and Faber, 1985.
Bowie, David. *The Rise and Fall of Ziggy Stardust and the Spiders from Mars*. RCA, 1972.
Bradley, Simon. *The Railways: Nation, Network and People*. London: Profile Books, 2015.
Bronco Bullfrog, directed by Barney Platts-Mills, EMI Films, 1969.
Bushell, Gary. *Time For Action: The Mod Revival 1978–1981*. London: Bertrams, 2012.
Cain, Maureen. *Society and the Policeman's Role*. London: Routledge 1973.
Coates, Ken and Silburn, Alan. *Poverty: The Forgotten Englishman*. Harmondsworth: Penguin, 1970.
Cohn, Nik. *I Am Still the Greatest Says Johnny Angelo*. Harmondsworth: Penguin, 1967.
Connolly, Ray. *That'll Be The Day*. Glasgow: Harper Collins, 1973.
Cosgrove, Stuart. *Young Soul Rebels: A Personal History of Northern Soul*. London: Polygon, 2016.
Cox, Barry, Shirley, John and Short, Martin. *The Fall of Scotland Yard*. Harmondsworth: Penguin, 1977.
Davey, Kevin. *English Imaginaries: Six Studies in Anglo-British Modernity*. London: Lawrence and Wishart, 1999.
Davies, Dave. *Kink: An Autobiography*. London: Boxtree, 1996.
Deakin, Michael and Wills, John. *Johnny Go Home*. London: Futura, 1976.
Denselow, Robin. *When The Music's Over: The Story of Political Pop*. London: Faber and Faber, 1989.
Doggett, Pete. *There's A Riot Going On: Revolutionaries, Rock Stars and the rise and fall of the 60s Counter Culture*. Edinburgh: Canongate, 2007.

Donoghue, Bernard and Jones, George. *Herbert Morrison—Portrait of a Politician*. London: Littlehampton Book Services, 1973.
Dunn, Nell. *Poor Cow*. London: Macgibbon and Kee, 1967.
Dunn, Nell. *Up The Junction*. London: Macgibbon and Kee, 1963.
Fowler, David. "Teenage Consumers? Young wage-earners and leisure in Manchester, 1919–1939". In *Workers' Worlds: Cultures and Communities in Manchester and Salford, 1880–1939*, edited by Andrew Davies and Steven Fielding, 133–155, Manchester: Manchester University Press, 1992.
Freeman, Gillian. *The Leather Boys*. London: New English Library, 1969.
Frith, Simon and Horne, Howard. *Art into Pop*. London: Methuen, 1987.
Gialiano, Geoffrey. *Behind Blue Eyes. A Life of Pete Townshend*. London: Hodder and Stoughton, 1996.
Gildart, Keith. "From Dead End Streets to Shangri Las: Negotiating Social Class and Post-War Politics with Ray Davies and the Kinks", *Contemporary British History*, 26, 3 (2012) 273–98.
Gildart, Keith. *Images of England Through Popular Music: Class, Youth and Rock "n" Roll, 1955–1976*. Basingstoke: Palgrave Macmillan, 2013.
Gilroy, Paul. *There Ain't No Black in the Union Jack*. London: Routledge, 1987.
Glynn, Stephen. *Quadrophenia*. London: Wallflower Press, 2014.
Glynn, Stephen. *The British Pop Music Film: The Beatles and Beyond*. Basingstoke: Palgrave Macmillan, 2013.
Harper, Sue and Smith, Justin. *British Film Culture in the 1970s: The Boundaries of Pleasure*. Edinburgh: Edinburgh University Press, 2012.
Herbert, James *The Rats*. London: New English Library, 1974.
Hill, John. *Ken Loach: The Politics of Film and Television*. London: Palgrave Macmillan, 2011.
Hill, John. *Sex, Class and Realism: British Cinema 1956-63*. London: British Film Institute, 1986.
Hinton, James. *Labour and Socialism: A History of the British Labour Movement 1867-1974*. London: Wheatsheaf Books, 1983.
Look At Life: Coffee Bars, Rank Organisation, 1959.
Lyddon, Dave. "Glorious Summer, 1972". In *The High Tide of British Trade Unionism: Trade Unions and Industrial Politics, 1964-79* edited by John McIlroy, Nina Fishman and Alan Campbell, 326–352. Monmouth: Merlin Press, 2007.
Lyddon, Dave. *Glorious Summer: Class Struggle in Britain 1972*. London: Bookmarks, 2001.
MacInnes, Colin. *Absolute Beginners*. London: Macgibbon and Kee, 1959.
Marsh, Dave. *Before I Get Old: The Story of the Who*. London: Plexus, 1985.
Marwick, Arthur. *The Sixties: Cultural Revolution in Britain, France, Italy and the United States*. Oxford: Oxford University Press, 1998.

McIlroy, John and Campbell, Alan, "The High Tide of Trade Unionism: Mapping Industrial Politics, 1964–1979". In *The High Tide of British Trade Unionism: Trade Unions and Industrial Politics, 1964–1979* edited by John McIlroy, Nina Fishman and Alan Campbell 93–130. Monmouth: Merlin Press, 2007.
McMichael, Joe and Lyons, "Irish" Jack. *The Who Concert File*. London, Omnibus, 1997.
Moorhouse, Geoffrey. *Britain in the Sixties: The Other England*. Harmondsworth; Penguin, 1964.
Music from the soundtrack of The Who film Quadrophenia. Polydor, 1979.
New Musical Express.
O Lucky Man!, directed by Lindsay Anderson, Warner Bros., 1973.
Osgerby, Bill. "Bovver Books of the 1970s: Subcultures, Crisis and "Youth-Sploitation" Novels", *Contemporary British History*, 26, 3 (2012) 299–331.
Pitt, Malcolm. *The World on Our Backs: the Kent Miners and the 1972 Miners" Strike*. London: Lawrence and Wishart, 1979.
Playfair, Guy Lyon. *This House Is Haunted: The True Story of the Enfield Poltergeist*. London: White Crow Books, 2011.
Powell, David. *The Power Game: The Struggle for Coal*. London: Duckworth, 1993.
Privilege, directed by Peter Watkins, Universal Pictures, 1967.
Quadrophenia, directed by Franc Roddam, The Who Films, 1979.
Quadrophenia: Can You See The Real Me?, directed by Matt O'Casey, BBC, 2012.
Repsch, John. *The Legendary Joe Meek: The Telstar Man*. London: Cherry Red Books, 1989.
Reynolds, Simon. *Shock and Awe: Glam Rock and its Legacy*. London: Faber and Faber 2016.
Robins, David and Cohen, Philip. *Knuckle Sandwich: Growing Up in the Working-class City*. Harmondsworth: Penguin, 1978.
Robinson, Lucy. *Gay Men and the Let in Post-war Britain: How the Personal got Political*. Manchester: Manchester University Press, 2011.
Rock Around the Clock, directed by Fred F. Sears, Columbia Pictures, 1956.
Russell, Ethan. *Dear Mr Fantasy. Diary of A Decade: Our Time and Rock "n" Roll*. Boston: Houghton Mifflin Company, 1985.
Sampson, Anthony. *The Anatomy of Britain*. London: Hodder and Stoughton, 1962.
Sandbrook, Dominic. *State of Emergency: The Way We Were, 1970–1974*. London: Allen Lane, 2010.
Sargeant, Mark. "Looking back with Irish Jack", *Scootering*, 163, (September 1999).

Savage, Jon. *England's Dreaming: Sex Pistols and Punk Rock*. London: Faber and Faber, 1991.
Scala, Mim. *Diary of a Teddy Boy: A Memoir of the Long Sixties*. London: Headline, 2000.
Shepherd, John. *Crisis? What Crisis? The Callaghan Government and the British Winter of Discontent*. Manchester: Manchester University Press, 2013.
Sillitoe, Alan. *Saturday Night and Sunday Morning*, London: W.H. Allen 1958.
Taylor, Andrew. *The NUM and British Politics Volume 2: 1969–1995*. Aldershot: Ashgate, 2005.
The Leather Boys, directed by Sidney J. Furie, British Lion, 1964.
The Who, *Quadrophenia*. Track Records, 1973.
The Who: Quadrophenia Live in London, directed by Chris Rule, UMC, 2014.
Tommy and Quadrophenia Live, directed by Aubrey Powell and Roger Daltrey, Rhino, 2005.
Townshend, Pete. *Quadrophenia: The Director's Cut*. UMC, 2011, CD.
Townshend, Pete. *Who I Am*. London: Harper Collins, 2012.
Turner, Alwyn W. *Crisis? What Crisis? Britain in the 1970s*. London: Aurum Press, 2008.
Unterberger, Ritchie. *Won't Get Fooled Again: The Who from Lifehouse to Quadrophenia*. London: Jawbone Press, 2011.
Waller, Robert J. *The Almanac of British Politics*. London: Routledge, 1983.
We Are The Lambeth Boys, directed by Karel Reisz, Graphic Films, 1959.
Weight, Richard. *Mod: A Very British Style*. London: The Bodley Head, 2013.
Wells, Simon. *Inside The Making of Britain's Greatest Youth Film: Quadrophenia A Way of Life*. London: Countdown Books, 2014.
Wharton, Gary. *Chasing the Wind: A Quadrophenia Anthology*. Somerset: Lushington Publishing, 2002.
Wilkerson, Mark. Who Are You. *The Life of Pete Townshend. A Biography*. London: Omnibus Press, 2009.
Wilky, Pete and Hellier, John. *I'm the Face: Pete Meaden*. Griffiths Books, 2016.
Wood, James. "The Kids Are Alright", *The Guardian*, 30 May 2009.
Young, Michael and Willmott, Peter. *Family and Kinship in East London*. Harmondsworth: Penguin, 1957.

CHAPTER 7

Quad to Run: The Crucible of Identity as Represented in *Quadrophenia* and *Born to Run*

Suzanne Coker

Identity is a shifting thing, forged in adolescence, but amended throughout life. Larger than self-opinion, identity is never formed alone; according to some psychological theories, it is a function of an individual's interaction with their world, especially their social world, whatever form that interaction may take.[1] More dance than diagram, this relationship is always changing, though there are certain moments when that change becomes obvious, central, perhaps even the nucleus of obsession. Throughout life, the growth of identity is a dark tide, sometimes shifting slowly, sometimes crashing on the rocks. In adolescence and beyond, this is likely to cause pain.

Music helps. It can serve not only as an anaesthetic but a voice, sometimes speaking for the permanently voiceless, sometimes borrowed until an emerging identity finds its own. Personal experience bears this out. I grew up in the Deep South of America in the 1970s, a time of cultural turmoil; for those unwilling to cling to poisonous and vanishing old

---

S. Coker (✉)
Birmingham, AL, USA
e-mail: smocker_hgb@yahoo.com

© The Author(s) 2018
P. Thurschwell (ed.), *Quadrophenia and Mod(ern) Culture*,
Palgrave Studies in the History of Subcultures and Popular Music,
https://doi.org/10.1007/978-3-319-64753-1_7

ways, identity had to be invented without local guidelines. So I looked elsewhere: books, mostly, and of course the radio. Occasionally a voice would stand out, one that spoke to me despite a strange accent, in a way that went beyond mere admiration or interest. Once in a while I'd hear something that explained me to myself, that I wanted to play for everyone I knew and say: *here, this, this is what's going on, can you hear it too?*

Born to Run, both the song and the album, was one of these. There were many songs by older bands, including the Who, that I liked a lot, but this was different. And it didn't matter that Springsteen was probably older, or that he was from New Jersey, a place strange enough to me at the time that it could just as well have been another country. Hearing these songs, though, I knew that it wasn't, or at least that whoever wrote them came from a similar country-within-a-country. It's easy to assume this place was adolescence itself, but the identification went deeper than that. It wasn't so much about being young together as feeling the same pain, feeling the same way *about* the same pain.

For me, it turned out to be a borrowed voice. In my early twenties I found peers, some in bands of their own. We were writing our own songs and poetry. This fragile, fleeting subculture not only helped me discover my own voice, but also taught me how to listen to older bands differently, to hear a sort of universality through time. Those voices from the radio, familiar but remote, became forbears, not competitors, who had experienced the crucible of identity in a completely different context, and survived it in their own ways; ways I could learn from, that might even save me.

During an especially volatile time in my mid-twenties, *Quadrophenia* was the album that got me through. It didn't matter that Jimmy, let alone Pete Townshend, was from a place even stranger than New Jersey, or that all the voices involved were emphatically male; I heard what I needed, a way to experience, survive, even learn from towering, self-destructive rage and inescapable despair.

Later still, listening to *Born to Run* on the occasion of Clarence Clemons' death, I was struck by similarities between these two albums, beyond the fact that I had loved and depended on them both; another type of universality began to come clear. Still hearing with passion but for the moment secure in identity, I could begin to hear universality working across cultures as well as through time.

There was a sense of delight and defiance in this. My identification was justified, and so was I. The worlds depicted in each album were so different, yet had so much in common. The value and impact of each album derived much more from their treatment of common topics and emotions than from any specific, even conflicting tribal markings; the value of each increased once I saw this. They were different from each other, and I was different from both, but we shared an emotional vocabulary, all the more valuable when coming from different worlds.

Universality supports identification. It was the emotions under the details that counted, and yet those emotions were shown in the details, the way wind is visible in the leaves of a tree or motion of a flag. Each album paints a portrait of youth at a particular place and time. For such a portrait to resonate, the details must be accurate; for it to have universality, to resonate not only for those who were there but for those far away in geography, culture, and time, the details must also be transcended. If it achieves this, a work can have value for years or even centuries after its creation, as well as at different stages of life. This effect is separate from nostalgia; a listener doesn't need associations from youth to benefit later. Such works become something beyond simple portrait or pop cultural commodity; universality is also characteristic of art.

A detailed comparison illuminates this. There are clear differences: *Born to Run* is as American as *Quadrophenia* is British, and fills a quite different place in Bruce Springsteen's career than *Quadrophenia* does in either Pete Townshend's or the Who's. Each album uses a different approach, although listening to each is a bit like listening into a conversation; in *Quadrophenia* it's a single character talking mostly to himself via the device of "quadrophenia," a sort of multiple personality. It's clearly the character speaking, not Pete Townshend. In *Born to Run* Springsteen directly addresses a number of characters, including the listener. Despite the differences, each album depicts a specific world in a way that inspires universal resonance. In this sense, what *Quadrophenia* does for and with London's Mods of the 1960s, *Born to Run* does for the less-defined and mostly anonymous denizens of backstreet New Jersey in the early 1970s.

Although *Quadrophenia* began as a far different project, a way to recap the first decade of the Who's career and give individual voice to each of its members, it became the story of one particular Mod, eventually named Jimmy Cooper in the movie adaptation.[2] While Springsteen doesn't use a single, named character's point of view or a narrative structure in *Born to Run*, both albums are portraits not so much of an individual, but of a world through an individual's eyes as they seek to find a place in it during the initial quest of youth. Both worlds are filled with conflict, loneliness, love, and the tension between cynicism and hope. Both require dealings with universal aspects of identity and community: gender roles, work, cultural expectations, authority.

Both worlds are boy's clubs, filled with the things that fascinate very young men (and, to be honest, older ones too.) Whether it's a "GS scooter" (*Quadrophenia*, "Sea and Sand") or something "hemi-powered" (*Born to Run*, "Born to Run") boys in both worlds seem to understand "faith in your machine." (*Born to Run*, "Night") Whatever the specific type of machine might signify, machismo or its opposite, these are a means not only of transportation but pride; faith in your machine is faith in yourself. The fate of Jimmy's, and later the Ace Face's scooters are pivotal points in *Quadrophenia*'s narrative, as Jimmy's world gets stripped down and he has to face himself without props.

There's also fashion and girls, which seem to hold very different places in each world. Concern with fashion famously pervades *Quadrophenia*, while in *Born to Run* it's only mentioned twice and never described in detail, relegated to "visionaries" who "dress in the latest rage" in "Jungleland" and used to court success in "Meeting Across the River": "change your shirt, 'cause tonight we got style."

Fashion in *Quadrophenia* serves as both a requirement of the subculture and a way to question gender roles. While specific outfits such as a "zoot suit, white jacket with side vents/five inches long" ("Cut My Hair") are more-or-less traditionally masculine, the exquisitely detailed concern with appearance calls tradition into question: "The mods undermined the conventional meaning of 'collar, suit, and tie,' pushing neatness to the point of absurdity."[3] The questions don't stop there, either, as the demands of fashion lead further, into "he man drag/in the glittering ballroom/greyly outrageous/in my high heeled shoes" ("5:15").

Roles in *Born to Run* are defined and questioned more by attitude than dress. Beneath a traditional veneer, there's deep ambiguity. This is most noticeable in "Backstreets," where a friendship is described in terms that traditionally would be reserved for a more romantic situation. The narrator's relationship to Terry, whose name could easily be a shortening of either Terrence or Theresa, is "a love so hard and filled with defeat," expressed by "slow dancing in the dark" in "endless juke joints and Valentino drag." Terry and the narrator may not be the ones dancing, the drag might only be seen in a movie, the friendship could really be just that; the song's last word on the subject is "we swore forever friends." Even so, it's a highly ambiguous friendship; refusing to pin the relationship down is itself a challenge to tradition and categorization.

Even when genders are defined and relationships clear, roles are not quite traditional. "The girls comb their hair in rear-view mirrors/and the boys try to look so hard," ("Born to Run") but by far the hardest character on this album is the unnamed heroine of "She's the One": "french cream won't soften them boots/and french kisses will not break that heart of stone." This is sung not with disgust, but admiration. The relationship here is at least a contest between equals; the girl actually seems to have a slight edge. Regardless of the actual power balance, she is clearly an active force in her own right, and the song is, among other things, a celebration of that fact.

In keeping with the "basic themes" of Mod life: "predominantly working-class, male-dominated, and centered on an obsessive clothes-consciousness," girls in *Quadrophenia* are pretty much objects; the only power they seem to have is as arbiters of fashion: "The girl I love is a perfect dresser/Wears every fashion, gets it to the tee/Heavens above, I've got to match her/I know just how she wants her man to be" ("Sea and Sand").[4] While they may be beautiful and desired, it's from a distance, with spurned cynicism flavouring even the most wistful longing: "I see her dance/across the ballroom/UV light making starshine/of her smile." ("Sea and Sand") There is talk of rape and deflowering: "Who is she? I'll rape it," "You say she's a virgin? Well I'm gonna be the first in." ("Doctor Jimmy") Even if only a boast, it's a very angry one. Though the character of Steph as Jimmy's love object in the movie adaptation does have a great deal of power, on the album, girls are ultimately not even objects of desire but targets of rage.

The girls in *Born to Run* have some rage of their own, as well as a range of other emotions and a fair amount of power, especially the almost terrifying heroine of "She's the One." That terror, and her power, comes from inescapable desire: "no matter where you sleep/tonight or how far you run/oh-o, she's the one." There's also the barefoot girl who (presumably) murders her lover in "Jungleland." Less threatening girls are named, if somewhat generically: Mary, Wendy, Cherry. They are coaxed and pleaded with and promised lasting love, desired not just as objects but as partners in a new life: "so Mary climb in/it's a town full of losers/ and I'm pulling out of here to win" ("Thunder Road").

That dream of a better life elsewhere distinguishes the two worlds, but the difference is deceptive. Solidly working class in setting, the action of both albums takes place in a sort of grim, shabby underworld where everything falls apart in the very shadow and process of blooming. *Quadrophenia*'s primary response is fight. *Born to Run*'s is flight. In Springsteen's world, there is always the option of just leaving town. But there's also the knowledge, implicit in the title phrase and certain beneath the fantasy and optimism, that escape is an illusion. You can fly, but there's nowhere to land.

In *Quadrophenia*, travel liberates in the triumphant pilgrimage of "Drowned," but Jimmy's desperate flight from London to Brighton lands him stranded on a rock. In both worlds, the fantasy of flight is ultimately a closed loop. Jimmy revisits Brighton because he remembers the glory of beach fights there; *Born to Run* depicts the joys of Saturday night cruising in the title song, but beneath that thrill is a sense of closed-in, repetitive horror: "the highways jammed with broken heroes/ on a last chance power drive/everybody's out on the run tonight/but there's no place left to hide."

Fighting happens in both albums, but it holds a very different place and employs different styles. Violence in *Quadrophenia* is mostly unarmed riots and fistfights; in *Born to Run*, it's switchblades and guns. In *Quadrophenia*, violence happens in groups, often very large ones, and seems to be almost a form of entertainment, "trouble-as-fun, fun-as-trouble."[5] It's something you build yourself up to and reminisce about after it's done, a sort of release from the tensions of daily living. Violence in *Born to Run* is pervasive, not exceptional, and at its most pure and decisive, deeply personal. Not resolution but source of daily tension, it goes hand in hand with loneliness: "no one watches when the ambulance pulls away" ("Jungleland").

Loneliness in *Quadrophenia* seems to come from being misunderstood, not fitting in, not even really being seen. Loneliness in *Born to Run*, like violence, is pervasive and almost taken for granted. Symbolized by night and darkness, it shows up in every song, sometimes explicitly in the lyrics: Roy Orbison sings for "the lonely" in "Thunder Road"; the narrator in "Tenth Avenue Freeze Out" is on his own, and he "can't go home," and in "Born to Run," of course, the singer is "just a scared and lonely rider." Every song is a nearly desperate attempt to reach out, to other characters, to the listener. In *Quadrophenia*, loneliness is social and at least theoretically curable. In *Born to Run*, it's existential.

In both albums, love and friendship are considered as solutions to loneliness. Despite some stretching of traditional roles, love in *Born to Run* is mostly the relatively straightforward type of most pop songs: guy and girl together against the world, gaining strength from each other, effective in direct proportion to their unswerving intensity. The song "Backstreets" is among other things a sort of meditation on friendship, keenly felt, fondly remembered, but ultimately betrayed "when the breakdown hit at midnight," apparently both a specific event and an effect of growing up. Until then, however, the song's narrator finds in his friend Terry a true and vital companion, a necessary ally in struggle with the world.

This sort of intense, personal, binding friendship doesn't seem to exist in *Quadrophenia*'s world, where Jimmy's peers are more competitors than companions and a source of much stress: "I have to work myself to death just to fit in" ("Cut My Hair"). Disillusion with his peers and with romantic love are at the heart of Jimmy's dilemma. Throughout the album, his life is systematically, almost ritually emptied of all he might hold dear or even aspire to. Love is actually the first thing to go: "The girl I used to love/lives in this yellow house/Yesterday she passed me by/She doesn't want to know me now" ("The Real Me"). But love comes to mean something else in the end. After emptying, healing, or at least a glimpse of it; this is consistent with "the idea of using music as a way to spiritually heal and elevate both himself and the Who's audience" arising from Pete Townshend's interest in the teachings of Meher Baba, an influence dating back to the composition of *Tommy*.[6] There is no equivalent on *Born to Run* for "Love Reign O'er Me," in function, presentation, or meaning. The transcendent, spiritual love referenced here is the ultimate answer to loneliness, social or existential, and Springsteen's characters never even imagine, much less cry out for it.

It's not that they don't want redemption, or feel the need for it, or that spirituality is absent from this world. References to religion are scattered throughout, though more subtly than in some of Springsteen's other songs (for instance, "I'll Work for Your Love" from 2007's *Magic*.) Churches are mentioned in "Jungleland" and "kneeling in the dark" in "She's the One" seems to be a reference to prayer. But the real faith here is in oneself, each other, and the chance to make good. "Thunder Road" says it most plainly: "All the redemption I can offer girl/Is beneath this dirty hood." Faith is not so much a means to resolve loneliness and sorrow, but a way to endure it: "Together Wendy we can live with the sadness" ("Born to Run"), "tying faith between our teeth" ("Backstreets"). Even that attempt fails and leads to helpless disillusion: "Back when her love could save you/from the bitterness" ("She's the One").

Disillusion springs from and reveals the tension between cynicism and hope. Jimmy's disillusion is total and dramatic; it makes an impact then begins to resolve, forged into the desperate, furious hope of the album's finale. Disillusion in *Born to Run* is more like that album's violence: pervasive, unsettling, never resolved. Springsteen's antiheroes aren't disillusioned by their own subculture; it's never trustworthy or consistent enough to inspire much faith to begin with. Whatever world of their own they have is fugitive, fleeting, it scatters and reforms and scatters again at the edges of a larger world, holding together only "until the local cops/Cherry Tops/rips this holy night" ("Jungleland"). The real disillusion in *Born to Run* is with that larger world, best summed up in the title song by the phrase "a runaway American dream." Runaway in two senses: it dangles always just out of reach, forcing believers to keep running after it, and it's out of control.

In both worlds, work is both a marker and function of class. *Quadrophenia* takes a combative tone toward this, especially in "The Dirty Jobs": "you men should remember how you used to fight." Jimmy's encounters with the workers in this song and with his former hero turned bell boy illustrate the interaction between larger culture and subculture at the heart of Mod. "More firmly embedded than either the teds or the Rockers in a variety of jobs which made fairly stringent demands on their appearance, dress, and 'general demeanour' as well as their time, the mods placed a correspondingly greater emphasis on the weekend. They lived in between the leaves of the commercial calendar, as it were… During these leisure periods…there was real 'work' to be done: scooters to be polished, records to be bought…"[7] This tension between "working for them" and "working for us" creates a dance between subculture and larger culture, expressed most clearly on *Quadrophenia* in the song "Bell Boy."

When Keith Moon sings "the secret to me/isn't flown like a flag/I carry it behind this little badge/what says/bell boy" it is not a comfort. Yes, the heart is what counts, but it remains hidden. The bell boy's uniform has replaced the Mods' "style which concealed as much as it stated."[8] The secrecy that was once subversive has become collaboration, however angry and unwilling; as style gives way to uniform, "working for them" wins out. Jimmy's perception of this leads to his ultimate disillusion, with mod itself. His rage and scorn lead to "The Rock", a wordless grand encounter with and through despair. On the album, the results are not clear, and while personal resolution is implied, the tension between heart and badge, subculture and culture, work and leisure remains unresolved. "Helpless Dancer," with its roster of social ills including unjust job loss, ends with an ambiguous statement that could be rebellion, resignation, or somehow both: "you realize that all along/something in us going wrong//you stop dancing."

In *Born to Run*, work is briefly alluded to at the beginning of the title track, and features in only one other song, where it's a necessary evil, best forgotten when not there: "you work nine to five/and somehow you survive/till the night" ("Night"). Class isn't directly addressed in *Born to Run* any more than it tends to be in daily American life, but is relentlessly implied throughout. The dreams of making it out and making it big are just that: dreams, the dangling carrot that keeps the donkey working, circling endlessly in its harnessed path. Here, the promise of "youth revolution (e.g., the beat boom, the mod explosion, the swinging sixties) [where] the relative success of a few individuals created an impression of energy, expansion, and limitless upward mobility" has become the foundation of an entire society.[9] The characters in *Born to Run*, as well as in Springsteen's other albums, see right through it: "and you're just a prisoner of your dreams" ("Night"). Cynicism about work, like loneliness, is for them simply a fact of life. While the topic is addressed more thoroughly in Springsteen's other works, on *Born to Run* it's treated as hardly worth mentioning.

Both albums display a sort of angry pity for their larger cultures. In *Quadrophenia*, this shows up both in "Helpless Dancer" and in the "country always starved" of "Is It In My Head." In *Born to Run*, it is stated most clearly in "Backstreets": "at night sometimes it seemed/you could hear the whole damn city crying." This attitude influences the characters' confrontations with cultural expectations, what they're supposed to be and achieve. For Jimmy, these expectations are relatively clear and modest: "get a job and fight to keep it." ("I've Had Enough") But the nastiness and hypocrisy of that fight put it out of reach; to do what's expected, he'd have to give up what's good inside him. Expectations for Springsteen's characters are more vague and grandiose; earnest efforts to live up to them cause little but trouble and pain. In Backstreets, they begin with a daunting task, "trying in vain to breathe the fire we was born in." They think they need to learn to walk like "heroes" but come instead to discover they are "just like all the rest/ stranded in the park/and forced to confess" ("Backstreets").

For most adolescents, authority is primarily represented by parents; each album's attitude toward authority is perhaps best summed up by how parents are described. Jimmy's parents are a key element of *Quadrophenia*. He fights with them at first half-heartedly, because he has to in order to fit in, though his affection for them gets in the way ("Cut My Hair"). It's only after they throw him out that he turns them into hypocritical villains. "They finally threw me out/my mom got drunk on stout/my dad couldn't stand on two feet/as he lectured about morality" ("Sea and Sand"). But parents make no appearance at all in *Born to Run*; they aren't even mentioned. While this might indicate an adolescent dream world where no one ever has to report home, it could just as easily represent a terrible vacuum, a world of latchkey children who are, ready or not, on their own and perhaps even homeless, "sleeping in that old abandoned beach house" ("Backstreets"). Authority in this world is represented more truly by the police, an impersonal force not to be trusted or confronted, only outwitted, evaded where it can't be ignored.

Their inhabitants confront universal problems, but these albums portray very different worlds. *Quadrophenia* is full of grand-scale violence and rage whose consequences are mostly internal and ultimately lead to redemption. The major symbol is water: vital and destructive, cleansing and threatening, it pervades and ultimately uplifts. The world of *Born to Run* is one of casual darkness, where unpredictable violence and corrosive cynicism lurk beneath and power a glowing dream. There is no plot, therefore no resolution; redemption is promised, hoped for, but never really arrives. The major symbol is night, a zone of both escape and threat.

Both albums are drenched in great emotion; each causes a sort of useful injury. *Quadrophenia* is blunt trauma; overwhelmed by sheer volume, power, and enormous grandeur on all fronts, the listener submits and learns. *Born to Run* is knifework. Honed to an edge of absolute intensity, it strikes and is done by the time you see you're bleeding.

Born to Run begins with a slammed door and a waving dress; it ends with a howl of soul-deep pain. *Quadrophenia* begins with waves on the beach and a snarling challenge; it ends with a crash of transcendence. In between, each presents its world in a way that takes both rock and the quest for identity into the realm of art.

Notes

1. Harke A. Bosma and E. Saskia Kunnen, Determinants and Mechanisms in Ego Identity Development: A Review and Synthesis, *Developmental Review* 21, (2001): 39–66. doi:10.1006/drev.2000.0514.
2. Richie Unterberger, *Won't Get Fooled Again: The Who from Lifehouse to Quadrophenia* (London: Jawbone Press, 2011), 184–193.
3. Dick Hebdige, *Subculture: The Meaning of Style* (London and New York: Routledge, 1979), 52.
4. Dick Hebdige, *Hiding in the Light: On Images and Things* (London and New York: Routledge, 1988), 110.
5. Hebdige, *Hiding in the Light*, 30.
6. Unterberger, 42–44.
7. Hebdige, *Subculture*, 53.
8. Hebdige, *Subculture* 52.
9. Hebdige, *Subculture*, 99.

Bibliography

Music

Springsteen, Bruce. *Born to Run*. CBS CK 33795. CD. 1975.
Springsteen, Bruce. *Magic*. Columbia 88697 17060 2. CD. 2007.
The Who, *Quadrophenia*, by Pete Townshend. MCA D2 11483. CD. 1996, 1973.
Quadrophenia, directed by Franc Roddam (1979; Who Films Ltd; Rhino Home Video R2 976624), DVD.

Print

Bosma, Harke A. and E. Saskia Kunnen. "Determinants and Mechanisms in Ego Identity Development: A Review and Synthesis." *Developmental Review* 21 (2001): 39–66. doi:10.1006/drev.2000.0514.
Hebdige, Dick. *Subculture: The Meaning of Style*. London and New York: Routledge, 1979.
Hebdige, Dick. *Hiding in the Light: On Images and Things*. London and New York: Routledge, 1988.
Unterberger, Richie. *Won't Get Fooled Again: The Who from Lifehouse to Quadrophenia*. London: Jawbone Press, 2011.

CHAPTER 8

Taking the 5:15: Mods, Social Mobility, and the Brighton Train

Tom F. Wright

Holding the gatefold sleeve of *Quadrophenia* in your hands for the first time, Ethan Russell's series of vivid black-and-white photographs provide an evocative commentary on the album's songs. Yet one of the images doesn't seem to fit. It is the frame of a young man slumped between two city gents in an upholstered first-class train carriage. The two men, in matching bowler hats, waistcoats, trousers of pinstripe, handkerchiefs in breast pockets, appear almost comically synchronized, immersed in the evening paper. Between them, in checked shirt and Carnaby Street tie, sits Jimmy, far enough down in seat and frame that he occupies a boyish position, disengaged from the news and from the scene around him, a symbol of generational alienation.

Upon listening to the songs, we discover that this oddly mundane image accompanies "5:15," the album's most famous track. The song relates a climactic moment of the album's narrative. Separated from his destroyed scooter yet desperate to escape London for the scene of his recent seaside skirmish, Jimmy alights the quarter-past-five "Brighton Belle" at Victoria. As Pete Townshend's liner notes tell us, this marked

---

T.F. Wright (✉)
University of Sussex, Brighton, UK
e-mail: Tom.Wright@sussex.ac.uk

© The Author(s) 2018
P. Thurschwell (ed.), *Quadrophenia and Mod(ern) Culture*,
Palgrave Studies in the History of Subcultures and Popular Music,
https://doi.org/10.1007/978-3-319-64753-1_8

the "the low point in his life ... he gets pilled up and takes the train to Brighton."[1] He finds himself coasting in an amphetamine haze through carriages of commuters returning home. The song abruptly shifts from the reflective mid-tempo intro to a churning Rocker whose horn chart conjures up, among other things, the rail rhythms of James Brown's "Night Train." As Townshend's plaintive vocal asks "Why Should I Care?" this becomes a song about detachment, a "sadly ecstatic" ride through a personal dreamscape as Jimmy recalls the concert-halls, the women and the confrontations that make up his own teenage wasteland.

This sequence of Jimmy taking the 5:15 was to become one of the most iconic moments in Franc Roddam's big-screen adaptation. In that film, we see Jimmy board the train, scoff pills and apply eyeliner in the toilet, before a key shot directly quotes the original album sleeve photograph, with the same actor even employed as one of the commuters. Here, the image becomes something else, fleshed out into a hallucinogenic music video, in which Jimmy edges woozily along narrow corridors that visually echo the Brighton and Shepherd's Bush alleyways from earlier in the film, and into compartments that serve as theatre for an interior series of confrontations and daydreams. The insistent 4/4 frenzy of the song soundtracks the low point in Jimmy's life, but is also undeniably exhilarating, a moment of grace and rebirth on board a locomotive hurtling its passengers coastward (Fig. 8.1).

Quadrophenia is a story told—fittingly—in four different media: songs and photographs, film, and finally as fiction, thanks to Alan Fletcher's 1979 novelization.[2] In each, the image of Jimmy taking the 5:15 exerts a powerful and mysterious force, for a number of reasons. There is the episode's sheer incongruity: a surreal juxtaposition of transcendence and despair amidst the routine everydayness contained within the song's title: an early train home, a time committed to memory by the commuter. There is also something of a mythic dimension, with our protagonist descending into a fantastical Brighton as if to an underworld for a final reckoning. It is also a scene loaded with ironies. Rather than unwinding on the early train homewards from the office, Jimmy is fleeing his own home in a state of escalating tension; rather than becoming a first-class commuter, he is a fake and a substitute, a pilled-up vagabond fleeing his mistakes in the capital for the promise of sea and sand.

This chapter uses the 5:15 scene as a way into *Quadrophenia's* most powerful theme: that of mobility, both literal and social. In its various incarnations, the treatment of issues of aspiration and thwarted social

8 TAKING THE 5:15: MODS, SOCIAL MOBILITY, AND THE BRIGHTON TRAIN 133

Fig. 8.1 He gets pilled up and takes the train to Brighton

desire in Jimmy's story are one of its most enduring legacies, and a theme whose tensions resonate ever more powerfully for its twenty-first-century audiences. All of these tensions are contained within the 5:15 image. The image of Jimmy aboard the Brighton train was one symbolic moment that allowed the album, film and novel to explore the connections between transport, identity and the meanings of Mod. In what follows, I pick apart the things that each medium does with this scene, and place them within the broader literary and cinematic history of the railway carriage as arena of class drama, and within broader debates over youth subcultures and social mobility. Debates that are essential to the meaning of the three different incarnations of *Quadrophenia*, and the distance between the historical moment of its mid-1960s setting and the later, more fraught years in which first album and then film met the world.

Going Mobile

British Mod was simultaneously an expression of, and rebuke to, post-war social aspiration. In its most characteristic incarnations, the subculture was a direct product of the unprecedented social and economic freedoms available for working and lower-middle-class youth, whose rising living standards allowed for the enjoyment of a consumer life their parents could only imagine. Mod was therefore a fascinating offshoot of what post-war sociologists heralded as the age of the "affluent worker," individuals with sharply increased spending power, leisure time and an unprecedented ability to define the parameters of their social and cultural worlds.[3] In part, this was about consumerism and the desire to live well on whatever budget one had possible. As chronicler of the subculture Richard Weight has argued, "Mod was the closest British have come to constructing their own version of the American Dream,—a mobilising, energising legend of opportunity which rebuked the snobbery and deference that conspired to give Britain one of the lowest levels of social mobility."[4]

This aspiration was most obvious in the Mod fixation with personal presentation. The archetypal stance of being strikingly neat and overdressed, smart both mentally and sartorially, gave off various messages. A generational dynamic was clearly important. Through styling oneself more deliberately, young men in particular could escape looking like their fathers and by doing so reject the confines of their parents' less cosmopolitan lives. It also led to class confusion, when Mods might be better dressed than their bosses. Yet this was aspiration as subversion. Mods might style themselves as well as their more affluent counterparts, but this went hand in hand with an apparent rejection of the values of what they saw as bourgeois conformity. For this reason, as the sociologist Dick Hebdige has argued, Mod was defined by its subversive appropriation of commodities, redefining the meaning of consumer items such as lavish Italian menswear. To dress even more smartly than one's betters was an act of socially mobile rebellion.[5]

Social mobility was perhaps even more obvious in the kinds of transport celebrated by Mod. The subculture seized in particular on the European scooter as an elegant expression of modern values. The upright, small-wheeled vehicle met demands for practical, elegant design whilst its Franco-Italian heritage and styling lent an air of conspicuous cosmopolitanism. Unlike motorbikes, scooters were defiantly urban machines. They were designed to zip around town, sometimes rather slowly, a product of style and convenience rather than speed or power. But practicality was rivalled in importance by transport as a means of self-expression. The scooter was a symbol moving at speed, both practical and distinctively modern, infinitely customizable, another instance of subversion through consumer choice.

Moreover, when driven en masse, the scooter was transformed into a symbol of solidarity. Driving in flocks through London, or to the legendary skirmishes at Clacton, Great Yarmouth and Brighton, scooter-riding Mods found an experience that cemented the kind of group identity whose spirit animates *Quadrophenia*. Here's the voice of Jimmy from Fletcher's novelization, remembering being part of the flock:

> At each junction and each roundabout we picked up more riders, by themselves or in groups, waving and smiling, joining the great sweep of the convoy as it headed in formation towards the A23, the Southbound road, picking up speed as it turned out of London. Towards Brighton. We gave a display for the towns along the way, like Lewes and Reigate, where people had come out of their houses to watch us pass by. It gave us all a great sense of power and pride, to be part of the convoy, to be mods ... in the sweep of the great convoy, in the middle of an event.[6]

There was a strange mixture of modernity and nostalgia at work in an "event" like this, summoning up the imagery and associations of cavalry from cinematic war films and Westerns. Riding in unison displayed a communal form of rebellion. It marked those who rode together out from the miners in the album's song "The Dirty Jobs" who get driven to work on "a local bus."[7] And whilst the very possibility of scooter ownership was the product of affluence, it also rebelled against what the sociologists of the period called the "embourgeoised" affluent worker, home-centred, and family-minded.[8] Post-war economic freedom and social mobility came together in a transport technology that was both means of escape and subversive icon of collective expression.

In all of these associations, scooters seem to offer a decisive alternative to the modernity symbolized by trains. The romance of the railway certainly still held great sway within mid-century popular culture; rail imagery is, after all, an enduring theme of the rock-and-roll and rhythm-and-blues music cherished in Mod circles. Paul Anderson's oral history of the movement helps flesh this out. One London Mod that he interviewed, named Pat Farrell, reports stories of a large disjoined crowd breaking into the number "Night Train" on the tube after pub closing time, "and the whole train started singing and dancing James Brown style."[9] Trains, particularly those whose timetables skirted the edges of the night, were also central to enabling the candle-burning excesses of Mod leisure. Think of Jimmy wailing, in the song "Cut My Hair," about "coming down / Got home on the very first train from town." But scooter riding challenged train riding in a number of ways. Where scooters were active, trains were passive. Railways represented an earlier, obsolete form of modernity, with its own outmoded codes of display. Scooters were European, cosmopolitan; the railway was English, even Victorian, tied up with an earlier industrial narrative of modernity. Trains led "backward" in history. Britain's role and pride in itself as the birthplace of rail was a collective expression and civic narrative that Mod attempted to frustrate.

The specific Brighton route depicted in *Quadrophenia* was a case in point. Sitting on the 5:15, Jimmy found himself on one of Britain's most well-known routes, amidst city workers commuting back to the towns that threaded the capital to the coast.[10] Thanks to the arrival of this line in the 1840s, Brighton had been transformed from louche seaside resort to perhaps the grandest of all "railway towns," and become a byword for railway modernity. The route through the South Downs involved one of Britain's largest cuttings; its viaduct across the Ouse Valley was one of the most elegant in the country. It was a remarkably *modern* route: becoming the first electrified mainline, and from the 1930s onwards, playing host to Southern Railway's iconic Brighton Belle service, delivering commuters and day-trippers to the coast in Pullman-carriage style. The 1953 film *London to Brighton in Four Minutes*, a sped-up version of a Belle journey from Victoria, captured the high point of this sense of the route's prestige.[11] It was a route that Mods even deigned to use. The London Mod Pat Farrell, quoted earlier, recalls witnessing the arrival from London through Sussex to the outskirts of the town in 1964: "the paper train had just pulled in and there were hundreds and hundreds of kids who had all got off at Preston Park and jumped over the fence because they never had tickets."[12] Another of Farrell's contemporaries added that "I think the first time we went to Brighton was when someone said 'We're all going to Brighton on the Mod train'. It was winter, just after Christmas as at the beginning of 1963. We all met at Victoria and bunked on the milk train."[13]

Yet compared with these romantic routes and daring journeys, Jimmy in *Quadrophenia* found himself on one of the line's more mundane services. "5:15" is as much a state of mind as a departure time. It spoke of the prudent early train home, the regimented escape from the temptations of the London evening in favour of domestic commitments. And this is why the 5:15 train, and in particular the train compartment, provided such an apt and powerful space and place in which Townshend and Roddam could dramatize their verdicts on the diminishing power of post-war myths of social mobility.

THE TRAIN COMPARTMENT

Since the arrival of the railway, writers had quickly seized upon the fascination of the railway compartment as a site for human drama.[14] They represented a new form of moving sitting rooms in which social games might be played out, in which every traveller is aware of being objectified and assessed. The setting looms in the background of major works such as Leo Tolstoy's *Anna Karenina* (1877) and Edith Wharton's *House of Mirth* (1905), and provides the foreground for sensation novels such as M.E. Braddon's *The Lovels of Arden* (1871), which exploited the sexual and social tensions implicit in such forced proximity. As literary critic Matthew Beaumont has argued, with their enforced contact, anonymity and false kinships, "these are spaces characteristic of modernity because structured by the most contingent of intimacies."[15] Stratified and segregated by class, these are places where we can act out our notorious genteel British unsociability in a curious suspension of public and domestic space—the dual "inside, outside" of Townshend's refrain in the lyrics to "5:15." Such dynamics have proved irresistible for filmmakers. Carriages could be the space of potential romance in *Brief Encounter* (1945), or in thrillers such as Alfred Hitchcock's *North by Northwest* (1959) could be transformed into a space of threat. In other genres, compartments could be more lighthearted. In the years leading up to Roddam's film of *Quadrophenia*, the most popular British reference point was the television show *The Fall and Rise of Reginald Perrin* (1976–1979), whose Pooter-esque hero anarchically disrupts the order of his Surbiton to Waterloo journey at the beginning of each episode.

More likely, however, *Quadrophenia* referenced not just this general setting but also a specific instance of youth culture invading the rail carriage: the opening sequence of Richard Lester's 1964 film *Hard Day's Night*. In that scene, the Beatles confront a gentleman in the first-class carriage, resulting in an exchange that playfully evokes the tectonic shifts at play around youth and social mobility.[16] Having taken their seats, Ringo switches on his portable radio, and an older passenger reacts angrily:

JOHNSON puts down his paper firmly.

JOHNSON

And we'll have that thing off as well, thank you.

RINGO

But I...

JOHNSON leans over and switches it off.

JOHNSON

An elementary knowledge of the Railway Acts would tell you I'm perfectly within my rights.

He smiles frostily.

PAUL

Yeah, but we want to hear it and there's more of us than you. We're a community, like, a majority vote. Up the workers and all that stuff!

JOHNSON

Then I suggest you take that damned thing into the corridor or some other part of the train where you obviously belong.

JOHN

(leaning forward to him)

Gie's a kiss!

PAUL

Shurrup! Look, Mister, we've paid for our seats too, you know.

JOHNSON

I travel on this train regularly, twice a week.

JOHN

Knock it off, Paul, y' can't win with his sort. After all, it's his train, isn't it, Mister?

JOHNSON

And don't you take that tone with me, young man!

GEORGE

But...

JOHNSON

(accusingly)

I fought the war for your sort.

RINGO

Bet you're sorry you won![17]

It is a light-heartedly staged scene but possesses an irresistible charge. The gentleman Johnson has recourse to the law and the war: the railway act and military service. McCartney ironically voices socialism; Lennon revels in acidic wit. The four use childhood, sarcasm and sexual ambiguity to dismantle the culture of deference. And we delight in it. As an opening flourish of the film, the scene offers a triumphant and cathartic moment of youthful rebellion, celebrating the new powers of upwardly mobile regional youth. However, the class dynamics were certainly more complex than they seem, and the entire exchange is confused by the musicians' status as newly affluent: flaunting their financial and social capital; wrong-footing the prior generation. It is an archetypal *nouveau riche* scene: the *arriviste* as man-child.

It is tempting to read the sequence of Jimmy on the 5:15 as a continuation of this defiant acting out. Taken out of context, Russell's album sleeve photograph is in keeping with this spirit. It seems to depict a fractious culture of deference on the cusp of eruption, folk devil slumped between the wary Establishment, eroding Britain's moral and cultural fabric.[18] The song supports this, reviving the stuttered vocal tic and the lyrics of "My Generation" (1965), making the song a self-conscious re-run of the youth culture battles of the previous decade: the call-to-arms of polka dot versus striped tie. Jimmy declares ownership: his legs thrust forward towards the viewer, seemingly invading the seats opposite, almost striding forward from the frame.

It is a scene of silent resentment at the affluent teenager, at his preening narcissism, and at the entitlement of Jimmy's generation of working- and lower-middle-class Londoners. Yet like John, Paul, George and Ringo, this well dressed barbarian is, as far as his fellow commuters know, a customer who has exercised a consumer right, and an "elementary knowledge of the railway act" tells them that they must tolerate his rise. Jimmy in the first image is an aspirant caught in a moment of Britain's short-lived economic and cultural boom, the high point of social mobility. And so Russell's image also seems to capture a moment of repose. The picture suggests a relatively settled, harmonious co-existence. The incongruity seems domesticated. All three travel silently in the same direction.

Roddam's film version dramatizes these ambiguities, and adds a few more. The shots make pains to relate back to the album sleeve. But there are key changes. Jimmy's suit is sharper, now more obviously Italian. The disdain, embarrassment and resentment at this interloper on the commuter's faces is more obvious and more pronounced as they try to ignore the arrival of the wired young man. Not only wired, but eye-linered: the makeup on Phil Daniels' face adds a fresh dimension to the scene. In the version of the song that plays over these shots, the verses are re-ordered to emphasise the "he-man drag" that Jimmy assumes as he is discovered in the ladies room applying eyeliner. Just as femininity was a central charge levelled at Mod, and just as Mod rejected the Rockers' crude conception of masculinity, Jimmy is here a feminized interloper into the homosocial world of the middle-aged male commuter. The train car becomes not a space of individual desire but an ultimate chance for controlled performance of fluid gender and sexuality that seems at points to owe much to the glitter of early 1970s glam as to the period in which it is set.

In this way, the sequence can be read as a darker replaying of the *Hard Day's Night* scene. It uses similar compositions; it draws upon a similar cast of characters, not least the schoolgirls who provide the audience for the protagonists' rebellion; it involves the same simmering notes of ambiguous sexual tension. Yet for Jimmy, the situation and outcome are quite different. Fletcher's novelization fleshes out Jimmy's thoughts in this scene:

> I went into the next first-class compartment (doing it with a bit of style) and settled in between two miserable types in dark suits and bowler hats. They seemed to shrink away, as I was a leper or something, though I realized it was probably my eyes – the liner really showed up – which unnerved them. They went back to their papers, and I thought about the kind of life they led, the horror of it. They'd never experienced nothing, never been in the street, never been blocked, nothing. They seemed hardly

real, and they hadn't got a clue about me, about the kind of life I was leading and why I was there, on a commuter train to Brighton flowing South.

Just as with the Fab Four, or with defiance of Sting's character Ace Face in the courtroom, Jimmy revels in his ability to unnerve. But this is the culmination not the onset of his journey; his train invasion is not triumph but defeat, a hollow defiance. A hollowness that is captured in the twin sense of the word "blocked" here. Drug lingo, but more broadly, a useful way of describing the growing social obstacles Jimmy faces—obstacles that ultimately provide the core subject of the album and film.

BLOCKED

Quadrophenia was a dialogue between three different periods of British life: the mid-1960s setting; the early 1970s of the album's composition; and the end of that decade, when Roddam's film was released. With this dialogue in mind, the meanings of Jimmy's story evolve in subtle ways. Let's begin with the first context. In the incarnation of high 1960s Mod that album and film depict, the subculture held most appeal and significance to a respectable urban working class that was, in the words of sociologist Phil Cohen, "caught and pulled apart by two opposed pressures of social mobility": upwards into the ranks of the new suburban working-class elite or downwards into the lumpen proletariat.[19] Mod's defiant stylization seemed to signify a positive answer to this impasse. Its optimistic, future-oriented aesthetic chimed with the spirit of years that were defined by empowerment and increased opportunity. As the overall standard of living continued to rise in line with a growing economy from the late 1950s onwards, young urban workers such as Townshend's Jimmy were symbolic of the fast pace of change, their experiences as liberating as they were disorientating. But this was a mood that changed dramatically in the early years of the next decade.[20] Global financial uncertainty, the 1973 oil crisis, and the industrial conflicts that led the Edward Heath government to declare repeated states of emergency all helped to put the brakes an earlier speed of social advance. By the time that Townshend was completing *Quadrophenia* in 1973, the national balance of payments was in deficit, and unemployment and inflation were rising. For the first time, a post-war generation might find themselves "blocked."

This second context helps account for the dark mood that hangs over the *Quadrophenia* album. It is there in the stark loneliness of Russell's monochrome shots of London, in the themes of work and employment that run through the songs and the liner notes. It is also there in the uneasy sense of guilt that the band projects, as they look back at the subculture and historical moments that nurtured and enabled their success. Both in the explicit reference to the Who's financial success ("Our Mums and Dads are all very nice and live in bungalows which we bought for them in the Outer Hebrides") and in the visual juxtaposition in one of the photographs of their situation with that of Jimmy: the former carousing post-performance, the latter forlorn and alone on the street. [21]

These qualities also lend a wistful nostalgia to the original 5:15 image and the social potential and ease of access it might represent. In 1964, the city gents Jimmy sits between might represent his own future, one of his *quad* of four potential personalities that smartness and ambition could lead him towards. But the later context also allows us to see the whole 5:15 sequence as extended mockery. It offers us the quietly recognized reality of Mod: that mobility is only surface; upward journeys are only clothes deep. In the words of Stanley Cohen, Jimmy is the archetype of the Mod as actor "not quite in their place," a bathetic replay of the triumphant railway rebellion of McCartney, Harrison, Lennon and Starkey.[22] And it chimes with the lesson Jimmy learns in perhaps the most fundamental moment of his journey towards disillusionment, as he alights upon Ace Face as bell boy ("He ended up working at the same hotel. But he wasn't the manager") and realizes that both rebellion and social empowerment had only been spectacle and show.[23]

Read through the more despairing lens of 1973, *Quadrophenia* therefore turns into a parable about the myths of social mobility, and the gains and losses of consumerism. As the liner notes said, "work wasn't worth the effort."[24] Some teenagers from poorer, semi-educated backgrounds never saw the point of aspiration in the first place. Mod was always a con; desires were thwarted; Mods found solace in their culture. This harshly ironic difference between appearance and reality was of course the subject of "Substitute". For all its association with modernity and futurity, Mod had never been an entirely optimistic worldview. Among the many oral histories of the movement, one 1964 interview that Weight quotes, with a London Mod called John Brady, then working as a mechanic, seems particularly apt, as he reflects that "There's a lot of hate in me … I suppose it's because I don't have a chance. I don't talk right and I haven't been to the right schools. I haven't had an education. That makes you sick, to see them preaching at you."[25]

These aspects were to come to the fore in the third context of 1979. During the remainder of the 1970s, the pace of social advance for young workers such as Jimmy had slowed even more. By the time of Roddam's film adaptation, the initial surge in mobility of the early post-war decades seemed doubly far away. Economic stagnation, the dismantling of whatever opportunities the grammar school system had offered, uneven access to the promise of higher education, and the institutional resilience of the British class system were taken as read as evidence of social malaise in a country that increasingly excluded the underprivileged urban young. This was the era of the breakdown of the affluent worker thesis, as working-class school leavers found themselves hit hardest by the economic changes. Understandably, one of the keynotes of Roddam's *Quadrophenia* was that of political nostalgia, taking that which was already latent in the original album and book and extending it further into a 1980s social imagination.

But the 1979 context also added a new layer of fury and alienation, and *Quadrophenia* has often been seen as re-imagining Mod through punk. Their potential for a shared emotional range was most obvious when the two came together, as in the Mod revival touchstones such as The Jam's "Eton Rifles" (1979), which took similar frustration with social mobility as their topic. Roddam's film took the muted disaffection and alienation of Townshend's view of the 1960s and ran with it, looking back at the events of fifteen years before through a punk-inspired lens of disillusion and nihilism that marks it out as far different from the flamboyance of Ken Russell's film re-imagining of *Tommy* (1975).[26] Both the spirit of punk rebellion and the full weight of punk nihilism were writ large in the courtroom scene. The obviously punk-inspired figure of Ace Face might be able to use disposable income to escape the situation, but he still fought the law and the law still won.

On one level, Roddam's repackaging of past rebellion might be seen as a cynical consumer act. But the film also took part in the dialogue that Townshend had started about the nature of the 1960s, offering a jaundiced view on what had been lost since in terms of social possibilities. Foreign audiences seemed to understand these meanings particularly clearly. A *Los Angeles Times* review of the film thought that it "threatens to explode at every turn. Given the limited social mobility in Britain, the future promised only more of the same frustration."[27] One of the ironies of the film version is that while it superficially celebrates Mod culture, and was central to its subsequent revivals, it was also a damning critique. Mod was presented as all surface, not a route out of one's social station. Through the figure of Jimmy, it dramatized a distinct disillusionment among sections of working-class youth with the democratic impetus of Mod, as consumerism failed to generate the social mobility that the precepts of the cult had promised. And it also dramatized a failure in the social solidarity that helped the subculture to coalesce in the first place. Many of the participants in oral histories testify to this powerful group identity. But as more than one came to recognise, such kinship was no match for the realities of class and the criminal justice system "When you're working class, it's them and us" argued one; another lamented "there's the powers, and then there's them that ain't got the power, unless we stick together."[28]

If *Quadrophenia* was Townshend's soundtrack of the frustrated hopes of a generation, his message resonated even more in 1979. And it certainly rings true for twenty-first-century viewers who have grown used to the kinds of stasis that album and film depict. The "5:15" scene remains at the film's heart, and offers a way of reading these shifting meanings. In 1973, Townshend's and Russell's imagery offered a glimpse of the nation as a rail carriage, heading forward into an uncertain future. By the end of the decade, the same scene encapsulates Roddam's dismantling of the myth that the young generation was, in fact, going mobile. By playing with ideas of movement, transport, social class and subcultural style, the "5:15" sequence allows us to think towards a more nuanced understanding of what social mobility might mean: not simply a question of movement up or even down the social scale, perhaps, but one of a mobile society that moves to meet its members, co-opting lifestyles and attitudes as part of consumer culture. And it tempts us to imagine an equivalent scene today. To reflect upon the new meanings it could have as ideas of transport, urban geography and social mobility have shifted once again. Within the modern metropolis, it is urban workers like Jimmy who have become commuters: travelling distances into the centre of cities whose cores have been re-defined economically and socially, and from which they are excluded. Moreover, we might say that, in the modern rail carriage, the concern of Mod with appearance and consumerism is now met most clearly in terms of the technology one holds in one's hand. The gradations of device we commune with during our journeys, and on which we might listen to or watch *Quadrophenia* itself, out of our brains on the train.

Notes

1. Pete Townshend, *Quadrophenia: Music from the Soundtrack of the Who Film* (London: Polydor, 1973) Sound recording, liner notes.
2. The four versions are as follows: Pete Townshend, *Quadrophenia: Music from the Soundtrack of the Who Film* (1973) incorporating Ethan Russell's images; Franc Roddam dir. *Quadrophenia* (1979); Alan Fletcher, *Quadrophenia* (London: Corgi, 1979). To this list we might also add the hit single "The Day We Caught the Train" (1994) by the Mod rock band Ocean Colour Scene, which revives the narrative of Jimmy on the 5:15.
3. Ferdinand Zweig, *The Worker in an Affluent Society* (London: Glencoe, 1961) and John H. Goldthorpe, *The Affluent Worker: Political Attitudes and Behaviour* (Cambridge: Cambridge University Press, 1968).
4. Richard Weight, *MOD: A Very British Style* (London: Bodley Head, 2013), 4.
5. See Tony Jefferson, *Resistance Through Rituals* (London: Routledge, 1993).
6. Fletcher, *Quadrophenia*, 120.
7. "The Dirty Jobs," *Quadrophenia*.
8. Zweig, *The New Acquisitive Society*, 1–12.
9. Quoted in Anderson, *Mods: The New Religion*, 61.
10. Andrew Martin, *Belles and Whistles: Five Journeys Through Time on Britain's Trains* (London: Profile Books, 2014), 171–175.
11. British Broadcasting Corporation, *London to Brighton in Four Minutes* (1953). The BBC repeated the exercise in 1983 and 2013, but the last version had to be a special service, as no non-stoppers now exist. All three can be viewed at http://www.bbc.co.uk/news/uk-england-23853863 [Accessed 4 July 2016].
12. Quoted in Anderson, *Mods: The New Religion*, 80.
13. Pat Farrell quoted in Paul Anderson, *Mods: The New Religion: the Style and Music of the 1960s Mods* (London: Omnibus, 2013), 61.
14. See Ian Carter, *Railways and culture in Britain: the epitome of modernity* (Manchester, UK; Manchester University Press, 2001), 212–220.
15. Matthew Beaumont, "Railway Mania: The Train Compartment as the Scene of a Crime" in Matthew Beaumont and Michael J. Freeman eds. *The Railway and Modernity: Time, Space and the Machine* (Bern: Peter Lang, 2007), 130.

16. Lester, Richard dir. *A Hard Day's Night* (1964). The film's script is available in public domain form at http://www.aellea.com/script/ahdn.htm [Accessed 4 July 2016].
17. *A Hard Day's Night* script, http://www.aellea.com/script/ahdn.htm [Accessed 4 July 2016].
18. See Cohen, *Folk Devils and Moral Panics* (1972).
19. Phil Cohen, 'Subcultural Conflict and Working-Class Community' in Ken Gelder ed., The Subcultures Reader (London: Routledge, 1997), 88.
20. Dominic Sandbrook, *State of Emergency: The Way We Were. Britain, 1970–1974* (London: Allen Lane, 2010).
21. The liner notes centre on an extended liner notes piece by Townshend entitled "Quadrophenia."
22. Stanley Cohen, *Folk Devils and Moral Panics: The Creation of the Mods and Rockers* (London: MacGibbon and Kee, 1972), 164.
23. Liner notes, *Quadrophenia*.
24. Ibid.
25. Quoted in Weight, *Mod*, 218–219.
26. Dave Allen. "Cultural Adventurers" in Forster, Laurel, and Sue Harper. *British Culture and Society in the 1970s* (Newcastle upon Tyne: Cambridge Scholars Publishing, 2010), 144.
27. Quoted in Christine Feldman, *We are the Mods: A Transnational History of a Youth Subculture* (New York: Peter Lang, 2009), 134.
28. Quoted in Paul Anderson, *Mods*, 70.

Bibliography

Allen, Dave. "Cultural Adventurers" in Laurel Forster and Sue Harper, *British Culture and Society in the 1970s: The Lost Decade*. Newcastle upon Tyne: Cambridge Scholars Publishing, 2010. 142–154.

Anderson, Paul. *Mods: The New Religion: The Style and Music of the 1960s Mods*. London: Omnibus, 2013.

Beaumont, Matthew. "Railway Mania: The Train Compartment as the Scene of a Crime" in Matthew Beaumont and Michael J. Freeman eds.. *The Railway and Modernity: Time, Space and the Machine*. Bern: Peter Lang, 2007. 125–154.

Carter, Ian. *Railways and culture in Britain: The epitome of modernity*. Manchester, UK; Manchester University Press, 2001.

Cohen, Stanley. *Folk Devils and Moral Panics: The Creation of the Mods and Rockers*. London: MacGibbon and Kee, 1972.

Cohen, Phil. "Subcultural Conflict and Working-Class Community" in Ken Gelder ed., *The Subcultures Reader*. London: Routledge, 1997. 86–93.

Feldman, Christine. *We are the Mods: A Transnational History of a Youth Subculture*. New York: Peter Lang, 2009.

Fletcher, Alan. *Quadrophenia*. London: Corgi, 1979.
Goldthorpe, John H. *The Affluent Worker: Political Attitudes and Behaviour*. Cambridge: Cambridge University Press, 1968.
Jefferson, Tony. *Resistance Through Rituals: Youth Subcultures in Post-War Britain*. London: Routledge, 1993.
Lester, Richard dir. *A Hard Day's Night*. Burbank, CA: Miramax Home Entertainment, 2002.
Martin, Andrew. *Belles and Whistles: Five Journeys Through Time on Britain's Trains*. London: Profile Books, 2014.
Roddam, Franc dir. *Quadrophenia*. Los Angeles, Calif: Rhino Home Video, 2001.
Sandbrook, Dominic. *State of Emergency: The Way We Were. Britain, 1970–1974*. London: Allen Lane, 2010.
Townshend, Pete. *Quadrophenia: Music from the Soundtrack of the Who Film*. London: Polydor, 1973. Sound recording, liner notes.
Weight, Richard. *MOD: A Very British* Style. London: Bodley Head, 2013.
Zweig, Ferdinand. *The Worker in an Affluent Society*. London: Glencoe, 1961.
Zweig, Ferdinand. *The New Acquisitive Society*. Chichester: Barry Rose, 1976.

PART III

Reading *Quadrophenia*: Genre, Gender, Sexuality

CHAPTER 9

"What are You Gonna Do Tonight?" "Wait for a Phone Call I Suppose": Girls, Mod Subculture, and Reactions to the Film *Quadrophenia*

Rosalind Watkiss Singleton

The above exchange between two young women in the film *Quadrophenia* (1979) evokes an impression of female passivity in the negotiation of romantic relationships; they are not making plans for the evening but will wait for the young men to take the initiative. Although McRobbie and Garner indicate "the high visibility of girls" within the Mod subculture of the 1960s, this scene suggests that they remained subordinate to the dominant males.[1] Consequently, this chapter will focus upon the portrayal of young women in the Mod scene using memoirs, autobiographies and oral testimony to examine the reality of the relationship between Mod "boys" and their "girls." It will attempt to ascertain whether the experiences of the Mods in the provinces were different to those who lived and worked in "Swinging London" and to establish the parameters of female involvement in the Mod subculture. The oral

R.W. Singleton (✉)
University of Wolverhampton, Wolverhampton, UK
e-mail: R.Watkiss@wlv.ac.uk

© The Author(s) 2018
P. Thurschwell (ed.), *Quadrophenia and Mod(ern) Culture*,
Palgrave Studies in the History of Subcultures and Popular Music,
https://doi.org/10.1007/978-3-319-64753-1_9

testimony will be drawn predominantly, although not exclusively, from the West Midlands region, but in order to provide a wider perspective and additional balance the memoirs and autobiographies will cover a wider geographical area.[2]

Criticisms concerning the fallibility of memory and oral testimony have been deliberated in numerous journal articles and books.[3] Fass and Nora have considered both the advantages and difficulties of utilising memoirs and autobiographies and Mills has recently reflected on the ways in which women reconcile their personal reminiscences of the 1960s with popular memories of the period.[4] In order to provide a wider range of Mod experiences, efforts have been made to interview individuals who have not previously told their stories, with two exceptions, both of whom were London-based Mods.[5] A number of respondents cited in this work were interviewed for other projects and were not consciously attempting to authenticate their allegiance to any subculture but merely relating aspects of their youth to the author who was working on earlier projects.[6] This chapter examines the experiences and perceptions of the Mod culture in order to establish the accuracy of the portrayal of Mod "boys" and Mod "girls" in the film *Quadrophenia* with the respondents' recollections of the period and establish the parameters of female involvement in the Mod scene. It will ascertain the extent to which girls and young women remained on the periphery of the Mod subculture, as onlookers or part of the supporting cast.

Simon, who lived in Birmingham, began our conversation by asking: "[i]n *Quadrophenia* they chant 'we are the Mods' but who were the Mods? I often say I used to be a Mod but I'm not sure others would agree with me. Everyone has different ideas about what makes a Mod."[7] This is a perennial question with a multiplicity of answers. Mods and Modernism remain nebulous concepts with a membership that has defined itself in numerous ways over an extended period and has far outlived most other similar youth groups, in the sense that subsequent generations of Mods are still emerging. When musing upon class, Jerry White, a historian who has written extensively about areas of London, concluded that, "[w]e all know class and classes exist, but it and they elude both scientific definition and enumeration."[8]

The definition of Mods and Modernism are similarly elusive. Precise details of when the movement began and how it spread and modified are the subjects of continuous and sometimes passionate debate; Paul Anderson argues "everybody's take on … [the Mod culture] is different."[9, 10] Every aspect of this group is contested, from the origins to definitions and locations, through to the time scale of the movement. As Osgerby correctly claims, "[h]istorical precision is not easy in the field of youth culture. The styles and music that shape its existence evolve and mutate in ways that defy easy generalisations."[11]

Original Modernists have argued that the Mods appeared on the London scene in 1959 and finished in 1966.[12] Pat Farrell, a London Mod, recalled that "[t]he true Mod I remember was from around '62."[13] Others, however, would agree with April who claims that the movement "transcends time…[as] every decade sees its own Mod revival."[14] Nevertheless, there have been numerous reincarnations and modifications since then, with specific revivals in the 1970, 1980, and 1990s. It is claimed by many of the Original Modernists, and most of today's Mods, that Mod was, and remains, a way of life for some of its adherents, in the sense that they retain the same sense of style, listen to the same music and perceive themselves as "Mods."[15]

Youth subcultures are generally perceived as almost exclusively masculine affairs, a platform for rebellion and the focus of societal concern. The exploits of males dominate media coverage and have been the theme of most academic research.[16] Young women are deemed to be peripheral to the main account of historical, sociological and ethnographic studies into youth culture. To use Rowbotham's oft-cited phrase, females are mentioned in "footnotes to the main text, as worthy of the odd reference."[17] McRobbie and Garner have drawn attention to the presence of women in youth subcultures and suggested that girls were indeed visible in the Mod subculture as they "*did* much more openly and directly participate,"[18] albeit in a subsidiary role. Their arguments require further research and this chapter will build on their work.

The historiography of the Mod subculture is quite sparse, but there are a sizeable number of non-academic texts.[19, 20] Given the localised and somewhat anonymous beginnings of Mod, and the fact that "the primary sources available on the Mod movement are few and far between," recollections and reminiscences, interspersed with images of club flyers and membership tickets, form the bulk of these texts.[21] Much of this popular literature has been produced by participants of the early Mod scene themselves, often self-published, and frequently consists of semi-autobiographical novels and/or the reminiscences of other group members.[22, 23] Almost inevitably, this can prove to be problematic for serious research as the authors of this type of publication tend to draw on a limited number of individuals, often acquaintances, for their interviews.[24] To some extent, although these volumes do reach wider audiences, they are produced by the Mods for the Mods, insular, and according to a minority of Mod critics, containing a level of exaggeration or self-aggrandizement. "Jacquie" claimed that "a lot of them are fantasists" and "Lee" agreed; he felt that "they look back to their glory days, their youth and on these forums (Facebook groups—Modculture and Original Modernists 1959–1966) some of them do have a tendency to exaggerate their involvement. They can't bear to admit they missed out on an event incident, or "gig."[25] Nevertheless, these publications are often beautifully produced glossy books with fascinating images (sometimes replicated), and can be both informative and enlightening, as they are eyewitness accounts of this specific era.

Perceptions of Mod Girls

Writing in 1965, in the wake of the previous year's bank holiday clashes between Mods and Rockers, Laurie described a fifteen-year-old Mod girl whom he classed as part of the *Teenage Revolution*.[26] He compared her looks unfavourably to the women in the 1940s whose "[l]ips were ripe like fruit for biting" while her face white and devoid of expression and her "Mod lips are almost painted out."[27] As he mused upon juvenile behaviour, he concluded that she, as a member of the revolutionary postwar generation, "is not going to be a woman in the traditional sense."[28] Laurie described the Mod girl in general as a "self-reliant entity" who would expect to enter a relationship with a boy on equal terms.[29] McRobbie and Garber have indicated that the Mod boys' obsession with their look and image produced a somewhat softer and feminised subculture; particularly when contrasted with the harsher and more exaggerated masculine styles of the Teddy boys, or Rockers, Mod facilitated a culture that was more suited to female participation.[30] In their estimation, there was a "greater visibility of girls" within the Mod subculture as the movement's focus upon style gave females a justifiable reason for entry into the Mod scene.[31, 32]

Bearing these observations in mind, it is strange to note that girls are woefully under-represented within the academic literature. A brief look at the index for Weight's book on Mods, consisting of more than 400 pages and published in 2013, shows that girls are mentioned, albeit briefly, on approximately 17 pages.[33] Osgerby, focusing on the Mod "invasions" of the south coast touched only on the somewhat inflated media coverage inducing moral panic concerning increasing sexual freedom of the era.[34] Similarly, Fowler's examination of the Mod culture, which he describes as a "largely male youth cult," excludes women other than a dismissive paragraph on Cathy McGowan, the presenter of the television programme *Ready Steady Go!*[35]

Quadrophenia

The film *Quadrophenia*, based upon the album *Quadrophenia* by the Who (1973), was released in 1979 although it was set in 1964. Focused upon Jimmy Cooper and his quest to escape the tedium of his job and the monotony of his home life, the film follows Jimmy's attempts to find meaning and excitement, with much of the action taking place on the August bank holiday on Brighton's seafront. Jimmy has a fleeting love/lust relationship with supermarket employee Steph, which culminates in a sexual encounter in an alleyway during the mayhem of a clash between the Mods and Rockers in Brighton. But women in the film are generally relegated to the periphery of young men's lives, far less important than clothes, scooters and adolescent allegiances. Girls in *Quadrophenia* appear in clubs, parties and coffee bars, in dance scenes, as pillion riders of the ubiquitous scooters, as well as check-out girls and consumers; they are present but certainly secondary players in a masculine struggle for identity and change. The gender stereotypes bear some similarity to those in the 1964 film *The Leather Boys*. The focus of the film is male angst, Jimmy's attempts to reconcile the reality of his life with his hopes and dreams.

Steph (played by Leslie Ash) and Monkey (played by Toyah Wilcox) are the only two female characters named in the cast list. Other than his mum and Yvonne, Jimmy's sister, the remainder are relegated to anonymous descriptions such as Girl with Steph, Disco Dancer, Biker Girl, and Chief Rocker Girl. These anonymous young women materialise at parties and dance scenes in the clubs and discos, which were familiar leisure-time locations for many young women in the 1960s but are portrayed as little more than accessories to the adolescent men—"pillion fodder," according to Weight.[36] On leaving the supermarket, where she is employed as a cashier, Steph enquires of a colleague, "What are you going to do tonight?" and the response to the query is "Wait for a phone call I suppose."

The subtext is clear. Despite the increasing independence of young women in the post-war era, the new employment opportunities, and increasing disposable incomes leading to increased consumption, they remain passive and submissive on the fringes of the Mod scene, partial rather than full participants.[37] For girls like Steph and her colleague, decisions concerning their social life and leisure activities were dependent upon the vagaries and moods of the young men in their lives; waiting for a phone call from a boy shaped their evenings and weekends. Their expectations of romance and attitudes to the opposite sex reflect the experiences of previous generations in that in the 1960s, the girls were still waiting for existing, or prospective, boyfriends to signal their availability.[38] Female emancipation was still a work in progress.

Reactions to the Film

Perceptions and opinions about *Quadrophenia* were, and remain, based upon the age and experience of the audience, in the sense that first-generation Mods, or the Original Modernists, as they are sometimes styled, are generally adamant that the movement originated in the outer suburbs of London in 1959 and ended in the mid-1960s. Sheila Laslett O'Brien felt that Mods "only lasted a handful of years. I think by late 1965 it was over."[39] Barnes, and other eyewitnesses, conclude that 1964 and 1965 should be regarded as the "peak of the Mod look" and the halcyon years of Mods.[40] However, Christina, Steve and Andy, who all lived in the West Midlands, identified 1966 to 1967 as the time when Mod fashions and music "really took off." Andy regretfully acknowledged this "was a bit late for me to enjoy properly" as it was a time when "we were all growing up, thinking of the future, perhaps even settling down. A time when we were saving for mortgage deposits and weddings so youthful fads went onto the backburner, financial priorities lay elsewhere. That was it we were just growing up."[41] Perhaps, inevitably, "ideas change when you reach a certain age and anyway we all got married much younger in the 1960 and early 70 s."[42] However, subsequent generations of Mods believe that the movement is fluid and constantly evolving, with new cohorts materialising at regular intervals.[43] Inevitably, given the discrepancies in accounts of the Mod scene in its various reincarnations, opinions of the film vary widely. Hewitt and Baxter are quite clear that the inaccuracies in *Quadrophenia* render it inconsequential, as for Mod purists it "has no value whatsoever."[44] Original Modernist

Roger McQueen wrote: "I was in Brighton wasn't like the film all I can remember is being cold and being moved on by the police good fantasy film (sic)."[45] Indisputably, many of the original Mods queued to see the film, although their impressions were not entirely favourable.[46] Described by respondents as "disappointing," "a let-down," "bleedin (sic) rubbish," and "a travesty," the film frustrated many of those expecting an accurate portrayal of the period, at least according to their perceptions.[47] Christina is quite clear that the film "was not really a reflection of our experiences in Wolverhampton and I found it quite boring. It didn't do it for me."[48] Amongst other Mods from the provinces, the views were similar, with Andy and others implying that "it [the film] was entertaining enough but *Quadrophenia* didn't really have many points of reference for us. We rarely went to the coast and fighting, what there was of it was localised and fairly rare."[49] "When we travelled from the Midlands to the south coast we were looking for fun, excitement but certainly not trouble. We wanted to get away from the area for a laugh, nothing more. More than likely I would have lost my job in the bank if I'd got into trouble."[50] Some respondents from the West Midlands actually recalled using the same venues as the Rockers: "Fights? Not really, they [Rockers] had their nights and we had ours, we didn't go looking for trouble but could take care of ourselves if we had to."[51] While in 1979 the film attracted new adherents to the Mod scene, the new generation of Mods had already begun to emerge two years earlier in 1977, as an alternative to the Punk scene.[52] Newer, or second-wave Mods, found some inspiration in the film. As Brian from Bilston explained his reception of the video in the early 1980s, "it was so different to the Punk scene, so smart and cool. We saw it a couple of times when it was released and later referred to the video for tips."[53] As Stephen, who was thirteen when the film was released, recalled "it [the film] was our video Bible; it was a template to aspire to."[54] Similarly, Gil explained that "[w]e could watch the film, copy their clothes and style as far as possible and to emulate their behaviour. *Quadrophenia* was a blueprint for our young lives; it was as real as we were."[55] His views were endorsed by all the second-generation Mods that were interviewed. This was corroborated by Vicky who remembered "watching the film endlessly to pick up tips on how to look cool, admire the boys, and dream."[56] The film appeared to be particularly influential with teenagers who were still at school, with Paul and Sue agreeing that "we were all really excited by the film and everyone in our group felt the same. It played a major role in our lives for a few years at least."⁵⁷ Rather worryingly, Stephen also admitted that he and his school friends watched the film "endlessly" believing that "Jimmy and Steph were the ultimate couple. We all wanted to be like Jimmy and Steph."⁵⁸ These comments give some insight into how the film was consumed by subsequent generations of self-identified Mods, with young teenagers appearing to be captivated by the romantic entanglements and excitement rather than the teenage angst and despair. Nevertheless, amongst some Mods there remains a sense of embarrassment concerning the film, with Sasha (born in 1988) admitting "the minute I saw *Quadrophenia*—I don't like to say it—but it did influence me in a way and a lot of people don't like saying that."⁵⁹

ARM CANDY OR FULLY FLEDGED MEMBERS?

To answer this question it is necessary to examine the views of the Original Modernists as well as the subsequent generations. Barnes, who was part of the original scene, has stated quite clearly that that "Mods were more interested in themselves and each other than the girls."⁶⁰ This is very much echoed by other Mod opinions cited by Barnes and many of the interviews in the non-academic literature.⁶¹ Cohn described Mod boys as "curiously self-contained. They tended not to be interested in girls, nor in anyone else." Furthermore, he dismissed the girls as "camp followers" who were virtually disregarded as they "trailed behind the boys."⁶² "It wasn't that we didn't want girls, or want sex come to that, but they could be an encumbrance in the sense that they wanted attention when you were with your mates and having a laugh. Girls were great in their place."⁶³ Second-generation Mods such as Terry Rawlings went further arguing that in the 1970s "[t]here were no girls and I mean none whatsoever (well there were one or two but they were few and far between)."⁶⁴ Girls were deemed an unnecessary expense to young boys who were struggling to buy the necessities of Mod life. "Lee" admitted that maintaining high standards of grooming and constantly buying clothes was so expensive that "girls were always second fiddle as my wages were always spoken for in advance—no money left to date girls."⁶⁵ These views were corroborated by Sara Brown who recalled that "[the] lads were so preoccupied with their clothes" and Janet, from Walsall, who said "you had to work hard to attract a Mod.⁶⁶ Dull boys were easy to come by but they were the sort your mum wanted you to settle down with. They were easy to entice but the Mods were always distant and obsessed with themselves."[67] "Lee" (who moved to London from Wolverhampton) and Steve agreed when they admitted "it wasn't that we didn't like girls but they weren't so important, at least until you met the sort you might like to settle down with. You didn't really have time, money or energy until then."[68] The girls very much endorsed this, with Jean agreeing that "[i]t was very difficult to get the attention of the boys who were pretty much caught up with their clothes, their mates and acting cool, so you really had to try very hard to get noticed."[69] Chris had similar experiences recalling that "we girls very much played second fiddle to the boys who met us early on in the evening and went off later with their mates. We weren't at all important to them."[70] The secret was to "dress well, look good, and pretend you weren't interested. It wasn't always easy, because obviously you were [interested] but we tried really hard to be cool, subtle, that sort of thing. Sometimes it worked and sometimes it backfired. I remember a lad called Steve, one I really fancied, telling me some twenty years later that he was frightened to approach as I always seemed disinterested and self-contained. What a blow! (laughter)."[71]

Christina recalled that clothes were as important as attitude for the Mod girls hoping to attract the right boy—"There was one girl who stood out. She never wore the same clothes twice. She married a footballer and she got your attention and that of the lads in Wolverhampton. She stood out the way I imagine Marianne Faithfull stood out in London. To me she seemed like a main Mod and you could see the latest fashions and trends by what girls like her were wearing."[72] Janet agreed that "you could see what the top Mod girls were wearing. Trendsetters you'd probably call them now. And you had to keep up if you wanted male attention; you couldn't be wearing things that were a couple of weeks out of date. No one would give you a second glance if you were behind the times. Mum used to go mad at what she called me wasting money. But I had a job and once I'd paid my board I could do what I liked. It didn't stop her creating though."[73] Sue used to "sneak new things in when my parents weren't looking. I needed to keep up with the trends, no chance of netting a decent lad otherwise, but they would have called me a wastrel. The cost was phenomenal but I didn't want a boring boyfriend—it had to be a Mod."[74]

Young women had their place in the Mod subculture but it was more as an accessory for the males. Elms for example, stressed the importance of the "right girl on your arm."[75] Johnny smilingly agreed that "a good looking girl wearing the right clothes would boost your image at times. But girls came much lower in the pecking order, after clothes, hair, and transport."[76] "Jacquie," whose antecedents were decidedly middle class, recalled that working-class boys were often looking for a girl whose presence would enhance their status: "Boys from the Peckham housing estate were looking for something different."[77] This, and other testimony from middle-class Mods, certainly questions claims that Mods were overwhelmingly working class.[78] Carlo Manzi confirmed this. Although initially stating that "[i]n Modernism you dressed for other blokes. You were far more interested in a guy coming up to you and saying 'great suit', than a girl coming up to you and saying 'great suit'"; he later admitted that "you would look at a girl if she looked like she'd spent a few bob" on her clothes.[79] So, in that sense the 'right' girlfriend was a means of enhancing status and kudos but "you couldn't let a sort stand in the way of the time with your mates, they were the priority. It was nice to have one around but in her place if you know what I mean? Clingy and persistent could just be a pain, so the balance was good enough to make your mates envious but someone willing to wait until you had time for them."[80] Si agreed that "a girlfriend is nice, fill in an hour or two with them when you were at a loose end. Problem was when they kept trying to find out where you'd be after college and then they'd just appear, usually with a tug, you know a fat or ugly mate, and then they'd keep trying to get your attention. Then they became an embarrassment and you'd get stick from the rest of the lads."[81]

In *Quadrophenia* Monkey is one such girl; she is besotted with Jimmy, who rarely notices her. On screen for approximately 10 minutes over the entire film, she appears to be one of the crowd, but her eyes and attention are usually focused longingly on Jimmy. She is constantly aware of him, gravitating towards him and often just at his shoulder, waiting, pleading to be noticed but constantly spurned. The audience can recognise her devotion, but he remains oblivious to her, using her to supply his drugs from the chemist where she works and for a careless fumble when Steph is not available. As Jimmy drives off on his scooter when he is finally spurned by Steph, Monkey tries to offer words of consolation, but he tells her to "shut up and piss off."' She is nothing to him and we, the audience, know that.

Some of the female respondents had similar experiences. Jenny and Jean both described occasions when "it was hard to pin some of these good looking lads down. You know, get some commitment. They'd say see you again and you'd either have to wait for them to get in touch, phone call or note through your door, or take the initiative and try and track them down. Find out where they'd be and appear. This was risky as it could backfire—you'd be there with a friend and sidle over to the group of lads and he'd virtually ignore you."[82] Unrequited love is an almost inevitable part of teenage life and was just the same in Mod circles, as Sue admitted 'there would be lads you sighed over and did your best to attract their attention but sadly some of them were impervious to my charms (laughs). We sort of followed them about, at a distance of course, and we hoped that eventually we would be noticed. Often when you were noticed it was by someone that you didn't fancy but *c'est la vie*. You grow up and sort yourself out but the teenage years can be difficult."[83] Janet recalled humiliation when she and a girlfriend went to the Milano, a Wolverhampton coffee bar, "I wanted my friend to see how good-looking and smart he was. All the Mods went to the Milano so we decided to pop in and meet him as if by accident. He was there with a group of lads laughing and joking. Our eyes met and he looked away and carried on talking. We got a coffee and sat at another table and I said 'he'll come over in a minute', but he never did and that was that so to speak. I was so sad and humiliated."[84] In the right circumstances a forthright girl could have success. Christina met John at work but "he didn't properly ask me out although we got together at times but I never knew where I stood until the New Year when I said "I want to know where I stand. I want to be your girlfriend but if not…"[85]

Girls' position in Mod culture, as with many other youth subcultures, was measured largely on their sexual attractiveness.[86] A number of interviews insinuate that many Mod girls, possibly because of the "unisex" look with somewhat masculine clothing, were not particularly attractive. Statements such as, "Mod girls were never as attractive as the Mod boys," "there were not that many good-looking Mod girls to go round," "to be honest there weren't a great many lookers, so we didn't bother," and "a girl would need to be something special for me to even notice," typify attitudes to these girls.[87, 88, 89, 90] In her autobiography, Janet Street Porter blamed her failure, by 1963, to attract male attention on her façade as a "cool, miserable looking Mod."[91] There was certainly a degree of arrogance amongst some males who felt that their status gave them access to the prettier girls. Jimmy, "Lee," and Andy all stated that their style and panache gave them access to the most attractive young women. Andy made it clear that "basically, girls hung around with the group and they wanted to go out with you. They didn't push exactly but it was more that they loitered, hovered, you know, hung around."[92] "Lee" described it "as an ego thing—you wanted them to fancy you but not to make a nuisance of themselves."[93] Ian Hebditch's experiences were similar and he claimed that "we felt we could more or less have anyone."[94] Mark Timlin's opinions encapsulate the views of many Mods: "I hate to say this but, girls were just appendages. Geezers were the most important people. You wanted a girlfriend but at the same time you didn't want them around because they didn't understand the music. They might pretend but what would they know about 'Green Onions'?"[95]

Robert Wyndham Nicholls, who describes himself as a "participant observer" in Soho's scene club, poses this very question in his article "'What would they know about Green Onions?': Musical lifestyles of the London Mods."[96] He challenges the idea that women were merely subordinate members of the Mod entourage arguing that "some girls took the lead, serving as conduits for Mod aesthetics."[97] In his estimation, and drawn from his direct experiences, Nicholls suggests that some girls did take the "lead and were admired for their personal autonomy, their role as conduits of mod aesthetics, and their skills in music and dance."[98] Undoubtedly, there is some truth in this, as Mod girls, much like the boys, retained their individuality. However, his evidence appears to be based solely upon his relationship with Pat Beckett and the behaviour of the fictional character Kay Miller in Tony Parsons' novel *Limelight Blues*.[99] Nicholls finds similarities between his admiration of Pat and the adoration given to Kay Miller and in the two women's personas. But it seems as though his attraction to Pat, fuelled by her musical taste and the fact that "we looked good together," resulted in a somewhat unequal relationship where she "set the boundaries" and he "was doomed to pursue her."[100, 101] The scant evidence points more to a young man in the first flush of youthful love than a true verification that many young women held prominent roles in the Mod scene. The fact that a girl can introduce her boyfriend to specific music tracks does not necessarily mean that girls were trendsetters and more than "arm candy." Inevitably, as in any subculture, there were women who led the fashion trends and had an exceptional appreciation of trends in music. The evidence of the respondents tend to indicate a passion for particular bands or genres such as Motown; with Christina it was the Small Faces, for Jenny it was Georgie Fame, and for some of the Midlands-based Mods it was the

Spencer Davis Group.[102] Other girls affected to like music that might impress the boys: "well I had broad tastes in music but if I knew that a particular boy I had a 'crush' on liked a track or an album then I would make it my business to find out a bit about it or drop something into the conversation."[103] For Mods, in London and the provinces, it was important to remain casual and not show too much interest in the live musicians. For "Jacquie" it was vital "to impress everyone else with your cool. So, we just danced to whoever played, we never went to talk to the bands and never screamed at them as it didn't pay to show that you were excited by them."[104] Pam agreed that "to show interest in the band was really uncool. Even if you secretly like them you had to pretend otherwise. We tried not to be impressed by anyone or anything."[105] Patricia Finn Litchfield recalled the Who playing on *Ready Steady Go!* when she was one of the dancers and her efforts to appear unimpressed,—"we were totally in awe, staring at top pop stars but trying hard not to stare, if that makes sense."[106]

The promiscuity in the film was one area that respondents contended vigorously. In a 2006 interview about *Quadrophenia*, director and co-writer Franc Roddam spoke about a sexual revolution in the 1960s in which teenagers were "definitely having sex" and, because of the advent of the birth control pill, were "definitely having safe sex."[107, 108] Roddam claimed that in 1960s Britain "before there was the Summer of Love there was the summer of sex, drugs and violence," but the oral testimony disputes this.[109] Although it is implied that the autonomy experienced by teenagers in the 1960s facilitated sexual freedom, and certainly scenes in *Quadrophenia* appear to endorse this, the era remained one in which most girls and many boys expected the commitment of a wedding or at least an engagement before they engaged in sexual intercourse. "Jacquie," who described herself as a precocious fourteen-year-old, insisted that "sexual freedom was a load of old tosh" and that few girls were sexually promiscuous.[110] The three main fears were an illegitimate baby, the worry that they would *have* to get married, and the concern that their reputation would suffer if they slept around. In the film, Steph is aware of the problems of promiscuity when she asks Jimmy to keep quiet about their kisses. Jenny explained that "we didn't usually have sex before we were married, or at least engaged, the risks were too great—a 'shotgun wedding', a baby before we could afford one and the fear that you would be letting your parents down."[111]

In the opinions of most respondents, the risks of promiscuity were too great as "even in the sixties we didn't risk an unwanted pregnancy. It was alright for the boys who pressured you but as a girl it was you who took the risks and had most to lose. They might promise to marry you but you couldn't be sure. It always makes me smile when you hear so much about the 'swinging sixties', it certainly wasn't true for me or my friends. A white wedding was really important back then."[112] "This idea that by the 1960s girls were free to run around and do what they wanted without a care was a total fallacy. For most of us there were restrictions on where we went, who we went with and what time you had to be home, so opportunities for sex were limited. That's why most of us married so early, to get some freedom."[113] There is scant evidence to suggest that attitudes to sex had transformed as much as the activities in the film suggest, particularly Steph's actions or the general party scenes. Certainly, kissing and heavy petting may have taken place at some of the parties that the respondents attended, but few young women "went all the way as it was just too risky."[114]

Conclusion

The actual definition of "Mod" remains a contested area, with scant agreement on periodisation or region. These are disputes that may never be reconciled. Nevertheless, despite anomalies in the areas of sexual freedom or sexual liberation and Roddam's claims of sexual emancipation, the oral testimony endorses the portrayal of young women in *Quadrophenia* as subsidiary to the Mod subculture. The film depicts the girls as very much on the periphery of the boys' lives and this was true for many of the respondents. Girls became Mods attracted by the clothes, the music, and often the musicians themselves, but for some the overriding factor was the appearance of the Mod boys as "they looked so smart and cool. They were different and the air of confidence was certainly attractive."[115] Jenny's memories of the 1960s indicate that "Mod venues were the place to go as the sort of boys you might want to date, possibly marry, went there. It was about being in the right place and mixing with the right crowd."[116] The respondents, both male and female, recognised Mod as a predominantly male subculture and there was negligible evidence to suggest otherwise.

It is indisputable that the Mods originated "in and around Soho" in 1959, but the fashions, music and culture permeated the rest of

Britain over several years and have witnessed several reincarnations since that date.[117] Reactions to the film *Quadrophenia* depend, to a large extent, on when individuals became Mods as well as their geographic location. As, original modernist Stuert Kinglsey-Innes wrote, "*Quadrophenia* has only given the world a distorted glimpse of one moment in time."[118] A true reflection of the Mods would be impossible to entirely verify because opinions vary so widely, with Ted Leigh arguing that "the only people who know were the one's (sic) who were there, and they are all in their late 60t's and early 70t's (sic)."[119] Mods from the 1970s and subsequent decades were more likely to consider the film as an instruction manual "to find out what you need to know about Mod fashions and lifestyles."[120] The most vociferously contested scenes by the oral testimony were the ones involving sex, with respondents making it clear that although some teenagers indulged in sex outside marriage it was still comparatively unusual in the early 1960s as "the consequences were too awful to consider."[121]

The film *Quadrophenia* marginalised women, depicting them as little more than subordinate characters on the Mod scene, and this is clearly corroborated within the oral evidence. However, the experiences of the respondents indicate that the extent of their sexual freedom was misrepresented by the filmmakers, due at least in part to Roddam's conviction that the sexual revolution reached further than it did in the early 1960s. Although ideas were slowly changing, young women who belonged to the Mods in the 1960s were largely unaffected by the ideas of a permissive society. The availability of the birth-control pill and claims of the "Swinging Sixties" did not affect the behaviour of the respondents who tended to adhere to traditional societal expectations of acceptable feminine conduct. Their views and actions did not differ from young women of earlier generations and they remained on the periphery of a male-dominated subculture, as followers not leaders.

NOTES

1. Angela McRobbie and J. Garber, "Girls and Subcultures," in *CCCS Selected Working Papers Volume 2*, A. Gray et al. (eds) (London: Routledge, 2007), 225.
2. Thirty-four respondents were interviewed (16 males and eighteen females) between 2014 and 2016. Four additional females had mentioned relevant topics, in 2010, in an unconnected project. See footnote 6.

3. Paul Thompson, *The Voice of the Past: Oral History* (Oxford: Oxford University Press, 2000, 3rd Edition); A. Hoffman "Reliability and Validity in Oral History," in *Oral History: An Interdisciplinary Anthology*, eds. D.K. Dunaway and W. Baum (London: Sage Publications, 1992, 2nd Edition); L. Layman, "Reticence in Oral History Interviews," *The Oral History Review*, 36, no. 2 (2009): 207–230; D.A. Boyd and M. A. Lawson eds., *Oral History and Digital Humanities: Voice, Access and Engagement* (New York: Palgrave Macmillan, 2014).
4. Paula S. Fass, "The Memoir Problem," *Reviews in American History* 34: 1 (March 2006): 107–123; Pierre Nora, "Between Memory and History: Les Lieux de Memoire," *Representations* 26 (Spring 1989): 7–24; Helena Mills "Using the personal to critique the popular: women's memories of 1960s youth," *Contemporary British History* 30, no. 4 (2016): 463–483.
5. "Jacquie" and "Lee" both of whom are using pseudonyms. The remainder of respondents are from the Midlands and North of England. Jacquie (London) in discussion with the author, December 2016. Lee (London) in discussion with the author, May 2016.
6. Rosalind Watkiss "Today I met the Boy I'm Gonna Marry: Romantic Expectations of Teenage Girls in the 1960s West Midlands, in *Youth Culture and Social Change: Making a Difference by Making a Noise*, ed. Worley, M; K. Gildart (Basingstoke: Palgrave Macmillan, 2017); *Women of Wolverhampton Oral History Project*; Rosalind Watkiss "Old Habits Persist, Change and Continuity in Black Country Communities: Pensnett, Sedgley and Tipton, 1945–c.1970" (Ph.D. diss. University of Wolverhampton, 2011).
7. Simon (Coventry) in discussion with the author, March 2016.
8. Jerry White, *The Worst Street in North London: Campbell Bunk, Islington, between the wars* (London: Routledge and Kegan Paul plc., 1986), 27.
9. Paolo Hewitt, *The Soul Stylists: Six Decades of Modernism—From Mods to Casuals* (Edinburgh: Mainstream Publishing Co. Ltd., 2008).
10. Paul Anderson, *Mods, The New Religion: The Style and Music of the 1960s Mods* (London: Omnibus Press, 2014), Preface.
11. Bill Osgerby, *Youth in Britain since 1945* (Oxford: Blackwell Publishers, 1998), 97.
12. Although it has been suggested that the television programme *Ready, Steady, Go!* (1963–1966) led to the demise of the Mods as it popularised their culture around the country, leading to the dilution of the original tenets of the movement. Robert Hall cited in Hewitt, *The Soul Stylists*, 87.
13. Pat Farrell cited in Paul Anderson, *Mods*, 28.

14. April Folan cited in *Ready, Steady, Girls: The Other Half of the Mod Equation*, Mark Baxter, J. Brummell and I. Snowball eds. (London: Suave Collective Publishing, 2016), 62.
15. "It's still an important part of the way I dress and think. Once a Mod always a Mod"; Brian (Walsall) in discussion with the author, April 2015.
16. Stanley Cohen, *Folk Devils and Moral Panics: The Creation of Mods and Rockers* (Oxford: Basil Blackwell, 1980, First Published in 1972).
17. Sheila Rowbotham (1973) cited in Stanley Cohen *Folk Devils and Moral Panics*, xxi; McRobbie and Garner 'Girls and Subcultures' in A. Gray et al. (eds.) *CCCS*, 219.
18. McRobbie and Garner, "Girls and Subcultures," 223. See also Angela McRobbie, *Feminism and Youth Culture* (Basingstoke: Macmillan Press Ltd. 2001, First Published in 1991), 19.
19. Richard Weight, *Mod! A Very British Style* (London: The Bodley Head, 2013); C. J. Feldman "We Are the Mods: A Transnational History of a Youth Subculture" (PhD diss., University of Pittsburgh, 2009); Peter Lang; Richard Barnes, *Mods!* (London: Plexus Publishing, 1979); David Fowler, *Youth Culture in Modern Britain, c.1920–c.1970: From Ivory Tower to Global Movement—A New History* (Basingstoke: Palgrave Macmillan, 2008); Cohen *Folk Devils*.
20. Keith Gildart, *Images of England Through Popular Music: Class, Youth and Rock 'n' Roll* (Basingstoke: Palgrave Macmillan, 2013), 89.
21. Fowler, *Youth Culture*, 128.
22. For example, see, Howard Baker, *Sawdust Caesar: Omnibus Edition* (HB Publishing, 2015).
23. Baxter, Brummell and Snowball *Ready Steady Girls*; Tony Beesley, *Sawdust Caesars: Original Mod Voices* (Days Like Tomorrow Books, 2014); Gareth Brown, *Mods and Rockers: The Origins and Era of a British Scene* (Church Stretton: Independent Music Press, 2010).
24. For example, a number of the same names may be cross-referenced in Anderson, *Mods*; Baxter et al. *Ready, Steady Girls*; Beasley, *Sawdust Caesars*; Hewitt, *The Soul Stylists*.
25. Jacquie Original "Mod." Jacquie was clear the members of first phase of the group (1959–1966) did not refer to themselves with this sobriquet and indicated that the word Mod should always be in inverted commas. She also indicated that there was a measure of exaggeration or hyperbole in some accounts. Similar criticisms were levelled by Joan (Tipton) in discussion with the author January 2011; Jim (Coventry); Rose (Bilston) and Andy (Stoke-on-Trent) in discussion with the author, July 2016.

26. Peter Laurie, *The Teenage Revolution* (London: Antony Blond Ltd., 1965), 7.
27. Laurie, *Teenage Revolution*, 27.
28. Laurie, *Teenage Revolution*, 7.
29. Laurie, *Teenage Revolution*, 27.
30. McRobbie and Garber, 'Girls and Subcultures', 19.
31. McRobbie and Garber, 'Girls and Subcultures', 20.
32. McRobbie and Garber, 'Girls and Subcultures', 17.
33. Weight, *Mod!*
34. Osgerby, *Youth in Britain since 1945* (Oxford: Blackwell Publishing, 1998).
35. Fowler, *Youth Culture*, 134–135.
36. Weight *Mod*—Image Caption.
37. Osgerby *Youth in Britain*, 31 and Chap. 5, 51–55.
38. For a detailed examination of these attitudes see Watkiss, "Today I Met the Boy" in Gildart, (ed.) *Youth Acts.*
39. Baxter et al. *Ready Steady Girls*, 106.
40. Barnes, *Mods!*, 128.
41. Christina (Wolverhampton) in discussion with the author, November 2016; Steve (Wolverhampton) in discussion with the author, June 2016; Andy (Halesowen) in discussion with the author, May 2016.
42. Janet (Coventry) in discussion with the author, September 2014.
43. Rawlings *Mod*, 159–209; Respondents in Baxter et al.
44. Paolo Hewitt and M. Baxter, *The A-Z of Mod* (New York, Munich, London: Prestel, undated), 208.
45. Roger McQueen *The Original Modernists Facebook Site*, 6 March 2016.
46. 'Lee'; Terry (Leicester); Pete (Coventry); Johnny (Leek); Sandra (Dudley); Chris (Wall Heath); Sue (Old Hill) in discussion with the author, May–June 2015.
47. Terry; Pete; "Lee"; Johnny.
48. Christina.
49. Andy; Steve; Jim (Wednesbury) in discussion with the author, March 2014.
50. Darren (Wednesbury) in discussion with the author, March 2014.
51. Mel (Wolverhampton) in discussion with the author, June 2016; Steve; Jim.
52. Weight, *Mod* Chap. 7, 243–277; Rawlings, *Mod*; Vicky (Old Hill); Stephen (Halesowen); Gil (Bilston) in discussion with the author, March 2015.
53. Brian.
54. Stephen S, in discussion with the author, November 2016; Feldman's book examines the Mod revival, 43–54.

55. Gil.
56. Vicky.
57. Paul (Birmingham) in discussion with the author, January 2015; Sue.
58. Stephen S.
59. Sasha cited in Feldman "'We are the Mods'".
60. Barnes, *Mods!*, 15.
61. Barnes, *Mods!*, 15.
62. Nik Cohn "Mods," in *The Sharper Word*, ed. P. Hewitt (London: Helter Skelter Publishing, 1999), 141.
63. Brian.
64. Terry Rawlings, *Mod: A Very British Phenomenon* (London: Omnibus Press, 2000), 164.
65. "Lee."
66. Barnes *Mods!*, 15.
67. Janet.
68. "Lee"; Steve.
69. June (Wolverhampton) in discussion with the author, January 2014.
70. Chris.
71. Pat (Wolverhampton) December 2010. The term "cool" was used in a number of interviews and its definition is almost as elusive as "Mod." In Weight's opinion, "cool" is inextricably linked to working-class aspirations and upward mobility within the Mod subculture (p. 390). Respondents, however, used the term to define Mods who were "slightly aloof," "those who set the trends," "fashionable," or "role-models." Terry, Sandra, Pete, Gil, and Vicky. As Steve explained, "Cool is indefinable, to some extent it's in the eye of the beholder."
72. Christina.
73. Pat.
74. Sue.
75. Robert Elms, *A Life in Threads: The Way We Wore* (Basingstoke: Pan Macmillan, 2005), 25.
76. Johnny.
77. "Jacquie."
78. Pat; Sue; Andy; Jimmy.
79. Carlo Manzi cited in Hewitt *The Soul Stylists*, 67.
80. Steve.
81. Si (Coventry) in discussion with the author, March 2015.
82. Jenny (Bilston) in discussion with the author, January 2015; Jean (Wednesfield) in discussion with the author, March 2015.
83. Sue.
84. Janet.
85. Christina.

86. McRobbie and Garber, *Girls and Subcultures*, 219.
87. Carlo Manzi cited in Hewitt, *The Soul Stylists*, 67.
88. Alfredo Marcontonio cited in Hewitt, *The Soul Stylists*, 75.
89. Pete.
90. Steve.
91. J. Street Porter, *Baggage: My Childhood* (London: Headline Publishing, 2004), 169.
92. Andy, Jimmy and "Lee."
93. "Lee."
94. Ian Hebditch cited in Hewitt, *The Soul Stylists*, 69.
95. Mark Timlin cited in Hewitt, *The Soul Stylists*, 75.
96. R W Nicholls, "What would they know about Green Onions?'; Musical Lifestyles of 1960s London Mods," *Popular Music History* 9 i.2 (2014): 155–172.
97. Nicolls, Abstract 155.
98. Nicholls.
99. Nicholls, 157; T. Parsons, *Limelight Blues* (London: Virgin Books, 1987).
100. Nicholls, 169.
101. Nicholls, 165.
102. Christina, Jenny, Sue and Pam.
103. Sue.
104. "Jacquie."
105. Pam, Sue and Jenny all expressed similar views.
106. Patricia Finn Litchfield *The Original Modernists Facebook Site*, 2 June 2016.
107. Franc Roddam, *A Way of Life: The Making of Quadrophenia*, Two Disc Special Edition, Universal Pictures (2006).
108. Roddam, *A Way of Life*.
109. Roddam, *A Way of Life*.
110. "Jacquie."
111. Jenny.
112. Janet.
113. Sue but similar views were expressed by most of the girls.
114. Jenny; Sue; June; Christina; Janet. See also Watkiss "Today I Met the Boy I'm Gonna Marry" in Gildart (ed.)
115. Pam.
116. Jenny.
117. Rawlings, *Mod*, 11
118. Stuart Kingsley-Inness *The Original Modernists Facebook Site*, 6 March 2016.
119. Ted Leigh *The Original Modernists Facebook Site*, 6 March 2016.

120. Stephen.
121. Sue.

Bibliography

Anderson, Paul. *Mods: The New Religion: The Style and Music of the 1960s Mods.* London: Omnibus Press, 2014.
Baker, Howard. *Sawdust Caesar: Omnibus Edition.* HB Publishing, 2015.
Barnes, Richard. *Mods!* London, Plexus Publishing. 1979.
Baxter, Mark., Jason Brummell and Ian Snowball, *Ready, Steady, Girls: The Other Half of the Mod Equation.* London: Suave Collective Publishing, 2016.
Beesley, Tony. *Sawdust Caesars: Original Mod Voices.* Days Like Tomorrow Books, 2014.
Boyd, Douglas A. and Mary A. Lawson, eds. *Oral History and Digital Humanities: Voice, Access and Engagement.* New York: Palgrave Macmillan, 2014.
Brown, Gareth. *Mods and Rockers: The Origins and Era of a British Scene,* Church Stretton: Independent Music Press, 2010.
Cohen, Stanley. *Folk Devils and Moral Panics: The Creation of Mods and Rockers,* Oxford: Basil Blackwell, 1980. First Published in 1972.
Cohn, Nik. "Mods." In *The Sharper Word,* Edited by Paolo Hewitt. London: Helter Skelter Publishing, 2014. 137–143.
Elms, Robert. *A Life in Threads: The Way We Wore.* Basingstoke: Palagrave Macmillan, 2005.
Fass, Paula S. "The Memoir Problem." *Reviews in American History* 34, n. 1 (2006): 107–123.
Feldman, Christine J. "We Are the Mods: A Transnational History of a Subculture", Ph.D. diss. University of Pittsburgh, 2009.
Fowler, David. *Youth Culture in Modern Britain, c.1920–c.1970: From Ivory Tower to Global Movement—A New History.* Basingstoke: Palgrave Macmillan, 2008.
Gildart, Keith. *Images of England through Popular Music: Class, Youth and Rock 'n' Roll.* Basingstoke: Palgrave Macmillan, 2013.
Hathorne, Carol. *Those Were The Days.* Dudley: The Kates Hill Press, 2014.
Hewitt, Paolo, ed. *The Sharper Word: A Mod Anthology.* London: Helter Skelter, 1999.
Hewitt, Paolo. *The Soul Stylists: Six Decades of Modernism—From Mods to Casuals.* Edinburgh: Mainstream Publishing, 2008.
Hewitt, Paolo, Mark Baxter and Martin Freeman. *The A-Z of Mod.* New York, Munich and London: Prestel Publishing, 2012.

Hoffman, Alice M. "Reliability and Validity in Oral History." In *Oral History: An Interdisciplinary Anthology* edited by Dunaway, D.K. and W. Baum, London: Sage, 1992.
Hyams, Jacky. *White Boots and Miniskirts.* London: John Blake, 2013.
Laurie, Peter. *The Teenage Revolution.* London: Antony Blond, 1965.
Layman, Lenore. "Reticence in Oral History Interviews." *The Oral History Review* 36: 2 (2009): 207–230.
McRobbie, Angela. and Jenny Garner, "Girls and Subcultures." In *CCCS Selected Working Papers Volume 2*, eds. Gray, A., Campbell, J., Erickson, M., Hanson, S. and Wood, H. 219–229, London: Routledge, 2007.
McRobbie, Angela. *Feminism and Youth Culture.* Basingstoke: Macmillan Press, 2001. First Published in 1991.
Mills, Helena. "Using the Personal to Critique the Popular: women's memories of 1960s youth." *Contemporary British History* 30: 4 (2016): 463–483.
Nicholls, R.W. "'What Would They Know About Green Onions?' Musical Lifestyles of 1960s London." *Popular Music History* 9, i.2 (2014): 155–172.
Nora, Pierre. "Between Memory and History: Les Lieux de Memoire." *Representations* n. 26 (1989): 77–124.
Original Modernists 1959–1966. Facebook Site [accessed May 2016–January 2017].
Osgerby, Bill. *Youth in Britain since 1945.* Oxford: Blackwell, 1998.
Parsons, Tony. *Limelight Blues.* London: Virgin Books, 1987.
Rawlings, Terry. *Mod: A Very British Phenomenon.* London: Omnibus Press, 2000.
Roddam, Franc. *A Way of Life: The Making of Quadrophenia.* Two Disc Special Edition, Universal Pictures, 2006.
Street-Porter, Janet. *Baggage: My Childhood.* London: Headline, 2004.
Thompson, Paul. *The Voice of the Past: Oral History*, Oxford: Oxford University Press, 2000.
Watkiss, Rosalind. "Old Habits Persist, Change and Continuity in Black Country Communities: Pensnett, Sedgley, and Tipton, 1945–c.1970" Ph.D. diss, University of Wolverhampton, 2011.
Watkiss, Rosalind. "Today I met the Boy I'm Gonna Marry: Romantic Expectations of Teenage Girls in the 1960s West Midlands." In *Youth culture and social change: Making a difference by making a noise.* edited by Keith Gildart. Basingstoke: Palgrave Macmillan, due out in 2017.
Weight, Richard. *Mod! A Very British Style.* London: The Bodley Head, 2013.
White, Jerry. *The Worst Street in North London: Campbell Bunk, Islington, between the wars.* London: Routledge and Kegan Paul, 1986.
Women of Wolverhampton Oral History Project (2014). Available at Wolverhampton Archives.

CHAPTER 10

"Poofs Wear Lacquer, Don't They, Eh?": *Quadrophenia* and the Queerness of Mod Culture

Peter Hughes Jachimiak

INTRODUCTION

This chapter considers the queerness of *Quadrophenia*—that is, the original 1973 double-album, the film adaptation and tie-in novel of 1979—and Mod culture. What is meant, here, by Mod culture is not only the origins of this very British youth subculture, but its multiple revivals since the post-punk era.[1] Furthermore, this chapter places *Quadrophenia* (all formats)—and, Mod (the original movement, and its subsequent revivals)—amid the context of queer politics. Thus, any critical queer reading of *Quadrophenia* will not only begin to aid our deeper understanding of Pete Townshend's working-class macho opus amid Mod itself, but within wider social and cultural structures above and beyond subcultures and gender politics.

Quadrophenia is a 1970s tale of a troubled young man of the 1960s, Jimmy, who encounters the tumultuous experience of the search for self/group identity in the late twentieth century. Furthermore,

P.H. Jachimiak (✉)
University of South Wales, Newport, UK
e-mail: peter.jachimiak@southwales.ac.uk

© The Author(s) 2018
P. Thurschwell (ed.), *Quadrophenia and Mod(ern) Culture*,
Palgrave Studies in the History of Subcultures and Popular Music,
https://doi.org/10.1007/978-3-319-64753-1_10

Quadrophenia—that is, the Who's original, twin-vinyl version from 1973—in many ways encourages the listener to reflect upon notions of gender and sexuality in relation to what is made obvious, and what is hidden, within a society that is dominated by a capitalist patriarchy. Think of the song "Helpless Dancer"—ostensibly a musical rant by Roger Daltrey about the harsh economic, social, and cultural conditions of a mid-70s United Kingdom—that includes the lines, "If you complain you disappear / Just like the lesbians and queers." Thus, the following discussion of the relationship between *Quadrophenia* (all formats) and Mod (original, and revivals) explores the development of a subculture in parallel with gay culture. It covers, among other topics, the appropriation of camp clothing into mainstream youth fashion, the gendered nature of two-wheeled transport, men's wearing of make-up, and the notion of Mod males as queer, mother-fixated "poster-boys." Furthermore, this chapter examines both male-female and male-male relationships amid both straight and gay Mod culture.

QUEER THEORY AND COMING OUT OF THE MOD CLOSET

Judith Halberstam, in applying queer theory to urban lesbian subcultures, not only highlights the male-centric-ness of the so-called classic studies of subcultures found in the collective works of the Chicago and Birmingham schools, but insists that looking at (what at first seem) straight subcultures through the prism of (more obviously) queer subcultures is advantageous.[2] As "some queer subcultures also provide a critical lens through which to revisit seemingly heterosexual youth cultures."[3] Thus, by teasing out the queer elements to be found in the Mod subculture, we are better positioned to be able to reappraise the more macho mannerisms of *Quadrophenia* as a hyper-Mod text. Quite crucially, then, queer politics is not restricted to conceptualising only the gay or lesbian community, or being used by those researching/writing purely in the areas of gay/lesbian and gender studies. Rather, queer theory/politics is not only on offer to—in the twenty-first century—all members of, now, a recognisable and global, lesbian, gay, bisexual, and transgender community, but those belonging to any form of subcultural grouping, be they gang-orientated (thus striving for a strength-in-numbers sense of self) or more individualised (suffering, perhaps, from that of an outsider syndrome). Moreover, the application of queer subcultural theory to *Quadrophenia*, allows us to not only conduct a nuanced analysis of its split-personality lead character, Jimmy, but to re-examine Mod in all its gendered multifariousness—that is, from the boasting bravado of a riotous "Doctor Jimmy" to the wistful romanticism of an in-love "Mister Jim."

The West, in the 1990s, was swept by a wave of queer politics. According to Chris Haywood and Máirtín Mac an Ghaill, this was fundamentally a set of deconstructive ideologies that, collectively, were concerned with the positive destabilisation of socially and culturally given forms of identities, classifications, and stereotypes.[4] At the heart of this destabilisation, Haywood and Mac an Ghaill stress, was the already recognised gay and lesbian movement. Yet, queer politics encouraged the members of this movement to re-evaluate their social identities further in line with a more extensive "range of political identifications/alliances that are in the process of being assembled."[5] In effect, this can be better understood as a more communal, concerted "coming out" of gay and lesbian individuals/movements into an intellectual arena. Thus, as a result of such a queering of identity politics, academics have been encouraged also to "come out" and produce a rich body of work on gay and lesbian issues and concerns that resonates with gender studies more broadly, providing "a philosophically rich range of concepts … including deconstructing the hetero/homo boundary, the heterosexual matrix and gender performativity."[6] Indeed, Haywood and Mac an Ghaill go on to insist that, as a typically utopian political stance, queer theory "celebrates the transgressive potential, both discursive and social, of the implosion of existing gender and sexuality categories, enabling us to reimagine inhabiting a range of masculinities and femininities," whereby "queer activists emphasize the openness, fragmentation and diversity that infuses contemporary ways of being."[7] Moreover, theorising upon both "out in the open" and "behind closed doors" male-male relationships, Eve Kosofsky Sedgwick asserts that the "epistemology of the closet" has not only "given an overarching consistency to gay culture and identity" throughout the twentieth century, but it is "on a far vaster scale and with less honorific inflection, inexhaustibly productive of modern Western culture and history at large."[8, 9] Moreover, any exploration of this "closet" can only take place following acknowledgment of, what Sedgwick terms, "binarisms" that are inherently unstable (for example, "secrecy/disclosure," "public/private," and so on). Thus, by adopting a "binarism" approach, that takes *Quadrophenia* out of the darkened "closet," and places it in the light, out along with all the other peacocking finery of Mod, we are able to achieve a true epistemology of subcultures—straight, queer, Mod, or otherwise.[10]

GAY CIRCLES AND CRUISING FOR A BRUISING

Richard Weight makes explicit the extent by which the rise of the Mod subculture, during the early 1960s, occurred during an era of continuing suspicion of, and outright hostility to, gays and gay culture.[11] Quite simply, even in the years leading up to the legalisation—in 1967 (in England and Wales)—of homosexual acts between consenting men aged over 21 years, being openly gay "risked derision, ostracism or violence."[12] Despite there existing a long-standing heritage of camp amid the bawdy humour of British vaudeville, Britain remained a nation entrenched in homophobia, with obviously gay men seen "as effeminate, predatory, immoral and a threat to the social order."[13] Indeed, to be both gay and a scooter rider must have been, come the mid-1960s, the very antithesis of British hegemonic masculinity. Thus, borrowing heavily from gay culture and fashions, male Mods' eventual wearing of pastel colours, low-rise trousers, and the like, "was therefore not simply a lifestyle choice but an act of defiance," whereby "Mods cut a path that British men have strutted down ever since."[14] Weight, citing Ken Browne, points out that the Mod subculture and the queer community were interlinked:

> There was a definite gay influence involved with the early Mods. The London clubs would have a lot of gays in them wearing outrageous white suits with big heels. Mods took that influence, it became a case of looking as pretty as possible, as nice as possible.[15]

Moreover, Peter Burton—remembering London's subterranean gay culture of the time—recalls, quite vividly, the extent to which both Mods and gays rubbed their immaculately tailored shoulders amid the clubs of Soho. According to Burton, the most high-profile Mod club, Ham Yard's the Scene (located to the rear of Shaftesbury Avenue), was understood as a straight equivalent of the gay-orientated Le Duce. Indeed, Burton stresses that, whilst Mods patronised the Scene, and gays went along to Le Duce, they were both not only from the very same working-class neighbourhoods of South and East London, but that "[b]oth groups took the same drug and shared the same music."[16] Furthermore, both Mods and gay men were clothes-obsessed in ways that, certainly to those outside of their respective subcultural groupings, looked identical to one another. In the formative years of Mod, during the late 1950s and very early 1960s, this was as a result of both groupings buying clothes from the same high-street stores—most notably Vince's and John Stephen's multiple outlets.

Richard Barnes, when considering the subculture's early shopping habits—and, perhaps more crucially, the subculture's intertwined relationship with Soho's gay culture—notes that, prior to Carnaby Street being transformed into a Mod mecca for clothes (thanks to the entrepreneurial skills of the young, Glasgow-born John Stephen), Vince's "had been selling flamboyant clothes to homosexuals and showbiz people since 1954."[17, 18] Thus, Vince's—or, more correctly, "Vince Man's Shop" (located around the corner from Carnaby Street, initially at 5, Newburgh Street)—was, with its revolutionary boutique-style format, not only the forerunner to what Carnaby Street was later to be world-famous for, but it was one of the few retail outlets from which the early Mods of the late 1950s and early 1960s could purchase outlandishly coloured, continental-styled clothing. However, as Jeremy Reed makes explicit, the Mods' discovery of Vince's occurred at a time when the shop—and the immediate vicinity within which it was located—was also being targeted by those who were far less enlightened and open to any form of revolutionary male fashions. Vince's, "located in an unattractive backwater behind Regent Street, was too marginalized and too branded by an overriding gay signature," to allow for any form of tolerance to be encouraged between the shop's clientele and the public more generally. Indeed, this eventual intolerance of those that shopped there meant that "Vince's customers were predominantly labelled queer."[19] Moreover, and in a far more sinister turn, "the precinct also attracted gay-bashers who hung out in the alleys looking for unsuspecting targets for their misplaced homophobic aggression."[20]

Indeed, following Vince's relocation to 15 Newburgh Street, and John Stephen's eventual opening, in 1956, of his first store, "John Stephen," nearby, trade proved frustratingly sluggish, with the latter's custom especially coming from "a cocktail of tentatively emergent Mods, gay hustlers from the Marshall Street Public Baths, actors and occasional pop stars looking to add significant colour to their stage clothes."[21] With Richard Barnes noting that "[i]t was all very St. Tropez," as, on display, there were "tight hipsters and white flared trousers and matelot shirts," it is significant that—for both "Vince Man's Shop" and "John

Stephen"—some of their customers frequented Marshall Street Public Baths, as it was "a popular cruising area in the 1950s for gay men who worked out."[22, 23] As, when Carnaby Street was in full swing during the mid-1960s—and Mod had caught on with the young male masses (or "Tickets"—later typified by *Quadrophenia*'s main character, Jimmy)— the subculture's obsessive conspicuous consumption, for some, was only attainable through an embrace of the illegal aspects of Soho's gay underworld: "This was especially true of those who had acquired serious pillhead habits without the funds to support them.[24] It led to a lot of larceny and, because Soho was also one of London's biggest homosexual cruising areas, considerable male prostitution."[25]

Pink Hipsters and Posing Pouches

One of the most notable recollections to be found within the book *Mods!* by Richard Barnes is when the author, accompanied by the Who's chief songwriter, first visited Carnaby Street. It is such an insightful passage—especially with regards to how the two young men, both infatuated with the embryonic Mod scene, first discover not only the precinct's most significant retailer on the cusp of success (that is, John Stephen), but the crossover between Mod subculture and gay culture amid that particular backwater of Soho—that it is, here, worth revisiting in full:

> I first went there with Pete Townshend. Somebody had told us about the street and one day, while we were in the West End we decided to have a look. We couldn't find it at first, it was really a back-street of London. It wasn't a very attractive street either. One side had a huge windowless brick-built warehouse owned by the Electricity Board or someone. There were four, or maybe five, men's clothes shops and a tobacconist's. I can't remember much else and I don't think there was much else. There was more than one shop called His Clothes, then, I think, Paul's and Domino Male and Donis. This day was wet and grey and the street was deserted. But when we saw the clothes we couldn't believe them. It was the more colourful clothes that amazed me: I mean, candy-pink denim hipsters for men? Fantastic. Outrageous.[26]

Such "fantastic," "outrageous," brightly coloured clothing was something that would, certainly by the early 1960s, come to define the Mod subculture. When recalling how he was dressed in a photograph dated

1963, Roland Kelly noted, in particular, that he was wearing "yellow-lensed shades" and "purple jumbo cord trousers."[27] In this way, of course, Mod helped usher in what was to eventually characterise the 1960s more generally—that is, the primary colours and geometric patterns of a youth-orientated culture shaped by not only Op- and Pop-Art, but advances in TV and cinema production and consumption.

"His Clothes"—especially when compared to the far more formal men's outfitters to be found in London at the time—was a forerunner of the boutiques that would come to characterise Carnaby Street, and the British high-street more generally, come the mid-to-late 1960s. John Stephen's shop was "crammed with clothes and accessories which were hanging up all around the door and everywhere," to the extent that Barnes concluded that, now, "[s]hopping was a lot easier and it was fun."[28] Although, with such—what Barnes' describes in breathless exaltation—fantastic, outrageous garments in mind, amid such a fun retail environment, it is worth noting that John Stephen's first trading outlet, "John Stephen" (located at No. 19, Beak Street, Soho, and opened in early 1956), proved revolutionary long before "His Clothes" offered pastel-coloured clothing to young male Mods of the early 1960s. An early best-seller—and imported, very exclusively, from the United States—were dark-blue denim Levi's. Stephen's was amongst the earliest shopkeeper's of the capital to introduce pre-shrunk Levi's into the United Kingdom (unlicensed that is); they were sold at No. 19 at the then astronomical price of £45. Moreover, and despite being advertised as pre-shrunk, Stephen's added to their allure by "advising customers to shrink them in the bath to achieve a tighter, sexier fit."[29] Furthermore, such at-home alterations were not only to achieve a slimmer silhouette when wearing such customised jeans, but it was also to attain a certain individualised quality with regards this mass-produced item of clothing, as "breaking in Levi's usually involved jumping into a hot bath and allowing them to dry-on for a personal contoured fit."[30] Thus, in *Quadrophenia*, the film, Jimmy is seen to be wearing around a dimly lit living room—whilst watching *Ready, Steady, Go!* in the bewildered company of his father—wet Levi's. In fact, to his uncomprehending father, this is all a clear sign of his son's queerness, as, in exasperation, he asks, "Gordon Bennett! What 'ave you got on? Some kind of new fashion that I 'aven't 'eard about? Soppin' wet trousers!" (Fig. 10.1).

Ken Browne makes explicit the considerable time and effort early Mods paid to the individualising of their newly purchased Levi's: "The

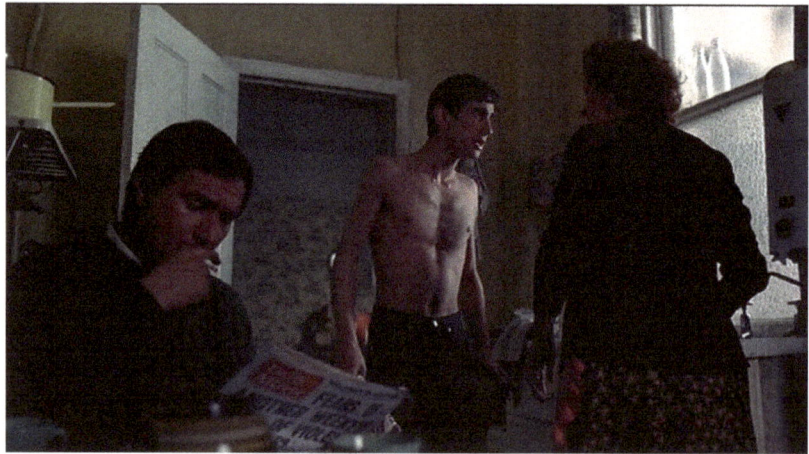

Fig. 10.1 Jimmy in his sopping wet Levi's

care you took with your Levi's was unbelievable. When you washed your jeans you didn't just put them in a washing machine, you used to place them on the draining board and scrub each knee and likewise the fly … The knees and crotch had to be white. That, believe it or not, was the look."[31] Of course, what underpins this vivid extract is the subcultural sexualisation of an item of leisurewear that, originally, was a purely functional item of work clothing. Furthermore, the lengths that young male Mods went to shrink and fade their Levi's—in order to, in the main, impress their same-gender group peers—meant that this, as a result, became a truly queer essential element of their casual wardrobes.

Of course, if both the stock and interior of John Stephen's Beak Street store of the early 1960s had caused a stir selling Levi's, the entrepreneur—when he already had premises at No. 5 Carnaby Street (which had opened in December, 1959)—offered other merchandise of an evocative nature. For, No. 5 Carnaby Street was "unapologetically camp in its colour-coding and use of body-beautiful male mannequins and blow-ups to promote minimally cut briefs."[32] As Eugene Manzi, press officer for London Records, makes explicit, catching a sight of such revolutionary underwear in a window of a Carnaby Street boutique was, yes, shocking. But, of course, their minimalism was an essential element of the Mods' skinny aesthetic: "You had to have briefs because the rise of the trousers were so low," as "[y]ou often only had a four-inch zip because it was such a low hipster."[33] However, this skinny aesthetic was (especially during the time in which *Quadrophenia* is set) no longer being perceived of as gay, queer, or even odd, as Irish Jack—the real-life character upon which *Quadrophenia*'s Jimmy is supposedly based—makes explicit: "The summer of 1964 really brought out the mod image … [as] half of England seemed to be looking for pink Sta-Prest Levi's, blue plastic macs, shoes by Raoul, college scarves … [and] Hong Kong nylon socks."[34] Quite crucially, then, that very moment—summer, 1964—is not only the year of *Quadrophenia*'s setting, but it is the very point at which the queerness of Mod went mainstream.

Aloof Guys and Independent Gals

Dave Marsh, in stressing the centrality of conspicuous consumption to the Mods' very being, states that they worked simply in order to spend their pay, each week, on off-the-peg and tailored clothes, scooters, American soul records, drugs, chewing gum, and so on.[35] In many respects, it was only this obsessive compulsion to spending that mattered, as, to many male Mods, "[f]ood, drink and girls hardly mattered."[36] Of course, sustenance was of little or no importance, as the Mods' drug of choice, amphetamines, were appetite suppressants. However, another side effect of such recreational drug use was that "speed" (such as Drynamil, or "Purple Hearts" as they were more commonly known) reduced one's libido—hence the notion that (again, to many a male Mod) girls hardly mattered. So, in Franc Roddam's cinematic version of *Quadrophenia* especially, Jimmy's nigh-on obsession with Steph— essentially the film's major love interest—is very much out of kilter with 1960s' (male) Mod more general perceived lack of interest in the opposite sex. As, quite simply, according to Barnes, "Mods were more interested in themselves and each other than in girls" because "girls were fairly unattractive and independent." That is, with the girls' rejection of the hyper-feminine signifiers of feminine beauty (red lipstick, bras that enhanced cleavage, corsets, petticoats, and so on), they were not only less attractive (well, in a conventional sense) but certainly less interested in being attractive in, what they now perceived to be, an out-dated manner.[37] Either way though, now "[i]t was a relief for them not to have to be feminine or painted up, and to be able to assume a more relaxed role sexually."[38] All of this, of course, is far more in keeping with Jimmy's on-off relationship with Monkey throughout the film. Monkey—played by Toyah Wilcox—is the absolute epitome of this less conventionally attractive, independent female version of Mod that, yes, by becoming one of the boys, has quite clearly adopted a more relaxed role sexually. Of course, another reason as to why male Mods seemingly ignored their female peers, was, perhaps, because "the smart [male] Mod was like a peacock strutting about in front of the peahens," whereby "[h]e used his apparent lack of interest to attract the girls."[39] Moreover, as Bill Norman states, it was all perhaps a result of the subculture's male-centric, style-fixated aloofness: "You had to be cool. To be chasing birds was seen as soft, a bit sentimental. You didn't want to lose face with the other guys."[40]

So, if Jimmy's obsession with Steph can be seen as rather overblown and contrived (when compared to the original male Mods' relationship with their female counterparts), and not in keeping with the subcultural times within which it is set, what other forms of love can we more accurately identify within *Quadrophenia*?

Stephen Glynn insists that *Quadrophenia*'s explorations of male-male bonding relationships goes far beyond that of "the monotone level of macho aggression."[41] Thus, whilst there is no open homosexuality on display within *Quadrophenia*, the first half of Franc Roddam's film alludes, quite strongly, to the close relationship between Jimmy and his former friend from his school days, Kevin. With the former now a teenage Mod, and Kevin a member of his subcultural nemesis, the Rockers, their all-nude, accidental re-acquaintance at a public bathhouse results, quite crucially, in them, first of all, aggressively confronting one another, only to "then reminisce as equals."[42] Thereafter, with an intimate dialogue taking place about subcultural allegiance and self/group-identity, a physical closeness is often reinforced by tender contact with one another. The two, at times, lock into a longing gaze into each other's eyes; all of this "serves to present Jimmy with his first moral dilemma," that is, "to choose Kevin or the gang."[43] However, this dilemma is something that Franc Roddam refuses to follow throughout in the second half of the film, as Kevin—following his severe beating by Jimmy's Mod gang (in retribution of the harassing of Spider and his girlfriend in an earlier scene)—is no longer seen, or even made reference to. Thus, as a result of Kevin's on-screen disappearance, "any hint of softness, let alone homosexuality, is suppressed."[44]

Indeed, the manner in which such queerness is suppressed in *Quadrophenia* is reinforced, again and again, when any form of non-masculine behaviour is pursued by Jimmy and his fellow male friends. Thus, when attending a fitting session of a bespoke suit, one Mod lambasts the harassed tailor with the casual comment "fuckin' rent-a-tent, innit?", whilst at the men's barbers having, collectively, their hair cut and styled, Jimmy recoils when he is offered a final squirt of hairspray. For, instead of a polite refusal, he shouts at to all that "Poofs wear lacquer, don't they, eh?" So, at the very least, this all "suggests a compensation for, if not a denial of, their own craving for the 'unmanly' pursuits of dressing up and looking good."[45] Yet, it is in the film's most aggressively masculine scenes—those depicting the Mods versus Rocker rioting at Brighton—where we find *Quadrophenia*'s most obvious moment of homoerotic closeness. Following their arrest and rough handling, as they are thrown into the back of a Black Maria by the police, Jimmy and the Ace Face (played by Sting) share a brief interlude of subcultural intimacy. For, this fleeting moment of ultimate Mod solidarity and male togetherness "contains a thin bat squeak of sexuality."[46] When Ace Face offers Jimmy a cigarette from a slim-line silver case, the parka-wearing teenager coyly accepts, but his eyes are barely able to meet those of older, peroxide-haired top Mod.

From Hairdryers to Mascara

Dick Hebdige (1988) insists that, right from the outset, the motor scooter was perceived of as a sexed object.[47] Noting that the earliest European motor scooters were produced in the period straight after World War I, the term motor scooter—or just scooter—referred to an under-sized motorcycle, with a horizontal board to rest the feet, and a rear-mounted engine that rested atop of the back wheel. Furthermore, the scooter was singled out from most other motorcycles due to its low-powered cubic capacity. All in all, such highly recognisable characteristics meant that the scooter very much stood apart from the rest of the two-wheeled motoring world, especially that of the far more highly powered, more traditional, more macho, motorcycles. Moreover, "[t]he demarcation between motorcycle and motorscooter coincided with and reproduced the boundary between the masculine and the feminine."[48] For, decades before hordes of Lambretta- and Vespa-riding Mods were to clog British inner-city roads during the early to mid-1960s, and, thus, challenge the dominance of British-made motorcycles industry: "the scooter was interpreted as an alien intrusion—a threat to the masculine culture of the road."[49] Thus, derided as mere hairdryers by those that refused to ride—to them—such an abhorrent form of two-wheeled transport, scooters and those who rode them were, certainly by the late 1950s, seen as "morally suspect" and "unmanly."[50]

If we move from so-called hairdryers (bikers' derogatory slang for Mods' motor scooters) to hair proper, we see that Mods continue to be associated with the unmasculine. David May not only verifies that— amid Mod—"[t]here was always a large gay element in it," but that "[o]n Saturday afternoon we'd go to get our hair done in the women's hairdressers."[51] Of course, the major reason as to why—certainly during the very early 1960s—male Mods visited women's hairdressers that normally catered for female clientele only was that a traditional men's barber, at that point, merely cut hair rather than styling it. However, a number of men took this notion of styling their hair to extremes. As Johnny Moke admitted, "I used to go to bed every night in hair rollers, to keep my hair in."[52] And it was not just with their hair that the male Mods demonstrated a certain queerness with regards their presentation of the self — their facial features, and eyes in particular, were also enhanced in a sexually ambiguous manner.

Alan Fletcher's film "tie-in" novel of 1979, *Quadrophenia* contains a highly illuminating insight into what is perhaps the queerest of all aspects of Mod: The male Mods' putting on of eye make-up. At a local Mod pub in Shepherd's Bush, in the washroom, Jimmy goes into great detail with regards his embrace of this feminine act of self-presentation:

> I went over to the mirror and started applying eyeliner, the stuff I'd "borrowed" from Yvonne, stroking it thickly on to the top of the lids. I'd borrowed the idea of lining my eyes from a mod singer I'd seen at Chislehurst ... The singer's name, with the gravelly voice he'd cultivated in mock reverence to the early blues men, was Rod Stewart.[53]

This passage not only places a young Rod "the Mod" Stewart centrally amid 1960s' Mod, but supports Richard Weight's insistence that it was not only through clothing and all-male dancing that Mods attempted to eradicate the boundaries between genders, but through their making-up of their eyes. As, it was the first youth subculture "to sanction the wearing of male make-up, mainly eyeliner and mascara which was quietly taken from sisters and girlfriends or bought for them by more understanding ones."[54] This, of course, allows us to make linkages between the more gender-less aspects of 1960s' Mod and the more "gender-bending" traits of 1970s' Glam. For, as Paolo Hewitt and Mark Baxter assert, "Mod helped build glam rock."[55, 56] Indeed, whilst acknowledging that this may be "[a]n outrageous statement," they note that "[t]hree of glam rock's major figures were heavily shaped and influenced by Mod in their formative years"—namely, Marc Bolan, David Bowie, and Bryan Ferry.[57]

Late on in the film, as Jimmy enters into his post-Mods and Rockers confrontations mental disintegration, he returns to Brighton by train in a vain attempt to rediscover his lost Mod grandeur—indeed, his true Mod self. Swigging gin from the bottle, and constantly popping pills—all purchased following his resignation's severance pay—Jimmy is, according to Glynn, "now at his most openly androgynous" as "he is caught topping up his eye-liner in the train toilet by an old woman."[58] Indeed, despite this being, for Jimmy, a potentially embarrassing intrusion upon his privacy, "he turns and, 'sadly ecstatic', flips his eyelashes."[59] Thus, in one fell queer swoop, Jimmy, from the claustrophobic confines of a train's toilet, dismisses the all-too-orthodox

Fig. 10.2 Jimmy topping up his eyeliner on the train

outside world. Then, arrogantly lounging in first class, seated between two rather uncomfortable-looking, bowler-hatted commuters, he is "[p]erfectly embodying the 'he-man drag' so 'greyly outrageous' announced by Daltrey on the soundtrack."[60] For, now quite acutely aware of the hierarchical nature of a stiflingly straight society that surrounds him, Jimmy enters a drink- and drug-induced melancholia, with his "eyes wide open yet opaque" and "the inflections at once distant and dreamy."[61] Moreover, "[t]here is an awkward grace here in an (emotionally 'moving') still passage, positioned spatially between the pinstriped symbols of adult conformity."[62] Significantly, then, "[i]t is with his eyes most defined with mascara that Jimmy finally sees that life is hideously wrong outside of himself and all that he has is 'Me!'" But perhaps, contra Glynn's interpretation, there may be something "hideously"—or, moreover, "un-hideously"—right in recognising the queer elements in Jimmy's identity in *Quadrophenia* (Fig. 10.2).[63]

No surprise, then, that those young, male Mod revivalists—following their watching of *Quadrophenia*—took on the 'Me!'-centric mannerisms of Jimmy's character, such as wearing eye make-up, for their own identity-forming purposes. Adrian Holder—of the 80s Mod band, The Moment (from Haverhill, Suffolk, UK)—explained to me, in interview, his wearing of eye make-up, both on- and off-stage, was absolutely central to his sense of Mod self-identity:

> The eye make-up came about because of an "I can be more Mod than you" mentality. I had an extended period, in my teenage years, of wearing the stuff. It would be applied if I went to a gig or if I was just going to the Pub. Make-up for men had been quite normal during the glam rock years and it didn't bother me that the local Haverhill pub homophobes called me a "queer." I liked the idea of being "different" and, to me, it seemed to sit naturally with the clothes and the blending of Mod male and female styles.[64]

Moreover, Adrian Holder makes explicit here that his wearing of eye make-up—as an essential element of his Mod look during the 1980s—was as a direct result of having watched the main character in Franc Roddam's film doing so:

> The fact that Jimmy, in the film *Quadrophenia*, applied make-up made it all the more authentic to me. Back then, I was a young Mod looking to

push things to the limit. I suppose I wanted to shock people or at least get some reaction … I'm not sure what I wanted to be back then but I am sure I wanted to be different from what was considered the norm. I thought it was funny that people assumed it was a statement about my sexuality. It wasn't. However, it was a very effective way of drawing bigots out of their shell and thus providing me with targets for my dissatisfaction with the social status quo.[65]

Holder's words—amid the context of a post-*Quadrophenia* Mod revival—suggests that the subculture's "he-man drag"—especially elements such as the wearing of eye make-up—was not just a stylistic nuance but was yet another Mod-centric, queer act of defiance in the face of stifling social conformity (be it sexual, gendered, or Capitalist/class based). Thus, whilst conventionally dressed, suit-wearing Mods very much adhered to the heterosexual conventions of the workplace locker room, a male Mod's applying of mascara could be a statement of public or private defiance.

Mod Poster Boys and Their Mothers

Phil Daniels—as a result not only of playing Jimmy but also the lead in the children's TV series *Raven* (ATV, 1977) and supporting role in *Scum* (1979) (with the latter two, notably, Borstal-based characters)—admits that, come the early 1980s, he was being typecast as an on-screen delinquent: "I suppose in my own small way I'd become a bit of a poster-boy for disorderly youth."[66] Whilst not conventionally photogenic, Daniels' urchin-like charm meant that—especially to those close to him—a certain deviant on-screen personae was being pursued: "I remember my mum wasn't too happy when *Quadrophenia* and *Scum* came out in quick succession. She was always saying, 'Why can't you play a good boy in all these films you do?'"[67] And such a "(bad) poster boy" image was not restricted to Daniels, as fellow *Quadrophenia* stars were also beginning, simultaneously, to achieve such a recognisable, mother-estranging social standing—even in their off-screen, private lives. For, Gary Shail and Mark Wingett—who, respectively, played Spider and Dave in *Quadrophenia*—befriended each other, following filming, to the extent that Wingett not only began lodging at the Shail family home, but, as a result, the pair began to socialise with one another in an inseparable manner:

One day Mark and I were walking up the road heading for the tube station. Following a few yards behind was my mother, who was off to the shops. Mark and I were dressed in exactly the same leopard skin tight trousers with matching shirt and black leather biker jacket and boots. (How fucking camp is that!) We walked past a woman standing at her gate and said "Good morning" …as my mother reached the woman at the gate she said, "I pity their poor mother." And my mum said, "I am their poor mother!"[68]

Here, then, Shail—in his autobiography, *"I Think I'm on the Guest List"* (2015)—not only makes explicit the camp nature of his and Wingett's post-Punk clothing, but that their New Wave, street-level queerness was something which both connected and disconnected them from their mothers' generation. In a podcast-based interview with the author, Shail acknowledged his mother's condoning of her son's outlandish outward appearance: "My mum used to stay up putting zips in my Levi's. And she loved it too …. She grew up in the late 50s, early 60s. And she had a bouffant hair and a pencil skirt. So, she sort of got it really, she sort of knew. She was never embarrassed by what I came up with."[69] Moreover, Shail makes obvious, with regards *Quadrophenia*'s wardrobe, that he very much possessed an exhibitionist's streak. As, overseen by a pair of original 1960s' Mods (Roger Burton and Jack English), "Contemporary Wardrobes" hired, sourced, and made costumes, whilst—all the while—reminiscing with the cast as to how such clothing should be worn and so on. However, whilst Shail acknowledges how vital such insights were in order for him to portray the role of Spider with any degree of accuracy," he also—in a typical post-punk dismissal—states "[t]hat's all bollox", as "I just liked dressing up!"[70] Indeed, Shail's love of dressing up allows us to draw direct comparisons between his character's on-screen flamboyance, and his off-screen, poster boy campness. Furthermore, such on-/off-screen posing also allows us to appreciate that Shail carried out such dressing up with a nigh-on catwalk-esque bent:

> I look back on those days and those photographs, and I think, "My God!" I didn't sleep. I didn't eat. But I was so particular about how I looked. Everything had to be different … I got to choose my own wardrobe, and I was very particular about what I wore. And also my mum was very good about that … I had a good idea for fashion. And I think I would have wanted to go into fashion if I had not been so lazy.[71]

Ultimately, though, both Daniel's and Shail's poster boy characters are, in *Quadrophenia* dwarfed by that of Sting. Franc Roddam—through Jimmy and Spider's on-screen adulation of Sting's character, Ace Face—makes explicit the homoeroticism to be found within *Quadrophenia*, and Mod more generally, with the Ace Face singled out by Shail's Spider at the scene set in a Brighton dancehall: "The geezer with the 'air, man, the geezer with the 'air. Oi! Dave! Dave! Dave! The one with the 'air. C'mon, let's go 'an watch 'im. Brilliant! Brilliant!"

For, after all, in a Mod world where girls didn't matter, this—surely—was the true love interest to be found within the film (and, thus, the tie-in novel, the soundtrack album, the original double album, and the rest). That is, not only Jimmy's relationship with other subcultural males (with male nudity replacing that of female), but his and Spider's nigh-on sexualized idolatry of Sting's Ace Face amid the context of 1979's geezerdom and post-punk/Mod revival queerness. This is made all the more explicit if we consider the following extract from Fletcher's tie-in novel:

> He saw the Face through the crowd. It wasn't difficult. He seemed to advertise his presence, his arrogance. The Ace Face, Jimmy thought, watching him dance and admiring the cool, slow self-conscious movements. Self-confident and assertive. Those around him tried to mimick [sic] or copy his steps, the sure sign of a Face, but they seemed clumsy and awkward beside him, only highlighting him the more.[72]

Conclusion: "Just like the Lesbians and Queers" … and Outsiders

Jonathon Green (1988) insists that—as well as an obsession with clothes, scooters, and the like—Mods (that is, Mod's very earliest originators, the so-called Stylists) strived to achieve an urbane European cool founded upon a certain high level of intellectuality—that is, an intellectuality "derived from reading the French existentialists popular at the time, the philosophic works and novels of Sartre and Camus, and by association the seminal writings of the openly gay ex-convict Jean Genet."[73] Indeed, David May, firstly, places great emphasis upon the significance of Camus to early Mod originals: "[O]ne did read Camus. *The Outsider*, there it was, it explained an awful lot."[74] Then, secondly, to May, Genet proved inspirational: "A sort of Jean Genet criminal lowlife was also important. These were the outlaw figures. People who went out and stole and so on."[75] As,

May—who, in his mid-to-late teens, lived a semi-legal life in Soho, during the early 1960s, amid homosexuality, drug-taking, and the emergence of Mod—admits that "[w]e lived in this whole other world."[76] This whole other world was, of course, one in which gay and Mod culture co-mingled, whilst being on the cusp of both coming out and going mainstream. For, John Stephen's clothing catalogues of the time utilised a particular image of a trendy young male, "with the gelled, meticulously constructed quiff, sweater-shirt, tight pegged French cotton slacks and suede Chelsea boots being instantly recognizable to readers as a gay stereotype."[77] Once very much outsiders, then, such young, gay men were—amid the Mod subculture of the early 1960s—being recognised as trendsetters. When Richard Barnes recalled his first visit to Carnaby Street, with Pete Townshend, on a rain-swept day in the middle of a week, the precinct was nigh-on deserted except for one notable—and highly noticeable—individual: "The only other person we saw was a tall, well-dressed young negro who bought a pair of the coloured denim hipster trousers.[78] This negro was obviously homosexual and I realized that homosexuals had been buying that stuff for years. They were the only people with the nerve to wear it."[79] Thus, *Quadrophenia* not only encapsulates the moment that Mod, quite notoriously, hit the headlines, but it is also a snapshot of a time when both an underground subculture and underground gay culture—once characterised by members who, in their own respective ways, thought of themselves as outsiders—emerged, simultaneously, into the light. Yet, at times, Mod (like gay culture) continues to be associated with an outsider mentality, as the author, in an essay entitled "Follow the Leader – Remembering the 80s Mod Revival" in *Heavy Soul!...* fanzine, insists.[80] Mod, certainly during its Revival period during the 1980s, was very much akin to being an outsider:

> So, being a Mod of the 1980s for me (and for many like me I suspect) had little to do with any form of a 'strength in numbers' mentality – far from it. Mod then had far more to do with living a life alone and on the edge ... I mean that, quite often, it would involve, geographically- and socially-speaking, living on the periphery ... In a world before "retro," being a Mod in the mid-'80s, certainly as far as "Joe public" was concerned, just looked sad; out of touch and out of time.[81]

Just a few years after the release of Franc Roddam's film version of *Quadrophenia*, Mod once again went underground. Very much at odds, fashion- and music-wise, with what was happening in the mainstream, its adherents were, once again, deemed outsiders, as those (such as the author) who clung on, quite desperately to Mod, looked—to those outside of the subculture—odd, and downright queer. In short, come the mid-1980s, Mod's uber-conservative, backward-looking style of neatly cut hair, 1960s-styled suits, and so on, was out of kilter with not only the far more radical "no future" look of punk, but the "revivalist" nature of Mod's guitar-driven music was also at odds with the "retro-futuristic" synthesized sounds of post-punk.[82]

However, let us also appreciate how Mod— more generally as a subculture, and as expressed, quite specifically, in *Quadrophenia*—widens our understanding of gender-based social relations. As, Bill Norman explains, for many a male Mod, "when you were at work, you were a nobody," whereby, most importantly, "you want to be a somebody to your mates" as "[i]t's your mates you want to impress, not particularly the girls."[83] Indeed, in relation to the Mod homosocial desire to impress one's mates, Barnes makes particular note of their queerness: "The boys *were* effeminate and used to fuss about and preen in front of the mirror, but they weren't homosexual. There might have been a homosexual element, but then there might also have been among Rockers, and it wasn't particularly important."[84]

Thus, whether homosexual or not, it was the Mods' defiant wearing of pink shirts, white suits, and so on—bought from Carnaby Street clothing emporiums that, beforehand, catered only for the flamboyant tastes of those from the theatrical and gay communities—that Richard Weight places great emphasis upon. As not only did this align the Mods' experience with that of other gay men (with both groups being beaten up by homophobic gangs as a result of merely looking different), but it placed them at the heart of gay culture—albeit, without the personal-as-political connotations, as "[t]his was no campaign for gay rights but Mod was the first youth movement to engage directly with gay culture."[85] Fundamentally, though, *Quadrophenia*—in all its formats (indeed, perhaps directly as a result of its now readily available multiple formats)—is best understood as a cultural mapping of both Mod and queerness amid both straight and gay culture. For, whether it is the original double album, Franc Roddam's widescreen version, Alan Fletcher's tie-in novel, or the soundtrack LP, *Classic Quadrophenia*, straightness, gayness, and queerness are all to be found amid the queer Modness of *Quadrophenia*.

This chapter goes beyond a study of Modness and queerness. For, this chapter—through its application of queer politics to the various texts of *Quadrophenia*—encourages us to re-evaluate our social and cultural identities in line with, what Chris Haywood and Máirtaín Mac an Ghaill insist are, a more extensive "range of political identifications/alliances that are [still] in the process of being assembled"; be they Mod, male, female, straight, gay, bi, or transgender.[86] And this re-evaluation of gender-based identities is very much needed within Mod today. As, once a subculture that was open to—and informed by—gay culture, it is now, arguably, in danger of becoming a subcultural bastion of heterosexuality and conservativism. Christine Jacqueline Feldman's interview and observation-based study, *"We Are the Mods" – A Transnational History of a Youth Subculture*, warns of such a trend whereby Mod seems to be ignoring youth culture's openness to queer possibilities: "[T]wenty-first-century Mod culture, given its past associations with gender and sexuality, is surprisingly unreflective of these social changes" as "there is nothing very radical about current Mod culture."[87, 88] This chapter has set out to encourage a re-queering of Mod, through a re-reading of *Quadrophenia*, in order that our continued awareness of subcultural identity formation is one that is based upon an appreciation that truly radical subcultures not only challenge the status quo, but—fundamentally—alter it.

Notes

1. See Terry Rawlings, *Mod—A Very British Phenomenon* (London: Omnibus Press, 2000).
2. Judith Halberstam, "What's that smell? Queer temporalities and subcultural lives," *International Journal of Cultural Studies* 6:3 (London: Sage, 2003): 313–333.
3. Halberstam, 'What's that smell? Queer temporalities and subcultural lives', 329.
4. Chris Haywood and Máirtaín Mac an Ghaill. *Men and Masculinities—Theory, Research, and Social Practice* (Buckingham: Open University Press, 2003).
5. Haywood and Mac an Ghaill, *Men and Masculinities*, 139.
6. Haywood and Mac an Ghaill, *Men and Masculinities*, 139.
7. Haywood and Mac an Ghaill, *Men and Masculinities*, 140.
8. Eve Kosofsky Sedgwick, *Epistemology of the Closet* (Berkeley: University of California Press, 1990, republished 2008).
9. Sedgwick, *Epistemology of the Closet*, 68.

10. Upon applying a queer "epistemology of subcultures" to both *Quadrophenia* and Mod, such an unstable "binarism" of "dark/light" is already, of course, akin to the Who's sympathetic ode to Mod at its apex—"The Kids Are Alright." A key track from the band's debut long-player, *My Generation* (1965), it includes the following lines: "But I know sometimes I must get out in the light / Better leave her behind with the kids, they're alright."
11. Richard Weight, *Mod—A Very British Style* (London: The Bodley Head, 2013).
12. Weight, *Mod*, 74.
13. Weight, *Mod*, 74.
14. Weight, *Mod*, 74.
15. Browne cited in Weight, *Mod*, 74.
16. Burton cited in Weight, *Mod*, 75.
17. Richard Barnes, *Mods!* (London: Plexus Publishing Ltd., 1979, republished 1991).
18. Barnes, *Mods!*, 10.
19. Jeremy Reed, *The King of Carnaby Street—The Life of John Stephen* (London: Haus Publishing, 2010), 18.
20. Reed, *The King of Carnaby Street*, 18.
21. Reed, *The King of Carnaby Street*, 30.
22. Barnes, *Mods!*, 11.
23. Reed, *The King of Carnaby Street*, 7.
24. "Tickets" were scooter-less Mods, so named for their reliance upon public transport (thus having to resort to purchasing bus and train tickets). Indeed, other derogatory terms for the younger, "pack"-orientated Mods were "Numbers" (as they wore T-shirts with numerals on the front); "Seven and Sixes" (for, again, wearing T-shirts—this time those purchased from Woolworths, costing "7/6d"); and "States" (literally, dressing in such a poor manner that—especially when compared to other, trend-setting Mods termed "Faces," "Stylists," etc.—"they looked a 'bit of a state'" Barnes, *Mods!*, 123.
25. Dave Marsh, *Before I Get Old—The Story of the Who* (London: Plexus Publishing Ltd., 1983, republished 2015) 118.
26. Barnes, *Mods!*, 10.
27. Paul 'Smiler' Anderson, *Mods, the New Religion—The Style and Music of the 1960s Mods* (London: Omnibus Press, 2013), 118.
28. Barnes, *Mods!*, 11.
29. Reed, *The King of Carnaby Street*, 29.
30. Reed, *The King of Carnaby Street*, 30.
31. Reed, *The King of Carnaby Street*, 30.
32. Reed, *The King of Carnaby Street*, 39.

33. Carlo Manzi cited in Paolo Hewitt, *The Soul Stylists—Forty Years of Modernism* (Edinburgh: Mainstream Publishing Company Ltd., 2000), 52.
34. Irish Jack cited in Marsh, *Before I Get Old*, 101.
35. Marsh, *Before I Get Old*.
36. Marsh, *Before I Get Old*, 18.
37. For one of the earliest insights into the female Mods' rejection of "conventional" forms of feminine beauty, see Colin MacInnes, *Absolute Beginners* (London: Ace Books, 1959, republished 1961). In the author's description of the "Dean" (a Modern Jazz-fixated, heroin-addicted precursor to Mod), his un-named female partner is described thus: "[H]air done up into an elfin style. Face pale—corpse colour with a dash of mauve, plenty of mascara," 51.
38. Barnes, *Mods!*, 15.
39. Barnes, *Mods!*, 15.
40. Bill Norman cited in Barnes, *Mods!*, 15.
41. Stephen Glynn, *Quadrophenia* (London: Wallflower Press, 2014), 75.
42. Glynn, *Quadrophenia*, 75.
43. Glynn, *Quadrophenia*, 76.
44. Glynn, *Quadrophenia*, 76.
45. Glynn, *Quadrophenia*, 76.
46. Glynn, *Quadrophenia*, 77.
47. Dick Hebdige, *Hiding in the Light—On Images and Things* (London: Routledge, 1988).
48. Hebdige, *Hiding in the Light*, 84.
49. Hebdige, *Hiding in the Light*, 84.
50. Hebdige, *Hiding in the Light*, 104.
51. David May cited in Jonathon Green, *Days in the Life—Voices from the English Underground, 1961–1971* (London: Pimlico, 1988) 35.
52. Johnny Moke cited in Barnes, *Mods!*, 11.
53. Alan Fletcher. *Quadrophenia* (London: Corgi Books, 1979), 69.
54. Weight, *Mods*, 77–78.
55. Paolo Hewitt and Mark Baxter, *The A to Z of Mod* (Munich: Prestel, 2012).
56. Hewitt and Baxter, *The A to Z of Mod*, 122.
57. Hewitt and Baxter, *The A to Z of Mod*, 122.
58. Glynn, *Quadrophenia*, 77.
59. Glynn, *Quadrophenia*, 77.
60. Glynn, *Quadrophenia*, 78.
61. Glynn, *Quadrophenia*, 78.
62. Glynn, *Quadrophenia*, 78.
63. Glynn, *Quadrophenia*, 79.

64. Interview between Adrian Holder and author, via Facebook message, July 7, 2016.
65. Interview between Adrian Holder and author, via Facebook message, July 7, 2016.
66. Phil Daniels, *Class Actor* (London: Simon and Schuster UK Ltd., 2010), 134.
67. Daniels, *Class Actor*, 136–137.
68. Gary Shail, *"I Think I'm on the Guest List"* (Newhaven: New Haven Publishing Ltd., 2015), 33.
69. Gary Shail, 'The Quad Goose' podcast, November 9, 2015.
70. Shail, *"I Think I'm on the Guest List"*, 33.
71. Gary Shail, 'The Quad Goose' podcast, November 9, 2015.
72. Fletcher, *Quadrophenia*, 133.
73. Jeremy Reed, *The King of Carnaby Street—The Life of John Stephen* (London: Haus Publishing, 2010), 27.
74. David May cited in Green, *Days in the Life*, 35.
75. David May cited in Green, *Days in the Life*, 35.
76. David May cited in Green, *Days in the Life*, 35.
77. Reed, *The King of Carnaby Street*, 36.
78. Barnes, *Mods!*.
79. Barnes, *Mods!*, 10.
80. Peter Jachimiak, "'Follow the Leader'—Remembering the 80s Mod Revival," *Heavy Soul!* 18. (2013): n. pg., accessed July 18, 2016.
81. Jachimiak, "'Follow the Leader'", n.p.
82. In order to sonically orchestrate the experiences and frustrations of 1960s Mod, Pete Townshend had chosen to bring to the fore of the Who's sound, amid the *Quadrophenia* long-player, state-of-the-art, 1970s 'synthesizers such as the ARP 2500 and 2600 models. Ironic, then, that such modern—or, even, "futuristic"—instrumentation was rejected by post-1979 Mods who, instead, tended to adhere increasingly to traditionalist forms of song-writing and musicianship. For a criticism of this "revivalist" trend in Mod, see Simon Reynolds, *Retromania—Pop Culture's Addiction to its Own Past* (London, Faber and Faber, 2011, republished 2012), 229.
83. Bill Norman cited in Barnes, *Mods!*, 15.
84. Barnes, *Mods!*, 15.
85. Weight, *Mod*, 74.
86. Haywood and Mac an Ghaill, *Men and Masculinities*, 139.
87. Feldman, *"We are the Mods,"* 142.
88. Feldman, *"We are the Mods,"* 142.

Bibliography

Anderson, Paul 'Smiler'. *Mods, the New Religion—The Style and Music of the 1960s Mods.* London: Omnibus Press, 2013.
Barnes, Richard. *Mods!.* London: Plexus Publishing Ltd., 1979, republished 1991.
Daniels, Phil. *Class Actor.* London: Simon and Schuster UK Ltd., 2010.
Fletcher, Alan. *Quadrophenia.* London: Corgi Books, 1979.
Feldman, Christine Jacqueline. *"We Are the Mods"—A Transnational History of a Youth Subculture.* New York: Peter Lang Publishing, Inc., 2009.
Glynn, Stephen. *Quadrophenia.* London: Wallflower Press, 2014.
Green, Jonathon. *Days in the Life—Voices from the English Underground, 1961–1971.* London: Pimlico, 1988, republished 1998.
Halberstam, Judith. 'What's that smell? Queer temporalities and subcultural lives', *International Journal of Cultural Studies* 6:3 (2003): 313–333.
Haywood, Chris and Máirtín Mac an Ghaill. *Men and Masculinities—Theory, Research, and Social Practice.* Buckingham: Open University Press, 2003.
Hebdige, Dick. *Hiding in the Light—On Images and Things.* London: Routledge, 1988.
Hewitt, Paolo. *The Soul Stylists—Forty Years of Modernism.* Edinburgh: Mainstream Publishing Company Ltd., 2000.
Hewitt, Paolo and Mark Baxter. *The A to Z of Mod.* Munich: Prestel, 2012.
Jachimiak, Peter. "'Follow the Leader'—Remembering the 80s Mod Revival," *Heavy Soul!* 18. (2013): n. pg. Accessed July 18, 2016.
MacInnes, Colin. *Absolute Beginners.* London: Ace Books Ltd., 1959, republished 1961.
Marsh, Dave. *Before I Get Old—The Story of the Who.* London: Plexus Publishing Ltd., 1983, republished 2015.
Rawlings, Terry. *Mod—A Very British Phenomenon.* London: Omnibus Press, 2000.
Reed, Jeremy. *The King of Carnaby Street—The Life of John Stephen.* London: Haus Publishing, 2010.
Reynolds, Simon. *Retromania—Pop Culture's Addiction to its Own Past.* London: Faber and Faber Ltd. 2011, republished 2012.
Sedgwick, Eve Kosofsky. *Epistemology of the Closet.* Berkeley: University of California Press, 1990, republished 2008.
Shail, Gary. *"I Think I'm on the Guest List",* Newhaven: New Haven Publishing Ltd., 2015.
Weight, Richard. *Mod—A Very British Style.* London: The Bodley Head, 2013.

Electronic:
Music from the Soundtrack of the Who Film Quadrophenia. Various Artists, Polydor Ltd.: 1979.
My Generation. The Who, Polydor Ltd.: 1965.
Pete Townshend's Classic Quadrophenia. Various Artists. Eel Pie Recording Productions Ltd.: 2015.
Quadrophenia. Franc Roddam (Dir.), Universal: 1979.
Quadrophenia. The Who, Polydor Ltd.: 1973.
'The Quad Goose'. Loose Goose Radio podcast, University of South Wales: November 9, 2015.

CHAPTER 11

The Drowning Machine: The Sea and the Scooter in *Quadrophenia*

Brian Baker

As a teenage Mod, in the lee of the 1979 Mod revival, I asked my father, who was born in 1947 and therefore seventeen years old at the height of Mod's popularity, whether he had been a Mod or a Rocker in that period. (I knew that he'd had a motorcycle and sidecar at age sixteen, but had quickly traded this in for a car at seventeen. He also, in the odd photos I saw of him in as a young man, had something suspiciously like a quiff, but his clothes didn't look like Rocker gear). He said, "I wasn't a Mod or a Rocker, I was in-between – a Mocker," and not knowing that he'd stolen this from a Ringo Starr line, I took it for a nice witticism. Of course, as a young man living in suburban Essex, my Dad was far from the centres of subcultural vibrancy, though he had moved with his family from North London in the mid-1950s. In my own teenage naivety, I had presumed that he would have been one thing or the other, Mod or Rocker, and it was something of an eye-opener to realise that he had occupied a pop-cultural space somewhere in between. Yes, he'd liked the Stones, and yes, he'd watched *Ready Steady Go!*, but no, he hadn't been a Mod. He had been just an ordinary Essex teenager. That was okay; I was pretty ordinary

B. Baker (✉)
Lancaster University, Lancaster, UK
e-mail: b.baker@lancaster.ac.uk

© The Author(s) 2018
P. Thurschwell (ed.), *Quadrophenia and Mod(ern) Culture*,
Palgrave Studies in the History of Subcultures and Popular Music,
https://doi.org/10.1007/978-3-319-64753-1_11

too. It didn't stop me from asking him recurrently about *The Avengers* or *Danger Man*, though, until they were repeated on Channel 4 (as was *Ready, Steady, Go!*).

Ordinary as I was, I've never owned a scooter. As a teenager and a student, I couldn't afford one, and now I suspect I might look a little silly riding one. (This doesn't stop many men of my generation cruising the seafronts of seaside towns on their Vespas and Lambrettas on bank holidays). I remember the classifieds in the local paper advertising a Lambretta for £50 in the early 1980s, and daydreaming about buying it and "doing it up," but £50 was far out of my financial reach. I would have had to wait until I was sixteen to ride it, in any case. But I have always been fascinated by the designs of the Lambretta and the Vespa, the streamlined monocoque of the Vespa and the bulbous engine panels, the sleek and long-shanked Lambretta and its shark-like front mudguard. In this chapter, I will concentrate on the importance of the scooter to the album and film versions of *Quadrophenia*, and to Mod culture more generally. I will read the scooter as a particularly Modern object, one which embodies particular tensions to do with masculinity and modernity, and whose streamlined shape connects the Mod to a European, mobile and stylishly clean future promised by Modernism but which would fail by the end of the 1960s, never coming into being.

BACK TO FRONT

In the story told by the Who's album *Quadrophenia*, Jimmy, the young Mod, suffering from a personality disorder that Townshend dubs "quadrophenia," has a kind of breakdown, and travels from his South London home to Brighton, where he has an epiphany at the seaside. The album ends ambiguously: the listener doesn't know whether Jimmy ends his life in the sea (one of the songs is called "Drowned") or whether he simply throws off the burdens of being a Mod:

> Why should I care
> If I should cut my hair
> I've got to move with the fashion
> Or be outcast[1]

That it is Brighton Beach upon which Jimmy has his epiphany—with its stony strand on which the opening track, "I Am The Sea," falls with a roar and billowing hiss—is of course a historical sign for the listener who understands or recognises the place of the Mod in post-war British popular culture. Brighton's is the symbolic beach upon which Mods engaged in a series of semi-theatrical fights with Rockers, who rode motorcycles (mainly British BSA and Triumph bikes) and wore leathers, were identified with 1950s rock 'n' roll. Mods, who rode Vespa or Lambretta scooters and wore suits, sharp styles and American army parkas, were oriented towards Italian fashions and listened to soul, Motown, bluebeat, and R&B. Dick Hebdige, in his essay on the scooter in *Hiding in the Light* (1988), argues that Mod subculture was localised—mainly in London and the South-East of England—and represented a kind of resistance *as* consumption. Using data taken from a survey conducted at Margate in 1964 (one of the scenes of Mod/Rocker confrontation), Hebdige suggests that "the mods tended to come from London, were from lower-middle or upper-working-class background and worked in skilled or semi-skilled trades or in the service industries. [...] The Rockers were more likely to do manual jobs and to live locally."[2] Where the Rocker, Hebdige argues, inhabited a "traditional" and working-class subjectivity, the Mod (who he associates with office work rather than manual labour) was aspirational, potentially socially mobile, and oriented towards a new, Modern future; hence the name, Modernist.

Since the Mod revival of the early 1980s, Mod has been less oriented towards the future, and more towards the past. It has also been oriented away from the South-East, where the battles between Mods and Rockers began in Clacton on the Easter bank holiday in 1964, then flared up in Brighton and along the South Coast on the following Whitsun weekend. The continuity of Mod revivalism with the remains of the Northern Soul circuit (centred on the North-West of England), albeit an uneasy continuum as identified by Terry Rawlings in *Mod: A Very British Phenomenon*, and the importance of the phenomenon of "scooterist" rallies to the contemporary Mod scene, has lent it a more nostalgic structure of feeling, somewhat at odds with the emphases and aspirations of the original Mods.[3] The early 1960s Modernists have their antecedents in the hip, consumption- and display-oriented young metropolitans documented in Colin MacInnes's novels, most notably *Absolute Beginners* (1959), the geographical epicentre of which was Soho, a part of London with a distinct and Italian-influenced everyday/night life (in delicatessens, restaurants, coffee bars). This youth culture, and its extension into the Modernists/Mods, pointed away from the Britain of austerity, rationing and work towards hedonism, consumption and leisure. The Mods were oriented towards a future Britain of spectacle, the "white heat" of technology, and one of productivity and full employment, of the road out of the metropolis towards the periphery. Except in the case of the post-war British condition of London's centrifugal energies (dispersal of working-class populations in new towns and LCC estates) and centripetal dynamics (post-consensus acceleration of London's economic predominance), that future did not come to pass.

In "The Meaning of Mod," Dick Hebdige makes a more tentative connection between the "Italianate style" of "working class dandies [...] known throughout the trad [jazz] world as mods and who were dedicated to clothes and lived in London" of the 1950s, and the successor youth subculture of the early 1960s.[4] MacInnes's *Absolute Beginners* enumerates this style: "the grey pointed alligator casuals, the pink neon pair of ankle crêpe nylon-stretch, my Cambridge blue glove-fit jeans, a vertical-striped happy shirt revealing my lovely neck-charm on its chain, and the Roman-cut short-arse jacket."[5] While *Absolute Beginners* ranges across London, from Belgravia, where the narrator meets Suzette, to Pimlico where his parents live, it is one part of London in particular that becomes identified with the Italian style, with coffee bars, with nightlife, with youth culture: Soho. Soho had, in the middle decades of the twentieth century, been associated with Bohemian life: literary culture, little magazines and periodicals, heroic drinking, and what Ian Hamilton calls "Sohoitis": "you will stay there always day and night and get no work done ever."[6] According to Dominic Sandbrook, "In the years before the Second World War, Soho became well-known for its swing and jazz clubs, clustered among the French and Italian restaurants and delicatessens of Frith and Dean Streets"; "Soho in the fifties meant cosmopolitanism, sex, and above all, coffee bars."[7] On the cover of the film tie-in edition of *Absolute Beginners* from 1986 (the same image was used on the cover of the film soundtrack album), Eddie O'Connell as Colin and Patsy Kensit as Suzette sit astride Colin's silver Vespa, which is somehow suspended in the air, front wheel higher than the back. Behind is a stylized silhouette of the London skyline, as if Colin and Suzette (in a strange reprise of Spielberg's *E.T.* (1982) or scenes from the Disney *Peter Pan* (1953)) were magically flying through the night sky of the city. The scooter here not only signifies actual mobility but a fantasy of symbolic, and very stylish, escape. The streamlined side-pods of the Vespa become a kind of "jet-set" fabulation, and the city itself (just as in the film adaptation, which infuses MacInnes' novel with the colour and fantasy of the 1950s musical) is made fantastic, kaleidoscopic, spectacular. The scooter, sharp blue suit and loafers clearly anticipate and retroactively signify Mod style; Soho becomes the launching point for the scooter and the Mod imaginary.

Hebdige goes on to suggest further elements of the Mod style in "The Meaning of Mod": "to consciously invert the values associated with smart dress"; "a desire to do justice to the mysterious complexity of the metropolis in his personal demeanour, to draw himself closer to the Negro whose very metabolism seemed to have grown into, and kept pace with that of the city"; and a "unique and subversive attitude towards the commodities he habitually consumed."[8] Hebdige's understanding of Mod is of a performative obsession with style: "Mod was pure, unadulterated STYLE, the essence of style," a style constructed through appropriated commodities whose codings were altered through relocation to a different context (Italian motor scooters, Italian suits, even amphetamines).[9] In Mod, the affordable mobility of the scooter becomes an emblem of a different orientation towards post-war British life: one in which consumption, affluence (albeit mediated through the availability of easier credit for those in work) and autonomy is articulated through sub-cultural affiliation and a stylish performativity. In *Hiding in the Light*, Hebdige identifies the scooter precisely with a post-war "Imaginary of affluence":

> The mirrors and the chromium of the "classic" Mod scooter reflected not only the group aspirations of the mods but a whole historical imaginary, the "Imaginary of affluence." The perfection of surfaces within Mod was part of the general "aestheticisation" of everyday life achieved through the intervention of the image, through the conflation of the "public" and the "personal," consumption and display.[10]

Quadrophenia offers a critique of the idea of performative autonomy when Jimmy returns to Brighton and meets the "Ace Face" ("I don't suppose you would remember me/but I used to follow you back in '63"), who works as a bell boy in a Brighton hotel:

> I got a new job
> And I'm newly born
> You should see me
> Dressed up in my uniform [...]
> Bell Boy

> Gotta keep runnin' now
> Bell Boy
> Keep my lip buttoned down
> Bell Boy
> Carry the bloody baggage out
> Bell Boy
> Always running at someone's heel
> You know how I feel…[11]

"Bell Boy" emphasises the deadening work, the alienating and humiliating work that lies behind (and provides for) the Mod image of leisure, display and autonomy: "the Dirty Jobs" Jimmy encounter with the bell boy reveals the logic of the "Imaginary of affluence," one that underpins Mod. As Hebdige notes, Mod's orientation towards consumption as a form of resistance makes it all too easy to recuperate as a "lifestyle," to fold the Mod back into sanctioned cultures of productivity and sanctioned leisure time. The beach, however, is different, a liminal space where Jimmy's own implication in the world of work (notably, on the LP booklet of Ethan Russell's photographs, he is shown carrying bins: he is a dustman, not an aspirational clerk or executive-to-be) is dissolved, transcended. Not only is this form of Modernism a suit of clothes, but so is the subjectivity of post-war British masculinity that he finds difficult to negotiate. While the Ace Face accepts his humiliation as part of the economy of Mod-ism, Jimmy rejects it.

That the Ace Face/Bell Boy works in a hotel by the seaside is a telling indicator of the shifting economies of leisure and mobility during the post-war period in Britain. That he works in a *hotel* is also crucial: the hotel is a locus of *other people's* leisure time, the circuits of labour and service that structures this "holiday" time becoming all too apparent. The seaside hotel, and in particular the streamlined modernity of Art Deco landmarks such as the Midland Hotel in Morecambe or Ocean Hotel in Saltdean, along the coast from Brighton, is an emblem of a spectacular (and aspirational) representation of the British seaside masking the labour that enables it to function. (Residential and cultural buildings such as the De La Warr Pavilion in Bexhill, or Marine Court in St Leonard's, have similar Modernist design principles).[12] The buildings also suggest a utopian futurity of leisure and pleasure. I would like to suggest, however, that Art Deco housing, with its *maritime* emphases on white surfaces, glass, porthole windows, polished metals, is found in towns next the sea co-exists with the "seaside" but is notably different from it. The modernism of the Midland Hotel, for example, its geometrical regularity standing out against the wash of the sea on the beach, dissolving horizon, blue or grey-brown of the bay, is at once a spectacular resistance to the peculiarities of location and an organisation of point of view: of the rail passengers whose first view of Morecambe when disembarking from the train would be the hotel, *and* the perspectives across the bay (away from the town) offered by the hotel's tearoom and accommodation. If you arrive, like Jimmy or the Ace Face, on a scooter, however, you are more likely to be serving customers or subject to exclusion and the rather more disorderly pleasures of the street.

The shape of the Vespa—its streamlined and chromed body echoing the emphases of the aviation- and maritime-inflected architectural seaside Modernism—is a symbol of Mod-ism's connection to a vision of the future that offered a radical break from the British past. Paradoxically, when the Mods travel from Soho down to Brighton, from urban centre to seaside, they are enacting a long-established dream of leisure space and time, of new configurations of mobility and class proposed by the Modernist seaside architecture of the 1930s. The lines of the scooter promise speed, mobility, modernity, the future: a future that Jimmy can only embrace, ironically enough, by sloughing off his Mod costume and driving his Modernist scooter into the sea.

Two Faces of the Scooter

In the BBC documentary on *Quadrophenia, Can You See the Real Me?* (2012), it is revealed that because of problems with Ramport Studios (then still under construction while the album was being recorded) and different technical specifications for quadrophonic sound systems, there was only ever stereo mix of *Quadrophenia*. Townshend's plans to tour the album with quadrophonic sound systems were abandoned due to lack of time and preparation (he had seen and heard Pink Floyd using quadrophonic live sound prior to recording the album), and when the quadrophonic system was used at Ramport, it was so loud that it produced the same decibels as the supersonic airliner Concorde on take-off, rupturing eardrums and making people's noses bleed. The overall symbolic structure of the 4 faces, 4 band members and 4 sides of music was then reduced to stereo, to two channels. The album itself plays with binaries as well as the "quad" symbolism (as in the song "Doctor Jimmy"), and is also found in the dual scooters used in the film of

Quadrophenia. Where, in the booklet of the album, Jimmy rides a Vespa GS, which he crashes before taking the train to Brighton, in the film, Jimmy (Phil Daniels) owns a Lambretta. The GS is owned by the Ace Face, a scooter that Jimmy steals and rides to the cliffs before launching it into the air (though very differently from Colin in the film poster of *Absolute Beginners*). This ending differs markedly from the near drowning experienced at the end of the album booklet's narrative. In publicity stills and posters for the film, Jimmy usually rides the Vespa; he also does so in the shot in the gatefold of the film soundtrack double-album of *Quadrophenia*. Curiously, although the Ace Face's GS is very similar to the one featured in the original 1973 album photography, in the film publicity, Jimmy is more usually presented riding a scooter that *is not his own*. He is even alienated from his own machine. (The Lambretta is "killed" when it slides under a lorry on a suburban street; the GS is "killed" when it is accelerated off the cliff-top). In this section, I will analyse more closely the presentation of the scooter in both film and album booklet to explore the shifting significations of the scooter across the *Quadrophenia* texts.

The presentation of the Vespa *and* the Lambretta in the film of *Quadrophenia* indicates the film's greater connection to the historical and cultural circumstances surrounding Jimmy's life as a Mod. The album, in contrast, tends to play as a traversal of a largely interior landscape (where Brighton beach is as symbolic and internal as it is "real"). In the third section, I will concentrate on the representation of Jimmy's Vespa GS on the album cover, as a symbol of his own psychological armature and dissolution, but here I would like to quickly note the importance of the two makes of scooter. As both Hebdige and Terry Rawlings note, the Vespa was both imported from Italy (the GS) and built by the Douglas company in the United Kingdom (the somewhat derided Sportique); while the GS was the more coveted machine, Douglas concentrated on marketing the Sportique for economic reasons. By comparison, all Lambrettas were imported from the Innocenti factory in Italy. Rather than diverting resources into production in the United Kingdom, Lambretta instead developed a much stronger network of dealers and servicing centres and "could concentrate on importing and marketing Lambretta's entire range of bikes, with brilliant and enthusiastic promotion campaigns that were effective, stylised and above all, successful."[13] Both Rawlings and Paul "Smiler" Anderson in *Mods: The New Religion* (2013) feature interviews with Mods who identify their hierarchy of scooters, from desirable to derided; these interviews also reveal their effect on the young men's social and sexual capital. Roland Kelly, in *Mods: The New Religion*, is quoted as saying "In 1964 I got my chrome [Lambretta] TV200 from London. Now, that scooter cost the earth but it was worth it because when you went to the village halls and you had a scooter you were the top dog. Blokes didn't want to pick a fight with you; they wanted to ask questions about your scooter. All the girls fancied you; it was like, 'Cor, who's that?'"[14] Browne, interviewed in *Mod: A Very British Phenomenon*, says about talking to "a girl in a club" that "You'd have to say you had a GS or a GT200, because they knew they were the ones to have. Boy, if you said it was an LD150 or whatever, you had no chance. There were scooters that were totally passé, like the LD and the Sportique, you just didn't want one of those."[15] While the scooter, with the crazes for modification (and thereby individuation) such as chroming, mirrors and headlights, offered a sense of mobility and freedom, it also adhered to the strict codings of the Mod social hierarchies. While in some senses gendered as female—Rawlings notes "the bike's sleek lines and bosom-like curves (on the Vespa, anyway) also gave the bike an almost feminine quality,"[16] and Hebdige notes the scooter's "androgynous qualities ("feminine" and sleek but also able to climb mountains, cross continents...)"—the scooter also became identified with the production of successful masculine heterosexuality, the ability to "pull" a young woman.[17]

This is certainly borne out in the film of *Quadrophenia*. Jimmy owns a middling scooter, a Lambretta LI150, not an embarrassing LD nor a top-of-the-line TV200. When he stops on the street to talk to Steph (Leslie Ash), the girl he is infatuated with (and keen to take away from her boyfriend), he sits neatly astride the LI. It's a respectable emblem of sexual and social capital, but it certainly does not have the spectacular power of the GS160 that he sees the Ace Face riding in Brighton. His act of stealing the GS is, in a sense, the culmination of Mod aspiration: sitting astride the GS, he has ceased to be a "Number" and has become a "Face," at the top of the Mod masculine hierarchy. While many of the publicity shots and posters from the film picture Jimmy riding the GS, the *mise-en-scène* of the film often portrays the Mods riding en masse, from Jimmy pulling up in front of the ranks of scooters in front of the club at the beginning of the film, to the shots of the group riding down to Brighton. In fact, several scenes in the film demonstrate the vulnerability associated with being separated from the group of riders: then, you become prey to gangs of Rockers on their British motorcycles. *Quadrophenia* interrogates the tensions between individuation and difference in Mod subculture (not wanting to be part of the "mass" or conforming to conventional desires and behaviours) while also exhibiting anxieties surrounding that individuation (loss of ties to family, isolation, psychological breakdown). While the film emphasises the group, the album more generally portrays Jimmy alone.

In stark contrast to the *mise-en-scène* of the film, when Jimmy is depicted with his scooter in the photographs in the album booklet, he is isolated. In three photographs, down a street heading away from Battersea power station, sitting alone as a group of Mod kids talk on a street corner, or kneeling beside the scooter as the Who emerge from the Hammersmith Odeon, his distance from others is emphasised. In the fourth, he sits with his back to a wall, the damaged fairing and lights of the "smashed-up" scooter visible at it rests on the pavement in front of him. Far from a symbol of belonging, or of affluence and mobility, the scooter in the Who's *Quadrophenia* signifies alienation, isolation and psychological damage. As I will explain in the final section, the image on the back cover of the album provides a crucial index of Jimmy's emotional, psychological and spiritual trajectory (Fig. 11.1).

The Drowning Machine

On the front cover of the Who's *Quadrophenia* (1973), the scooter has four faces. Jimmy sits on his Vespa GS, facing away from the camera, his parka almost a shroud. His face is hidden. The four faces presented to the viewer are those of the band, from the top: Townshend, Moon, Entwistle, Daltrey. The faces are reflected in four mirrors that, in Mod fashion, extend from a chrome frame attached to the fairing of the Vespa. These faces, of course, reflect Townshend's plan for the musical structure of *Quadrophenia*: that the "quadrophenic" motif reflected Jimmy's fragmentation, the sonic production in quadrophonic sound, and that key songs and leitmotifs would correspond to each of the members of the band: "Is it me?" for Entwistle, "Helpless Dancer" for Daltrey, "Bell Boy" for Moon, and "Love Reign O'er Me" for Townshend himself. Although Jimmy appears to look into the scooter's mirrors and see four reflections, with the absence of his own face completing a geometric alignment (one becomes four), if you study the photograph closely, you can just make another reflection in the chromed

11 THE DROWNING MACHINE: THE SEA AND THE SCOOTER ...

Fig. 11.1 Jimmy's smashed-up scooter: not a symbol of affluence or mobility. Photograph by Ethan Russell. Copyright © Ethan Russell. All rights reserved

side-pod of the Vespa. Is this the photographer? Is this the viewer? The front cover of *Quadrophenia*, staged by Graham Hughes (from an idea credited to Daltrey) isolates Jimmy, unlike Ethan Russell's photobook inside the album, where Jimmy is purposefully placed in a South London milieu. The front cover of the album is a moment of *reflection*, but one that is outside the diegesis: the black and white image, with a background that suggests a tarpaulin, is foggy, miasmic, perhaps internal. With a "Who" symbol on the back of the parka, this is an emblematic shot, working with a series of equivalences: "Who" = Jimmy = four faces = parka = scooter. The image on the back cover, Jimmy's GS half-submerged in the sea, seems to be "real" but is equally symbolic and extra-diegetic, for Jimmy's narration has it that he crashes the scooter in the "pissing rain" and gets the 5:15 train to Brighton. (The film, of course, solves this by Jimmy's theft of the Ace Face's Vespa, while Jimmy himself has a Lambretta). The fate of the scooter is inextricably linked with Jimmy's own; the scooter both reflects him and his own splitting.

In this section I am going to read this connection between Jimmy and the scooter through the work of Klaus Theweleit, whose *Male Fantasies* (2 vols, 1989) is a key work with regard to theorising masculinities and in particular the armoured masculine subject. The imagery that Theweleit analyses, taken from the writings of proto-Fascist *Freikorps* militiamen in the period following the First World War, opens up the symbolic register of *Quadrophenia* in an illuminating way, and in particular the relation between the sea—the flood, flux—and the scooter, which I will read here as Jimmy's armoured self, reflected also in Jimmy's 'wartime coat' which protects him from the "wind and sleet." I will suggest that the chromed, streamlined shape of the Vespa itself signifies the imperatives towards speed and violence that Futurism brings to the surface in Modernism, and that Jimmy's "Mod" subjectivity inherits the deeply anxious and troubled masculinity that is imperfectly armoured by the psychological and symbolic armour.

The very means by which *Quadrophenia* presents Jimmy's fragmentation seem confused. From the "Four Faces" (the name of one of the songs left off the original album release of *Quadrophenia* but subsequently released on the film soundtrack album), we have the image of binary splitting in "Doctor Jimmy," with its Hyde-like Mr. Jim produced by drinking gin; to the statement of unitary subjectivity in "I'm One" (which, in the lyrics of the chorus, alternates between "I'm one" and "you'll all see I'm *the* one," a rather different conception); to what seems to be a voice from the void, from dissolution, who can only recognise a fleeting embodiment or subjectivity: "Is it me, for a moment?" Of course, there is no "real me," no authentic Jimmy to be uncovered. This confusion about Jimmy's identity is reinforced in the resolution of the film, with its opening/closing shots of the scooter going over the cliff and Jimmy walking away from the edge. The sense that there *is* no "Jimmy" presupposes the need to construct him, to engage a psychic apparatus through which to produce and defend some kind of subjectivity in the face of a terminal fragmentation or dissolution.

This armour is theorised by Theweleit as being produced by social and cultural conditions that can be traced back much further than that of wartime Germany; the deep roots of the production of the armoured male subject are coterminous with the rise of an industrial and bureaucratic modernity. Theweleit, drawing upon Deleuze and Guattari, proposes an anti-Oedipal reading of masculinity, though he does accept the basic Freudian structure of the "drives." Indeed, Theweleit argues that:

> A psychic type whose basic structure was more or less "psychotic" may have been the norm in Germany (at the very time that Freud was writing), and that this type was far more "normal" and more common than Oedipus, for example. Oedipus seems likely to have been a highly unusual specimen: a fictional non-fascist citizen modelled on Freud himself.[18]

Theweleit proposes that there are numerous parallels between the "soldier males" he draws upon and the "average man": the soldier is merely an extension of the tendencies of the more general condition of masculinity. He further suggests:

> Since the "ego" of these men cannot form from the inside out [...] they must acquire an enveloping "ego" from the outside. [This is] a result of coercion; it is forced upon them by the pain they experience in the onslaught of external agencies. The punishments of parents, teachers, masters, the punishment hierarchies of young boys and the military, remind them constantly of the existence of their periphery (showing them their boundaries), until they "grow" a functioning and controlling body armour, and a body capable of seamless fusion into larger formations with armorlike properties. [T]he armour of these men may be seen as constituting their ego.[19]

This armour is particularly used in defence against the threat of dissolution, typed (in Fascist writings) as the "red flood." The "most urgent task" of the armoured masculine subject "is to pursue, to dam in, and to subdue any force that threatens to transform him back into the horribly disorganised jumble of flesh, hair, skin, bones, intestines, and feelings that calls itself human – the human being of old."[20] The flood is, of course, gendered; flow, flux, the "morass," is feminine, that which must be defended against: feminization, dissolution. At the same time, Theweleit suggests, the armour produces a desire to "explode" out of its confines in a violent moment of ecstasy.

Mod masculinity, with its suits, parkas and scooters, I would argue, inherits the psychological structures of the armoured male, and if not fascist, then perhaps a Modernist subjectivity that embraces the idea of the machine, the future, and in particular a form of masculine immaculateness that is bound up with separation and isolation.[21] Richard Weight, in *Mod: A Very British Style* (2013), writes that "Mods fetishized technology that accelerated physical mobility" and somewhat unconsciously opens up the terms of my debate in the short section about scooters, when he writes that

> The scooter's cleanliness augmented its appeal. Because the engines of Vespas and Lambrettas were covered, it was easier for machine and rider to stay spotless. Mods no more wanted oil on their jackets than wind in their hair and to protect smart suits and dresses from the weather and scooter dirt they made use of the parka.[22]

The relation between technology, mobility, and cleanliness is illuminating. As quoted on the back cover of the *Quadrophenia* soundtrack album, Pete Meaden defined "Mod-ism" as "clean living under difficult circumstances"; Weight quotes Giacomo Balla's "Futurist Manifesto of Men's Clothing" which declares "WE MUST DESTROY ALL PASSEIST CLOTHES and everything about them which is colourless, funereal, decadent, boring and unhygienic."[23] The idea of cleanliness, indeed of "spotlessness" or immaculacy, is surely part of this psychic armouring against dirt, against the morass, against the flood. If the flood is feminine, then Meaden's suggestion that "[we were] not too heavily into chicks […] because chicks you got to remember are emotional distressful situations for a man" takes on a rather different cast. Meaden continues: "we were totally free because your sex drives, your libido […] was turned right down low by Drynamil."[24] Here, even "leapers" become part of the defensive apparatus, one that is explicitly proposed as "freedom."

The Vespa, with its streamlined chrome pods, its armature of bars and mirrors, is the emblem of Jimmy's armoured self, a masculinity produced by the disciplinary structures of work and domestic life that he struggles against, but which at the same time protects him from a dissolution that is longed for. The shot on the back cover of *Quadrophenia*, with the scooter half-drowned in the sea, signifies a breach in that psychic armour. Jimmy's journey back to the sea can be thought of as an enactment of a desire to rupture his armoured subjectivity, to "drown" and dissolve the unsustainable fragmentation in a "oneness" that is without boundaries altogether, rather than the joining up of components in the Mod crowd that signifies further conformity and struggle. Theweleit, writing about water and the ocean, declares: "We use that substance, that 'pure mother', to cleanse ourselves of the dirt of the world, the dirt of our beds, of love, of women – the dirt that we are ourselves."[25] Jimmy, of course, has himself been involved with the "dirty jobs'" spending a few days as a dustman; immersing himself in the sea will cleanse him of everything.

Total dissolution, death by drowning, is implied in the shot where Jimmy is fully submerged under the water. This, of course, is not the last shot. Jimmy makes it to "The Rock," and the final shots in the booklet show him walking alone the shore, like the scooter, half-in and half-out of the water. I would argue that in these images *Quadrophenia*, the album, rejects the narrative of maturation that seems encoded in the beginning/ending of the film, while at the same time rejecting suicide as a means by which to transcend the disabling tensions produced by the psychic armour and the need to rupture it, to "explode" out of it (in the violence shown in the album where Jimmy and others overturn a Mark II Jaguar). Instead, Jimmy maroons himself on another beach, walking the tideline, *between* the sea and the sand rather than *by* it. The imagery of the rock, phallically protruding from the sea but deeply invaginated, echoes this concept of the beach not only as "the place where a man can feel/He's the only soul in the world that's real," but also one where the constructions of gender are themselves in flux.

The drowning machine is therefore the Vespa GS and, in a sense, Jimmy himself. Jimmy is machinic not only in the sense of an armoured body that can be conjoined with other masculine components in the Mod crowd (again, to be wished for and feared as another conforming mass), but also in a Deleuze/Guattarian sense, extending from Theweleit: Jimmy's drowning machine is a desiring machine, a body without organs, a point of flux *between* and prior to subjectivity: "desire and its object are one and the same thing: a machine, as a machine of a machine," in the way that "the beach is kissed by the sea."[26] Ultimately, the drowning machine is not just a thing, not the Vespa nor Jimmy, but a productive process of which they are both emblems. Jimmy desires to be "one," not a unitary subject but one *with* the world, to dissolve the boundaries of the masculine subject entirely.

In the three sections of this chapter, I have attempted to draw together different threads: legacies of Modernism, the significance of the scooter in Mod culture, masculinity and the splitting of the subject. The three sections, rather than a more appropriate four, suggest that one of the elements is missing, Pete's carefully worked-out quadrangulated structure undermined. The 4-as-1, 1-as-4 band symbology of

Quadrophenia was disintegrating even as the Who recorded it in 1973. Between the album and the film of *Quadrophenia*, the group recorded two more studio albums, but Keith Moon, struggling with alcohol addiction, became less and less reliable as drummer, and Daltrey and Entwistle considered replacing him during the recording of the 1978 album *Who Are You*. In September 1978, Moon, in increasingly poor health, tried to go sober with the use of clomathiazole, a sedative used to alleviate the symptoms of withdrawal. On 7 September, he took an overdose in his London flat, and died. *Quadrophenia* was made into a film that Moon, the Bell Boy, would never see: it was released just over a year after his death. If this chapter contains three sections rather than four, it is then necessarily so if it remains true to the project, to its complete incompletion, with Jimmy left on the beach. The last image of the album *Quadrophenia* is the back cover, the GS Vespa half-submerged in the sea. Ultimately, perhaps, the drowning machine, the four-faced scooter threatened by dissolution, was not only Jimmy but the Who itself.

Notes

1. The Who, "Cut My Hair," *Quadrophenia* (Track Records, 1973).
2. Dick Hebdige, *Hiding in the Light* (London: Routledge, 1988), 113.
3. Terry Rawlings, *Mod: A Very British Phenomenon* (London: Omnibus, 2000), 201.
4. Dick Hebdige, "The Meaning of Mod," in *Resistance through Rituals: Youth Subcultures in Post-war Britain*, ed. Stuart Hall and Tony Jefferson (London: Routledge, 2006), 71.
5. Colin MacInnes, *Absolute Beginners* (1959) (Harmondsworth: Penguin, 1986), 34.
6. Ian Hamilton, "Sohoitis," *Granta* 65 (1999): 297.
7. Dominic Sandbrook, *Never Had It So Good: A History of Britain from Suez to the Beatles* (London: Abacus, 2000), 139, 141.
8. Hebdige, "The Meaning of Mod," 72.
9. Ibid., 76.
10. Hebdige, *Hiding in the Light*, 113.
11. The Who, "Bell Boy," *Quadrophenia*.
12. For an overview of this kind of architecture, see Fred Gray, "1930s Architecture and the Cult of the Sun," *Modernism on Sea: Art and Culture at the British Seaside*, eds. Lara Feigel and Alexandra Harris (Oxford: Peter Lang), 159–176.
13. Terry Rawlings, *Mod: A Very British Phenomenon*, 142.

14. Paul 'Smiler' Anderson, *Mods: The New Religion, The Style and Music of the 1960s Mods* (London: Omnibus, 2013), 103.
15. Rawlings, *Mod: A Very British Phenomenon*, 134.
16. Ibid., 142.
17. Hebdige, *Hiding in the Light*, 95.
18. Klaus Theweleit, *Male Fantasies II: Male Bodies: Psychoanalysing the White Terror*, trans. Stephen Conway, Erica Carter and Chris Turner (London: Polity, 1989), 213.
19. Ibid., 164.
20. Ibid., 160.
21. While I am here suggesting the continuity of some aspects of Modernism with the Fascist imaginary (particularly in terms of Futurism), I would be concerned not to collapse all Modernist artistic and cultural practices into Fascism. Indeed, many Modernist avant-gardes (such as Berlin Dada) were explicitly anti-Fascist.
22. Richard Weight, *Mod: A Very British Style* (London: Bodley Head, 2013), 65, 64.
23. Ibid., 72.
24. Ibid., 67.
25. Klaus Theweleit, *Male Fantasies I: women, floods, bodies, history*, trans. Stephen Conway, Erica Carter and Chris Turner (London: Polity, 1989), 422.
26. Gilles Deleuze and Felix Guattari, *Anti-Oedipus: Capitalism and Schizophrenia*, trans. Brian Massumi (London: Athlone Press, 1983), 26. In *Anti-Oedipus*, Gilles Deleuze and Felix Guattari propose the "body-without-organs" as a figure for their metaphysics of flux and becoming. This "BwO" counters a Freudian narrative of a closed "organic" subjectivity in suggesting the priority of desire that *flows through* bodies: "Desire constantly couples continuous flows and partial objects that are by nature fragmentary and fragmented [and] causes the current to flow" (5). Connection and "coupling" rather than Oedipal conflicts or the "lack" of the phallus are the structuring of human (and other) life.

BIBLIOGRAPHY

Anderson, Paul "Smiler". *Mods: The New Religion, The Style and Music of the 1960s Mods*. London: Omnibus, 2013.

Deleuze, Gilles and Felix Guattari. *Anti-Oedipus: Capitalism and Schizophrenia*. Translated by Brian Massumi. London: Athlone Press, 1983.

Gray, Fred. "1930s Architecture and the Cult of the Sun". *Modernism on Sea: Art and Culture at the British Seaside*, edited by Lara Feigel and Alexandra Harris, 159–176. Oxford: Peter Lang, 2011.

Hamilton, Ian. "Sohoitis", *Granta* 65 (Spring 1999): 291–303.

Hebdige, Dick. *Hiding in the Light*. London: Routledge, 1988.
Hebdige, Dick. "The Meaning of Mod". In *Resistance through Rituals: Youth Subcultures in Post-war Britain*, edited by Stuart Hall and Tony Jefferson, 71–79. 2nd edn. London: Routledge, 2006.
MacInnes, Colin. *Absolute Beginners*. 1959. Harmondsworth: Penguin, 1986.
Quadrophenia. Dir. Franc Roddam. The Who Films, 1979.
Quadrophenia: Can You See The Real Me? BBC, 2012.
Rawlings, Terry. *Mod: A Very British Phenomenon*. London: Omnibus, 2000.
Sandbrook, Dominic. *Never Had It So Good: A History of Britain from Suez to the Beatles*. London: Abacus, 2000.
Theweleit, Klaus. *Male Fantasies I: women, floods, bodies, history*. Translated by Stephen Conway, Erica Carter and Chris Turner. London: Polity, 1989.
Theweleit, Klaus. *Male Fantasies II: Male Bodies: Psychoanalysing the White Terror*. Translated by Stephen Conway, Erica Carter and Chris Turner. London: Polity, 1989.
The Who. *Quadrophenia*. Track Records/Polydor, 1973.
Weight, Richard. *Mod: A Very British Style*. London: Bodley Head, 2013.
Wells, Simon. *Quadrophenia: A Way of Life*. N.p.: Countdown, 2013.

CHAPTER 12

"You Were Under the Impression, that When You Were Walking Forwards, that You'd End up Further Onwards, but Things Ain't Quite that Simple": Time Travelling and *Quadrophenia*'s Segues

Pamela Thurschwell

> *One of the most significant, but also one of the most painful psychical achievements of the pubertal period is…detachment from parental authority, a process that alone makes possible the opposition, which is so important for the progress of civilization, between the new generation and the old.* (Sigmund Freud)[1]

I saw the Who perform *Quadrophenia* in 2013 at the O2 in London. As a lifelong fan of the band and the album it was a big deal for me, but there was a man, probably in his late 60s, standing next to us, with his two adult sons, for whom it was an even bigger deal. Tears streamed down his face as he belted out every song. It was clear from his reaction, and what he drunkenly told us, as his sons tried to keep him upright, that he felt he *was* Jimmy; even the timeframe fitted. If Jimmy was

---

P. Thurschwell (✉)
University of Sussex, Brighton, UK
e-mail: p.thurschwell@sussex.ac.uk

© The Author(s) 2018
P. Thurschwell (ed.), *Quadrophenia and Mod(ern) Culture*,
Palgrave Studies in the History of Subcultures and Popular Music,
https://doi.org/10.1007/978-3-319-64753-1_12

nineteen years old in 1964 he would have been born at the tail end of the Second World War, and he'd be in his late 60s now, like the man at the concert. It struck me that *Quadrophenia*, my bible for getting through my teenage years, exerted an enormous nostalgic pull, whether that was toward an earlier time of life (youth) or an earlier historical period (the early 1960s), whether it was for one's own Mod youth, or a Mod youth that, for me, was utterly, attractively, alien in time and place.[2]

This outpouring of nostalgia might sit uneasily with the fact that the album is in fact an anatomy of a young man's mental distress and near breakdown, a despair about his life that drives him to the brink of real suicide or at least symbolic scooter-cide. *Quadrophenia*, in all its manifestations, is hardly an advertisement for carefree youth. But perhaps our longing for youth has never been simply about the fantasy of it as carefree. Throughout the twentieth century, adolescence has been constructed as a time in which the most intense experiences and emotions seem possible, are welcomed even; in which experiments with sexuality, style, identity, and politics are expected and sanctioned. Adolescence is when rebellion is allowed, when the old order is seen as needing to be overthrown so that the future can turn out differently from a present that has been grudgingly inherited. Both Freud's Oedipal theory, and arguably, literary and artistic Modernism, are based on the child's ongoing desire to kill off the values of the generation that spawned him or her, and create the world anew.[3] At a certain point, however, this desire to destroy one's parents and one's inherited circumstances is expected to cease; the adolescent is supposed to stop pogo-ing or throwing rocks at policemen on Brighton Beach, to take up a position in a world in which economic productivity and heterosexual reproduction—the values of a previous generation—are required. You re-enter the history you've inherited. You settle into that job as a bell boy or in an advertising agency, get married, have a kid, and forget about sleeping on the beach until you hear the Who play fifty years later and it all comes flooding back to you in a melancholic rush, and you're crying at a concert at the O2.

This is one story of adolescence, and how we might understand the nostalgia for youth, initiated by a blast of music from our past. The story I've just told chimes with the traditional plotline of adolescent development in the novel, the *bildungsroman*, in which a young man (usually a young man) has adventures and misadventures in love and life and work, before learning from his mistakes, and accommodating himself to adulthood and to his historical circumstances.[4] And we can find this story in *Quadrophenia* if we look for it. If we think Jimmy is older and wiser after he discards his Mod self for an unknown new one, then at the end we might see him as finally accepting an adult world and the process of growing up. The narratives offered by the film and album diverge, however, suggesting different relationships to a propulsion toward death—Jimmy's real or symbolic suicide and the end of his identity as a Mod. The ending of Townshend's liner notes to the album leave Jimmy stranded on a rock in the sea, having exchanged the speed and flash of Mod for a kind of slowness: "I'm stuck here in the pissing rain with my life flashing before me. Only it isn't flashing, it's crawling." There's not much accommodation to reality in this bleak picture. By contrast to this, the final photos in Ethan Russell's booklet are more hopeful, showing Jimmy walking on the beach, after a picture of him submerged under the water. These photos suggest that being "drowned" can be a temporary condition, something that can be returned from (the way in which a pop song might allow you to experience death for three-and-a-half minutes and then move onto the next song). The album itself ends with a kind of transcendence: the yearning, simultaneously desperate, and spiritually hopeful, "Love Reign O'er Me" suggests that maybe something might be learned, after all.[5] At the end of the film we watch the scooter crash on the rocks, however, since we saw Jimmy walking on the beach at the beginning of the movie, we can assume the entire narrative is structured as a kind of flashback, and that it was Mod and not Jimmy who died. But can we then presume that there is an older and wiser Jimmy flashing back? This is partly a question about whether we can easily match up an individual's life cycle with the ebb and flow of teenage subculture, hegemony, and rebellion. Narratives that fit one may not fit the other.

Quadrophenia's endings are obviously conflicted both about what lies ahead for Jimmy (immersion in some kind of adult world), and what lies behind him (his allegiance to Mod subculture). It's possible to retrieve a plotline arced toward growing up in *Quadrophenia*, however, neither the album nor the film make "growing up" look very appealing. Adult society is shown in both film and album to be rife with unhappiness. If Jimmy's Mod self is drowned, with the drowned scooter (on the back cover photo of the album) or the wrecked- on-the-rocks scooter (at the end of the film), what version of an adult self will take its place? Can there be a future for Jimmy, apart from submission to an adulthood of work in the junkyard or the advertising agency (both of these, in different ways "dirty jobs")?[6] I want to suggest in this chapter that rather than trying to chart a way out for Jimmy, it might be more productive to linger with the impasses that *Quadrophenia* dramatizes. *Quadrophenia*'s representation of Jimmy's situation (in terms of his fraught relationship to Mod subculture, class, masculinity, sex, work, the existential angst of the teenager) may create a potential dead-end for him in terms of one kind of narrative, the narrative of development, but might open up other possibilities that are enacted through *Quadrophenia*'s interventions into its various contemporary moments via its sometimes jarring leaps and transitions across space and time, its anachronisms, its nostalgia, its orientation toward a different kind of future—what I'd like to call its time travelling. To make this argument, I'm going to focus on the idea of transition in *Quadrophenia*, briefly from one place to another, and then from one time to another, and finally from one song to another.

Imbued with the Mod obsession with speed in various forms, *Quadrophenia* portrays many different kinds of transport and ways of moving through space; it's significant, however, that most of this movement is thwarted or arrested. In the album, Ethan Russell's accompanying book of photographs, and Franc Roddam's 1979 film, Vespas rev up only to crash at the side of London streets; the cliffs near Brighton promise freedom, but serve up only suicidal plunges onto the rocks or into the sea for people or scooters. In another example of motion that eventually goes nowhere, the 5:15 commuter train serves a double purpose—it transports middle-class men who work in the city back to the various suburban stops along the Brighton train line, but it only partly concealing the well-dressed, but pilled-out-of-his-mind time bomb in its midst, the working-class Mod Jimmy. Here Jimmy's movement is south to Brighton, but also back in time. With a nostalgia perhaps only available to the young, Jimmy is pining for the previous weekend. Returning to Brighton to try to relive the triumphant Mod collectivity of a few days' earlier—having sex with a girl he fancies and getting arrested with the Ace Face at the beach fight of bank holiday 1964—he finds only disappointment.[7] If Mods are supposed to be oriented toward a fast and shiny modern future, then Jimmy seems, by contrast, introspective and backward looking. His relationship with Steph dramatizes the fact that he is not fast or modern enough; she is only in it for a laugh, and quickly moves on to the next boyfriend, while Jimmy is sentimentally stuck on her, and their encounter in the alley.

Speed, then, of all sorts, is central to the story of *Quadrophenia*, and for Mod culture, where the right scooter is as crucial as the right cut of jacket. But from crashing the first-class section of the 5:15 train to Jimmy's stealing of the row boat in Townshend's liner notes ("I pinched this boat, first time I'd ever been on a boat at sea"), in the world of *Quadrophenia*, the possibility of getting from one place to another is never guaranteed; transport is often something you have to steal or sneak your way into.[8] Stealing transport happens most dramatically when Jimmy takes the Ace Face's scooter at the end of the film and wrecks it off of Beachy Head. The scooter for Jimmy, and for every Mod, it is implied, is, on the one hand, an extension of the unique individual self (the four mirrors on the scooter on the cover of the album reflect an image of each member of the Who), but on the other hand, also a sign of communal identity—the gleaming rows of scooters lined up on the Brighton seafront secure a place as one among many. Mod scooters traverse the space between London and Brighton, but also traverse the space between being an individual (adding that extra mirror or light to go one better than the other Mods) and being a part of the group.[9] If speed and mobility are key to the kinds of freedom that Jimmy values in *Quadrophenia*, then this freedom remains elusive. You can always lose or wreck a scooter, just as you might lose or wreck yourself.

These repeated scenes of transport trouble—stolen and wrecked scooters, stolen and drowned boats, trains full of businessmen on their way home to the suburbs sheltering the speeding but also backward-looking Jimmy—all help dramatize a central problematic movement for *Quadrophenia*; the abyssal crossing from adolescence to adulthood. How does one make it through that journey without crashing out? Can that journey be reimagined laterally, rather than toward growing up? If you are clever, can you find a way to go fast enough to achieve a kind of escape velocity from approaching adulthood?

As other essays in this collection point out, *Quadrophenia* is a text that refers to, and has been restaged in, many different historical eras, from the early 1960s' Mod moment it represents, to the early 1970s of the album, to the late 1970s' moment of the film, to the early 1980s' Mod revival spearheaded by Paul Weller and the Jam, and the dispersal of Mod style and subculture into other countries.[10] Stephen Glynn has suggested that both the album and the film of *Quadrophenia* jog between the early 1960s era they ostensibly represent and the contemporary moment in which they are made, with a refreshing disregard for documentary accuracy. As Glynn argues one can see the film's anachronisms and its apparent indifference to chronology (using "My Generation" before it actually came out, etc.) as an effective strategy for giving it an emotional truth that transcends its time.[11] Made in 1979, the film of *Quadrophenia* was aimed at, and also about, punks, and adolescent rebellion more generally, as much as it was "about" the minutiae of being a proper Mod in 1964. Glynn argues that the film's wayward and not always accurate evoking of Mod culture perfectly exemplifies Claude Levi-Strauss's "bricolage": "In cultural theory the term refers to the processes by which elements are appropriated from the dominant culture, and their meaning transformed, often through ironic or surreal juxtapositions, to challenge and subvert that culture."[12] Glynn goes onto suggest that the film's historical inaccuracies both celebrate and imitate the methods of the formation of subculture itself. Dick Hebdige argues that Mods were expert bricoleurs appropriating and subverting the mainstream culture of their parents, taking apart the previous meanings of a tailored suit or a respectable form of transportation such as a scooter to make it signify differently, as youthful, new, dangerous.[13] Mods stole from the past, while simultaneously orienting themselves toward a sleek, modern, European future. One thing that *Quadrophenia* might be about then is, in a sense, the uses of time travel for daily life. The film and album register clashing constellations of history and desire, around youth and age, subculture and hegemony, the early 1960s, the early 1970s and the late 1970s (the moment of punk). The power of both album and film (at least for the writers in this collection, and for that crying man at the O2) might lie, in some part, in how *Quadrophenia* manages to move the listener or the viewer through its various time periods.

Keeping these versions of movement across space and time in *Quadrophenia* in mind, I want to now turn toward might initially appear as a much less dramatic kind of movement, the transition between songs on an album. The segue is such a small thing that it is almost not a thing at all; the few seconds on any kind of musical recording through which the listener experiences the transition from one song to the next, or the running of one song into the next, when that space disappears.[14] Usually, the segue consists of a miniscule amount of empty time, but it can also collapse time, when one song flows seamlessly into another. I began to think about segues when I first encountered the shuffle button on my iPod, when, "Golden Slumbers" cut off abruptly instead of moving smoothly into "Carry that Weight" as it did on *Abbey Road*. Suddenly time and listening seemed out of joint. The pleasure of the surprise segue, where a familiar song is followed by one you are not expecting, was counterbalanced by the possibility of a bumpy listening experience.[15] Segues, whether empty transitional space or space filled with sound, create connections between songs, on albums obviously, but also through personal memories and associations; a good mix tape (a skill I spend a great deal of time mastering in the 1980s and early 1990s) was all about the segues. Segues on a concept album are as important; they function as transitions between one scene in the story, or one aspect of the concept, and another. Repeated refrains and riffs move the narrative forward but also remind the listener of how the album hangs together.[16] Listening to *Quadrophenia* from beginning to end, and thinking about its transitions between songs might lead us to think about the segue as a disappearing art form. The waning of the segue is bound up with the waning of the album; in the 1970s and 1980s, when you were more likely to listen to the songs on an album side in the order in which they were laid out, then there was more of a sense that that transitions between songs and sides mattered. The segue in the 1980s and 1990s became differently crucial to creative consumption for DJs who wanted to control the pace and emotional movement of a party or club scene. The segue was always key to the success of a playlist; the right segue made an album, or a mix, work.

Of course, many music fans still do carefully construct mixes, following an ideal order and paying careful attention to transitions, but with the advent of massive downloading possibilities, we are now much more likely to leave it all up to fate. Where once I carefully planned mixes for myself or for friends, I now hit shuffle and skip over songs I'm not in the mood to hear. The perfect segue has been replaced by different kinds of pleasure, instant gratification and the element of surprise. We might enjoy the clashes of genre and song that ensure from hitting iPod shuffle, but, some of us, at least, are less likely to take the time to line up our songs in an ideal order.

If segues on albums are now practically historical, it might be worth retrieving how the segues function for the listener on a carefully constructed album such as *Quadrophenia*. *Quadrophenia*'s segues help place Jimmy's story into different kinds of history, weaving together different strands of his experience. An example can be found at the end of "Drowned" on side three, which fades out into Townshend singing "Come sleep on the beach," a refrain from "Sea and Sand," while walking along the seafront. (The sound of beach pebbles underfoot is audible.)[17] The scene then shifts to Jimmy spotting his hero Ace Face, working at a sea front hotel as a bell boy in the song "Bell Boy." The reality of the setting, the plaintiveness and loneliness of Townshend's wistful voice channelling Jimmy's feelings, above the crunch of Brighton Beach, seems at first like an especially poignant contrast to the bombastic Rocker that follows. But that repeated refrain from "Sea and Sand" also foreshadows a similar sense of failure and insecurity haunting Keith Moon's alter ego; the once proud Ace Face, now servile bell boy at the hotel, "always running at someone's heels," hardly has time to notice the sea right outside the hotel's front door. The slow moving poignant wistful longing of "Come sleep on the beach"—so close and so far—becomes a yearned for horizon ("some nights I still sleep on the beach/remember when stars were in reach") when you are enslaved to a service economy, rushed off your feet carrying bags. The scene in the film, in which Sting clumsily drops a bag and is told off by a toff, serves to reinforce the fact that work time is humiliating and demanding compared to leisure time, where youth identity lives.

I'm arguing then, that the segues in *Quadrophenia* do a lot of narrative and emotional work, specifically, in relation to the way the album configures time. The album, released in 1973 attempts to represent a moment from recent history, the beach fights between rival gangs in 1964. That moment is experienced by Jimmy (in both the album and the film) as an exhilarating apotheosis—the moment when his individual identity merges successfully into a historical-collective one. (Acted out in the film as that ecstatic chant "We are, we are, we are the Mods!")

Quadrophenia is self-conscious about its relation to history, then, combining a gritty realism centred on Jimmy's home life, with a nostalgia partly cut through with an ironic understanding of the Who's Mod past. The Who were never very successful at inhabiting Mod and Townshend knows this; the album documents the failure to live up to an identity. Mod then is an idea and an ideal, more than a lived reality; if it exists at all, it only does so momentarily for Jimmy—a fleeting feeling of collective epiphany that immediately collapses into a melancholic loss.[18] Jimmy longs to be subsumed into the crowd; he wants to look the part ("My jacket's gonna be cut slim and checked/maybe a touch of seersucker with an open neck") and at the same time he fears losing his mind and his shaky individual identity ("Can you see the real me? Can you?")

As with its movements in space, time too, in *Quadrophenia*, moves toward a kind of impasse. Conceived post–*Who's Next*, at the height of a certain version of bloated fame, *Quadrophenia*'s divided time frame pits the young Jimmy of the 1960s' Mod scene against the rock star Who of the 1970s. This dissidence is captured in a central scene in the album's booklet of photographs in which the precisely dated 1964 Mod Jimmy kneeling next to his Vespa, watches, from a distance, as the successful 1970s' Who (weighed down with 1970s' facial hair) clown around in front the Hammersmith Odeon where they are playing a sold-out concert. This tension is also explored in "The Punk and the Godfather," the song that stages a confrontation between a young punk and a fallen rock star idol, which I will consider at the end of this chapter (Fig. 12.1).

Quadrophenia then takes its listener through self-conscious identifications across historical time. To some extent, all great pop songs do that. Hell, mediocre pop songs do that too. A song is extracted from its own time and embedded in ours. We hear it once, and then we hear it again; the song becomes a part of our lives, taking its place in our own personal histories. Pop songs remind us of an earlier time or place, often an earlier version of ourselves. Mechanical reproduction functions by allowing us to repeat experience, and pop music is where mechanical reproduction goes to make us cry; to contain our loneliness; to remind us how to love. For me, *Quadrophenia* was one of the first albums to makes that process seem historically embedded and self-conscious and this process is, at least

Fig. 12.1 The punk not quite meeting the godfathers, in front of the Hammersmith Odeon. Photograph by Ethan Russell

in part, lodged in the emotions of its segues; the time-travelling distance between the Mod moment of 1964, the Who of 1973, and the listener wherever and whenever she may be.[19]

I want to suggest that *Quadrophenia*'s segues usually construct a melancholic/nostalgic relation to history, while sometimes also nodding toward more nourishing relationships between pasts and futures. I will now consider two of *Quadrophenia*'s segues to flesh out these claims.

At the end of the short, carnivalesque, "Helpless Dancer," Roger Daltrey's voice cuts the song off abruptly, after a list of things that seem wrong with the contemporary world ("you get beaten up by blacks/who though they worked still got the sack/and when your soul tells you to hide/your very right to die's denied"). The ending builds to a crescendo, Daltrey's voice rising: "And when a man is trying to change, it only causes further pain/you realise that all along something in us going wrong.... You stop dancing." It cuts out, and in the background, faintly, we hear the Who's 1965 hit "The Kids are Alright." "Don't mind other guys dancing with my girl.... That's fine, I know them all pretty well..." Plaintive, and more than a little insecure, this is also optimistic, collective, hopeful. "The Kids are Alright" is an attempt to conjure a group of friends that will make everything ok for the singer—that won't run off with the singer's girl. "The Kids are Alright" speaks to a desire for friends who will function as a sustaining collective from which the singer can sometimes depart ("You know sometimes I must get out in the light") to a lonelier or more individualized identity, but then safely return. It's like a kinder idealized version of what Mod as an identity should do. The song's innocence makes a stark contrast to "Helpless Dancer's" suggestion that the dancing is done, and *Quadrophenia*'s sense that, in multiple ways, the kids are not all right. The line "I know if I go things will be a lot better for her/I had things planned but her folks wouldn't let her" I've always found extraordinarily poignant, speaking to a youthful innocence that still registers and respects what parents might want. Between "The Kids are Alright" and "Helpless Dancer" you can feel that the very meaning of dancing has changed as well. In "Helpless Dancer" it's not clear that the dancing is going on on the dance floor; it feels as if a gun is being pointed at the singer's head and he's being told to dance to the tune of hegemony.

In an interview with Pete Townshend from 2011, Jon Savage makes a similar point: "One of my favourite moments in *Quadrophenia* is at the end of Helpless Dancer, when you get the start of The Kids are Alright.

But if you play the original record, it doesn't sound like that, because of the context, that's where you get the difference between '64/65 and '73." Townshend responds, "It's that thing of sending it over the ether. We attempted to broadcast it, and then bring it back. I think I tried to get Radio Caroline, in its death throes, to broadcast it so I could record it off the radio, but we kind of synthesized it. It's literally music over the ether. That's how it was."[20] The radio is a transmitter for Mod time travel; the 1965 hit reminds the listener in 1973 of the route from one kind of dancing to another, more desperate one. "The Kids are Alright" with its tentative promise of a community of friends you could trust, is a nostalgic ideal, when the current context is Jimmy dancing alone, as fast as he can, to the impossible demands of modern life. If "Helpless Dancer" seems to be set more in a shaky 1973 than in 1964, the "The Kids are Alright" segue suggests that the earlier dancing might also be shadowed by a kind of insecurity.

Let's consider another transition between "Cut my Hair" and "The Punk and the Godfather" to make one final point about the ways in which *Quadrophenia*'s segues tell a story about the Mod in history. The song, "Cut my Hair" is a low-key lament about the misery of Jimmy's home life ("The kids at school have parents that seem so cool, and although I don't want to hurt them, mine want me their way"). The song ends on a harsh minor note, its final line marking the beginning of a devastatingly ordinary day, "my fried egg makes me sick first thing in the morning." Townshend's voice is intercut with the sound of a kettle boiling, and a BBC radio newscaster reporting on the Brighton Beach riots of May 18–19, 1964: "A gang of nearly 1000 youths entered the Grand Hotel in pursuit of two leather clad Rockers." As the end of this song slides into the next we find ourselves assaulted by Townshend's axe-like guitar chords—the defiant beginning of one of the album's centrepieces, "The Punk and the Godfather." Break this segue down and there is a story buried there: the boiling kettle is Jimmy, mired in his depressing quotidian home life with alcoholic parents who don't understand why he thinks, acts, or dresses the way he does. He, like the kettle, is ready to go off. This transition opens out a personal boiling point to a collective one in the news that's emerging from the radio—1000 Jimmies on the beaches of Brighton, ready to explode, 1000 adolescent kettles boiling over. The oh-so-proper BBC English of the news announcer also emphasizes the differences between the working-class Mods and the only venues through which their histories are told.

This is the perfect segue in an album full of brilliant segues. The movement from the defeated ending of "Cut My Hair" ("inside I'm still the same") to the riot going on is a movement from the inside to the outside, from the personal to the political. The kettle is an image of building pressure, but simultaneously a reminder that any explosion that happens is likely to be contained and deflected by domestic spaces and the dreary ordinariness of adult lives. However, this moment is also one of possibility. After the segue's movement outwards to the wider world (under the breakfast, the beach!), we are slapped in the face by the defiant chords of "The Punk and the Godfather," the album's manifesto for a punk future, just over the horizon: "You declared you would be three inches taller/you only became what we made you," Daltrey (by 1973, definitely a godfather, but voicing the punk) snaps at us. Jimmy's voice now seems to be a part of a potentially powerful "we."(Fig. 12.2)

Fig. 12.2 "Under the breakfast, the beach!". Photograph by Ethan Russell

This segue between the domestic quotidian and a reaching toward transcendence—individual or communal—echoes a transitional strategy used by James Joyce in another classic adolescent *bildungsroman*, *Portrait of the Artist as a Young Man*. In Joyce's *Portrait* his early twentieth-century, late-dandy, proto-Mod, the cocky, insecure, Stephen Dedalus, ends each chapter with an epiphanic moment of transcendence emerging from his experience of his ordinary working-class Dublin life; spotting a beautiful girl on the beach he feels hit by lightning: "My god, I will be a writer, and a lover!" he thinks (Joyce says it better, of course). Stephen vows to immerse himself in the worlds of the flesh and the pen and forsake the religious transcendence he was seeking earlier. Each of the five chapters of *Portrait* ends with a visionary or triumphant moment for Stephen, and each of the following chapters begins with a bodily reality that drags him back down to earth: his mother washing his socks or something equivalently embarrassing.[21] In the novel, there is always a moment in which an epiphanic discovery falls back into the degradations of the everyday, which is, for Stephen, his poverty-stricken, engulfing, family context.

The transition from "Cut my Hair" to "The Punk and the Godfather" works in the opposite direction to the Joycean segue, but I think in a similar way; the queasiness of Jimmy arguing with his parents, and the greasy egg he can hardly bear to face, builds up in the mounting tension of the teakettle's whistle, and explodes into history with the BBC report on Brighton Beach.[22] The kill-your-idols bravado of "The Punk and the Godfather" is the logical outcome of this encounter between the egg and the beach. This song makes it possible for the adolescent to talk back, to be heard; it embodies a transcendent moment when Jimmy, or the album, can at least imagine stepping out of his entrapped life. The song reaches for a different kind of vocabulary, one that abstracts and generalizes the generational dilemmas, the time-travel problems, which obsess the album. In the space of this song, Jimmy can tell the godfather that his reign is ending, that now, the old order needs to listen to the new. If we return to Ethan Russell's photograph in the *Quadrophenia* booklet, we see that this confrontation is across time in a different way as well. In the photo, the 1964 Mod Jimmy stares across a gulf at the 1973 rock star Who. The booklet glosses this non-encounter in 1964, still with a sense of this gulf, "After the show I hung around outside, waiting for them to come out. When they did they never bloody well recognized me. I shouted, and one of them turned round and said, 'How are you doing?' like he remembered me. 'Working?' he said. I hate it when people say that. Course I wasn't working. I was still at fucking school."[23] "The Punk and the Godfather" is the point where Jimmy insists on being recognized and heard. The strange temporal distortions, between the 1970s' Who and the 1964 Jimmy, between the songs on the album and the book of photographs, means that Jimmy represents both the past and the future for the Who; themselves as young, uncomfortable Mods and the usurpers who follow them, insisting that they are past their sell-by date. The segues on the album move the listener between times and between registers for Jimmy, from his entrapping family kitchen, to the riot on the beaches, to the place where the old idols, the rock stars, matter and don't to the young punks who want to be them and discard them.

A few years after *Quadrophenia* was released the Clash will sing "It's 1977" and blast a lot of what Townshend is doing out of the water, while simultaneously making his songs seem incredibly prescient. In 1982, I saw the Clash open for the Who. From my perspective, they were tiny dots on the horizon of Philadelphia's now torn-down JFK stadium, which seated a small city. Watching those dots in the distance, I thought a lot about "The Punk and the Godfather," the song in which Townshend predicts his own obsolescence. Johnny Rotten and Joe Strummer clearly wouldn't need him to explain themselves to themselves anymore, and anyway the Godfather will inevitably get it wrong. But the typically quavery Townshend-voiced bridge from "The Punk and the Godfather" still compels as a story of torch-passing; I imagined it compelled Joe Strummer: "I have to be careful not to preach/I can't pretend that I can teach/and yet I live your future out/by pounding stages like a clown…" Yes, you can see punk foreshadowed in "My Generation," in Keith's decimated drum kit, and Townshend's autodestruction, in "Anyway Anyhow Anywhere," but you can also find it here, in "The Punk and the Godfather," which moves toward a hope that the future need not replicate the past, even as we still turn to heroes for guidance. Here I have argued that you can find that future in the smallest of spaces, in the movement between the individual angry Mod and the joyous youthful mob, between 1964, 1973, and all the possible futures that haunt *Quadrophenia*'s brilliant segues.

NOTES

1. Sigmund Freud, *On Sexuality: Three Essays on the Theory of Sexuality and Other Works*, eds. Angela Richards, trans. James Strachey, Penguin Freud Library Volume 7 (Harmondsworth: Penguin, 1977), 150.
2. In this article, I move quite rapidly between the film, the songs that make up the album, and Pete Townshend's original story in the liner notes of *Quadrophenia*. All of these contribute to an overall narrative of *Quadrophenia*. I try to be clear about which version I am talking about when it makes a difference to my argument, but I also refer to a kind of amalgamation of the shared elements of all three as simply, *Quadrophenia*.
3. See Freud's "On Puberty" in *Three Essays on the Theory of Sexuality*. See Geoff Gilbert, *Before Modernism Was: Modern History and the Constituency of Writing* (London: Palgrave, 2004), Chap. 2, "Boys: Manufacturing Inefficiency" 51–73, on Modernism, adolescence, juvenile delinquency, and Oedipal rebellion.
4. See Franco Moretti *The Way of the World:* The Bildungsroman *in European Culture*. Trans, Albert Sbraglia. (London: Verso, 2000 (1987)) for a classic discussion of the *bildungsroman*, which emphasizes youth's relationship to modernity in the nineteenth century.
5. Pete Townshend, Liner notes to *Quadrophenia*. The first recording of "Love Reign O'er Me" predates the story of *Quadrophenia* and is part of a different aesthetic: Meher Baba/*Lifehouse* rather than the gritty realism of Mod. Townshend said of the song "It refers to Meher Baba's one time comment that rain was a blessing from God." It works perfectly as the grand finale to the album; perhaps Jimmy and Mod needs some kind of spiritual transcendence as well. (Richie Unterberger, *Won't Get Fooled Again: The Who from* Lifehouse *to* Quadrophenia (London: Jawbone Press, 2011), 175–176; 227–228).
6. Could he (as Keith Gildart points out in his chapter) access different kinds of adult communal possibility, along the lines of his father's involvement with trade unions or socialism? There is another rumour of a sequel happening as I write this.
7. In the film in an alley in Brighton; in Townshend's story it happens on the beach.
8. Pete Townshend, Liner notes to *Quadrophenia*.
9. See Brian Baker's chapter in this collection for more on the significance of the scooter.
10. Feldman, *We are the Mods: A Transnational History of a Youth Subculture* (New York: Peter Lang, 2009).

11. Stephen Glynn, *Quadrophenia* (New York: Wallflower Press, 2014), 63–67. The film's director Franc Roddam also makes this point, telling fans repeatedly to "never let the facts get in the way of the truth." (Ali Catterall and Simon Wells. *Your Face Here: British Cult Movies Since the Sixties* (London: Fourth Estate, 2001), 162.
12. Glynn, 64.
13. Dick Hebdige, *Subculture: The Meaning of Style* (London: Methuen and Co, Ltd., 1979), 104–105.
14. From the Italian for follows, as a musical direction, "segue" means continue the next section without a pause. I'm using it loosely here as a way of thinking about the spaces between songs whether they are empty or full of some other kinds of noise (as they often are on *Quadrophenia*).
15. Ratliff makes a related point that the way we experience music has changed drastically: "The unit of the album means increasingly little to us, and so the continent-sized ice floes of English language culture that were Beatles and Michael Jackson records are melting into the water world of sound" (Ben Ratliff, *Every Song Ever: Twenty Ways to Listen in an Age of Musical Plenty* (New York: Picador, 2016), 5).
16. Perhaps the concept album has merged into the phenomenon of the smash musical, like *Hamilton*. But also the concept album is with us strongly in video and audio events such as Beyoncé's *Formation*.
17. In *Quadrophenia: Can You See the Real Me?* Townshend talks about walking down the beach with a stereo and mike singing "Sea and Sand."
18. That epiphany is only true for the shortest amount of time. There's a substantial difference in focus between the film and the album, which has to do in part with a difference in format. The album, is almost by necessity, focused on the individual; the quadrophonic conceit explicitly sets the album up as about Jimmy's inner turmoil– the clashing personalities of him as a "bleeding quadrophenic," and his insecure sense of himself as a Mod ("How come the other tickets dress much better?/Without a penny to spare, they dress to the letter.")The entire album is retrospective in relation to the Brighton rumble, which was Jimmy's good moment, of being in love with Mod, part of a crowd. The film on the other hand, is able to portray the beach fight as it happens—it can have its collectivity and mourn it too. When we hear the joyous cry of "We are the Mods!" we are, at least partly, experiencing that epiphanic moment with Jimmy. Film can portray crowds and collective identity in a way that the more individual focus of the album does not.
19. In *Quadrophenia: Can You See the Real Me?* the critics Mark Kermode and Howie Edelson point out the uses the album makes of its soundscape. Edelson argues that the way in which the listener experiences pieces of songs, and refrains, means that songs are always returning as memories,

as part of Jimmy's internal dialogue. Kermode talks about the way the first song with lyrics on the album, "The Real Me" begins, "I went *back* to the doctor…" According to Kermode the first time he heard it he thought he'd mistakenly put on Side Two. *Quadrophenia* begins *in media res*. As Kermode says "you come right into the middle of a rush."
20. *Mojo*, December 2011 "Talkin' About My Generation" Jon Savage interview with Pete Townshend, pp. 76–83.
21. David Trotter points out that "All five chapters of *A Portrait* conclude with a moment of self-transcendence; four times, the next chapter opens with a harsh reversion to squalor and plain style." (David Trotter. *The English Novel in History, 1895–1920* (London: Routledge, 1993), 293).
22. The critic James Wood, in a moving personal article on his *Quadrophenia* fandom, begins with Ethan Russell's photography of Jimmy's greasy egg. "The Kids are Alright" *The Guardian*, 30 May 2009 www.theguardian.com/books/2009/may/30/quadrophenia-seminal-album-who.
23. *Quadrophenia*, Criterion Set, booklet, 28.

Bibliography

Catterall, Ali and Simon Wells. *Your Face Here: British Cult Movies Since the Sixties*. London: Fourth Estate, 2001.

Feldman, Christine Jacqueline. *We are the Mods: A Transnational History of a Youth Subculture*. New York: Peter Lang, 2009.

Sigmund Freud, *On Sexuality: Three Essays on the Theory of Sexuality and Other Works*, eds. Angela Richards, trans. James Strachey, Penguin Freud Library Volume 7. Harmondsworth: Penguin, 1977.

Gilbert, Geoff. *Before Modernism Was: Modern History and the Constituency of Writing* London: Palgrave, 2004.

Glynn, Stephen. *Quadrophenia*. New York: Wallflower Press, 2014.

Hebdige, Dick. *Subculture: The Meaning of Style*. London: Methuen and Co, Ltd., 1979.

Moretti, Franco. *The Way of the World:* The Bildungsroman *in European Culture*. Trans, Albert Sbraglia. London: Verso, 2000 (1987).

O'Casey. Matt. (director) *Quadrophenia: Can you see the Real Me?* BBC Four documentary, 2012.

Ratliff, Ben. *Every Song Ever: Twenty Ways to Listen in an Age of Musical Plenty*. New York: Picador, 2016.

Roddam, Franc. *Quadrophenia*. Criterion Collection DVD, booklet.

Savage, Jon. Interview with Pete Townshend *Mojo*, December 2011 "Talkin' About My Generation" pp. 76–83.

Townshend, Pete. *Liner Notes to* Quadrophenia, *Quadrophenia*, Fabulous Music Ltd, 1973.

Townshend, Pete. *Who I am*. London: HarperCollins, 2012.
Trotter, David. *The English Novel in History, 1895–1920*. London: Routledge, 1993.
Unterberger, Richie. *Won't Get Fooled Again: The Who from Lifehouse to Quadrophenia*. London: Jawbone Press, 2011.
The Who, *Quadrophenia*. Track Records, 1973.
Wood, James. "The Kids are Alright" *The Guardian*, 30 May 2009 www.theguardian.com/books/2009/may/30/quadrophenia-seminal-album-who.

CHAPTER 13

Interview with Franc Roddam

Pamela Thurschwell

As well as co-writing and directing *Quadrophenia* and creating *Masterchef*, Franc Roddam's works include the award-winning TV drama *Dummy*, and BBC documentaries *Mini* and *The Family*. Roddam graciously agreed to be interviewed for this book to talk about some of the influences and decisions that went in to making the film. A transcription of the interview follows.

PT: Can you tell me a little about what your relationship to Mod culture was when you came to make *Quadrophenia*?
FR: Talking about *Quadrophenia* now, it does seem like we're talking about the last century, and we are. The world seems to have changed so much and yet at the same time adolescence is adolescence, and adolescence remains forever. *Quadrophenia* was about an eighteen-year-old boy, who was eighteen in 1964. I myself was

---

This interview was conducted by Pamela Thurschwell on 2 December 2016.

P. Thurschwell (✉)
University of Sussex, Brighton, UK
e-mail: p.thurschwell@sussex.ac.uk

© The Author(s) 2018
P. Thurschwell (ed.), *Quadrophenia and Mod(ern) Culture*,
Palgrave Studies in the History of Subcultures and Popular Music,
https://doi.org/10.1007/978-3-319-64753-1_13

eighteen in 1964 and I was young enough to still have a memory of what it was like to be post-adolescent when I made the film. Also I grew up at a time when the Mod era was quite strong. All my friends were Mods, although I wasn't a Mod myself.

PT: Did you have another image which you identified with?

FR: I identified with Bohemians. I wanted to be a bongo-paying bohemian. I was a typical fifteen-year-old pretending to be older, going down to London to Ban the Bomb marches like Aldermaston. I loved the idea of being a beatnik—I was a baby beatnik, went to jazz clubs, travelled a lot. In Egypt and Istanbul and Afghanistan at the times when those places were very remote. I was much more radical in that respect. I remember being away on a trip for a few months and when I came back to my small town in England everyone had become a Mod. Boys and girls alike. Suddenly everyone was a smart Mod with sharp suits, and the girls had their hair short. It just clicked big time. So I was familiar with the Mods; I was best man at two Mod weddings. I had a couple of Mod girlfriends, so I knew the territory. When I was asked to make the film I had some inside knowledge about what it was like to be eighteen and about what it was like to be a Mod, and where it sat socially, politically, musically, stylistically so I was a good choice.

PT: Did you know when you were sixteen that you wanted to work in film? Did you always know that?

FR: No, I wanted to be a beat poet. I was reading the Russian poet Yevgeny Yevtushenko and Ginsberg and so forth. I wanted to be a poet, and then I was travelling through Greece and got a job on a film as an extra, and I hadn't realised that film was available to me. I come from a small town but I'd loved the cinema; I used to go to the movies often. There were two cinemas at the top of my street and I used to go from the age of eight onwards two or three times a week.

PT: What were your favourites? Were you into artsy films?

FR: In those days (early 50s) it was all westerns, Randolph Scott, but it was also Bogart. There was film noir that we'd sneak into. My love of cinema, John Ford and the American landscape. I lived in a small town in the north of England and the American landscape was magnificent.

So the affection for cinema was there and when I got this job as an extra, I suddenly saw the camera and the tracks and the lights and being an extra demystified it for me. I suddenly realised it was available to me. I went back to London and discovered that film school was a possibility. I applied, I went, I loved it, and devoted myself to it.

PT: You were brought into *Quadrophenia* because of *Dummy* and your credentials as a young, gritty realist filmmaker. From what I've read you had a really short amount of time between being brought into the project and beginning filming.

FR: It was an amazing thing. I was contracted the middle of June and we were filming by the end of September, and at that point there was no script, no casting, no locations, nothing. We put the whole thing together at great speed. When I did *Quadrophenia* I didn't have a director's chair, and the producer at the time said I'm not getting you a chair because you won't have time to sit down on it. And I think that's true; it happened fast. But if you think about the cinema in the old days, when people like Raoul Walsh were making three films a year, you just made them; you went for it. A lot of people second guess themselves; it's a form of pessimism, and that makes you passive. Whereas I was totally optimistic, totally positive, didn't have time to think. "We're doing this, we're doing that, it's done." Film is like a military operation; you cannot make half a decision. I liked the idea of moving at speed; I liked the idea of getting through it. *Quadrophenia* was the perfect start.

PT: And when you jumped in were you already a fan of the Who? Did you know the album?

FR: When I was asked to direct I was a fan of the Who, but not excessively. I'd seen them live and they were fantastic. I knew their music and I had great admiration for Pete's work, but I was going into the idea of making a film noir thriller at the time; I was writing a script. And then this came up out of the blue and I just leapt at it.

PT: When you were thinking about how to do to make the film what kinds of things influenced you?

FR: The album was a beautiful album; albums were works of art in those days and that was a particularly good album. But you have to embrace a good idea but not become a slave to it. I'm not a groupie—not a fan in that respect. I go into an art gallery thinking "I can do that" rather than with great reverence for the artist. It's not conceit; it's being engaged. I don't feel intimidated—you want me to write a screenplay, I'll write a screenplay. At the same time I have fantastic respect for quality art by other people. I can read something and be completely overwhelmed by its beauty.

PT: I think a hyperfan might have had a harder time having to go with what Townshend wanted, but it sounds like he actually gave you creative control.

FR: By working at the BBC and making documentaries, again having to be decisive, it gave me a period of higher objectivity. I was looking in an analytical way. I was thinking I'm not going to do *Tommy*—that's been done. *Tommy* was a rock opera with orchestration—I think *Quadrophenia* should be a different looking film completely. I was very quick to come to these decisions. It should be street; Mod is a blue-collar movement and I'm going to take the film in that direction. It also suited my style as I came out of a documentary background. I would give it a naturalism moving toward realism, rather than other directors at the time, like Alan Parker, who were into melodrama. I'm not someone who would go to melodrama. The strangest thing—I knew what I was doing, and I think that came from doing a series of documentaries where you had to be stronger than your subject and you had to protect your subject. I felt very clearheaded about it, and I had good people around me who were sympathetic to what I was trying to do. Orson Welles said making a film is like having a dream but everyone needs to be having the same dream.

I was fortunate to have Martin Stellman who was a great ally. Martin was a great writer and a smart bloke and our politics were similar.

PT: Did you write the screenplay together? Did you pass it back and forth?

FR: We were writing it together and writing it separately. We had the basic idea: guy goes off cliff in the end, guy loves girl in the beginning, but we would knock around incidents together. A lot of the incidents in *Quadrophenia* actually come from my youth—breaking in at the party and destroying the house, breaking in at the pharmacy. I was best man at the wedding of one of the guys who broke into the pharmacy—using the carjack to open the window. All these stories come from my life, and because of that it was what Pete and Roger would understand. And what Martin Stellman would understand. My friends used to get drunk and go and rob supermarkets; they would take off their shoes, put their socks on their hands and use the carjack. I gave that to Martin and Martin would craft that into a piece that works.

PT: One of the things that I find great about the film is that it comes from source material that is quite depressing but it's also incredibly funny. Were you consciously thinking about how to balance that out or did it just come naturally?

FR: That balance of action and humour in working-class communities of men, but women as well, there's a tremendous amount of humour. I worked in the shipyard, the humour's going on all day—it's the way they deal with work. I was talking the other day to Mini (this friend of mine who I did a documentary about) and I was trying to encourage him to write a play about jokes because we were telling outrageously non-PC jokes at the time, but that's how we integrated with people. We were very strong communities, and the humour was part of integration, but now it's part of exclusion. With the humour, Martin Stellman is a naturally funny guy… we just knew that to be honest, humour would have to be a big part of it.

PT: The phrase "*Quadrophenia*: a Way of Life" is a great phrase. Where does that come from? Thinking about the movie as a cult film—something that becomes something that people live, rather than just watch—that phrase seems to capture it.

FR: I can't remember where the phrase came from. Very interesting. It sounds like an advertising slogan. It might have come up as an advertising phrase. When we put the document together to get the money together—I think we used it—I can't claim it for myself. It's not on the original album?

PT: No. I was looking at Simon Wells's book, which is called *Quadrophenia: a Way of Life*, and it's great—it's exhaustive. It's clear that Mod was a way of life, and *Quadrophenia* became a way of life too. Were you thinking about *Quadrophenia* as a cult film from early on (if that concept even existed)?

FR: No. I think a way of life came from the idea that Mods had a code. Martin and I would talk sociology as well as script writing; when you're in a group like that, the group is everything. You look at adults and people and everyone else around you and they just don't count, because they're not in your way of life. I think it probably grew out of that. To be eighteen, to be a Mod, everything that wasn't Mod was bad. Mod was not just wearing a particular coat or suit; it was actually a way of life.

PT: It's interesting you brought up sociology and thinking about it from that perspective because one of the things that people in my academic book are writing about are sociologists who started writing about subculture in the 1970s, and particularly about Mod—Dick Hebdige, and Stanley Cohen's work on folk devils. Were you thinking about the fact that people were looking at Mods and teenagers as this sort of other species?

FR: I think we were objective about that. Martin and I had conversations about the phenomenon. I think we were more political. We had some sociology behind some of our theories. I would say this, and this was me standing apart from the Mods; one interesting thing about the Mods was that they weren't fighting to get out of prison, they were fighting for the top bunk. They were rebels not revolutionaries. It was an era in which people like myself were associating with revolutionaries—the Angry Brigade and radicals all over the world who wanted a revolution, and I was thinking in revolutionary terms, and when I looked at the Mods I had to define it for myself, and say these people are not politically conscious—they are Mods. We even put the lines in the film when he goes to see Pete and Pete says "you've got to work, if you don't work, you don't get money and clothes." It was an almost pre-Thatcherite devotion to conservatism in a strange sort of way. They were rebels—they wanted to spend their money on clothes and bikes and girls, and they wanted to have the top bunk and be the top Mod but they didn't want to change the world. Whereas Martin and I were much more radical in that respect—we were looking to see a change in the world.

PT: It does seem there's a critique of Mod in the movie even though it's also incredibly sympathetic to Mods. It always struck me as strange that the Mods and Rockers wanted to fight each other, rather than ganging together to fight the police.

FR: Yes, in Zola, in *La Terre*, there's a line where the schoolteacher who's an outsider gets drunk and suddenly starts cursing all the farmers and says "you're the majority—you could have had everything but you saved your best fights for each other," and that's always been a problem with the masses; they've turned on each other. Look at the people who voted for Trump; all the people who will least benefit from his policies, and they've picked up his banner.

PT: People are always talking about making a *Quadrophenia* sequel; at some point, in an interview, you said you thought Jimmy might have grown up to be a Thatcherite. But then of course there is also that relationship to punk which was happening at the time. Can you say some more about how punk fed into the movie?

FR: When I was asked to make the film the one thing that worried me was that we were in the middle of the punk movement and it made Mod-ism seem very old fashioned, and the punks were to some extent more interesting in that they were contemporary and had more radical ideas. But of course for punk as well everything seemed to get commercialized. Malcolm McLaren's son wanting to burn his collection. There's always been an ability of the institutions to absorb any new movement. I was interested in punk from an artistic point of view. Musically, it leaves me a bit cold, but the idea of deconstructing the fashion—the idea that I'm going to wear a jacket that's five sizes too big for me, I'm going to make it uneven. It's like Bunuel's film where he's re-arranging things on a mantelpiece and he goes—in the first line of the film—"I hate symmetry." I think that punk was very useful for that. It began to affect everything, even architecture. You don't have to be symmetrical, you don't have to have order; whereas the Mod thing was quite tight. For a lot of Mods, *Quadrophenia* was about the style; for me it was about love, sexual experience, individuality and also it was a socialist film. It really is an attempt to show the lives of working-class people.

PT: Thinking about that, the film is also so much about the crowd. If the album is about the individual—the inner life of Jimmy's breakdown, then what you're able to do in the film is show the great things and the terrible things about being a part of the crowd. What it means to be part of a group.

FR: Yes, when he's in the bicycle shed with his Rocker friend and he says "I want to be someone, I want to be an individual, that's why I'm a Mod, see?," I was very fortunate because of Pete Townshend and the Who's work because they wrote an album about teenage angst, and I was able to make a film about teenage angst because of that. I was able to give a lot of affection to the people I'd grown up with. This guy reminds me of this guy;

this guy reminds me of that guy. There's always the one girl who everyone fancies, and there's always the girl like Monkey who's devoted but gets left behind. We were able to look at the young stereotypes and also to bring in our own friends—I based the father on my father. The thing about him falling down a well—that's something that happened to my uncle. It was authentic; it was Pete's vision but we were adding flesh to the bones. Some of it comes from Martin, some from me. I felt very fortunate to be able to express my culture. It was like saying goodbye to my youth.

PT: I was thinking about what you were saying about socialism. There is a lot about work in the film and album. With Mod you always get the sense that you have the wild weekend in Brighton and you take the pills and then you have to go back into that work world.

FR: When I go to a Mod screening I wouldn't necessarily share this, but it still to this day annoys me that there are always complaints about what people are not doing for them; this person hasn't done this for us, and this person hasn't done that for us, but they're not doing it for themselves. Many of them have never got behind a political movement to change it. People complain about the disparity in wages, lack of facility in education, but did they vote for Bernie Sanders? No. I understand the fear of socialism, because I think it is passé in one sense, part of it, but that the idea that the masses allow themselves to be ruled has always been anathema to me.

PT: At the time you were making it, there was Paul Weller in the Jam making incredibly political music as well. There's always been contradictions between some of the music and some of the fans.

FR: Like the song "My Way"—people love it who don't have it their way. "I did it my way." No you didn't. This is all the political aspect of it, but I think it's helpful if you have layers of understanding in the film. First of all we had to deliver the Who album and turn it into a film, and we had to set it in the Mod movement, we had to talk about love. We had to talk about relationships and possible suicide. It didn't mean to say we couldn't have a layer of politics underneath that and a few social and political realities to deal with.

PT: But it does seem like Mod style might soak up some of the political energy—it takes money, it takes effort.

FR: It takes work. There's no reason why you can't be a Mod and you can't change society at the same time.
PT: Why do you think it is one of those styles that keeps coming back?
FR: It goes right back to the Rat Pack. Look at Sinatra and Dean Martin and those guys; they were incredibly smart and yet it was a restrained flamboyance. I guess it's just a convenient style for men and women. It's sharp.
PT: Mods are famously fussy about details. Issues about accuracy must have been going on in your mind when you were making the film, and of course people were going to call you out on getting things wrong when it was done. Did that bother you at the time?
FR: No, the only thing that bothered me were the tracks on the cliff at the end. Nowadays it would be a five-minute job just to wipe them clean. The other details were not so important for me.

There were certain interesting things about the details—the movie was about the beginning of the birth control era. Up until that time boys and girls didn't spend as much social time together. Where I grew up near Stockton the boys would all go out and get really hammered together on a Friday night, and on Saturday night they'd go out with the girls. Boys and girls started integrating more as a group—before that it was usually all guys or all gals. And early marriages through pregnancy, and then the pill came out, birth control. And the scooter was really great. It wasn't a dirty old bike; the engine was covered and it was clean, so the girls and the guys could hang out together. There was a vehicle to go together. For the first time young people had their own tailors; just a couple of years before that if you went to buy a suit you went to the same tailor as your father and you had a version of his suit. And suddenly there were Mod shops selling really nice shirts and sharp suits. The market place realised that youth was a great source of income for business, so Mod music, Mod shops, Mod clothes, Mod vehicles—it was a big social shift.

From that came precision; in this scruffy world of rock and roll, suddenly you had to have your suit cut in a certain way, your trousers had to be cut in a certain way. The girls' hair had to work in a certain way.
PT: Presumably that must have taken a lot of work for you in 70s when everyone's hair was long, to get everything right for the crowd scenes.

FR: Not really difficult. Of course there are people to this day who complain about the clothes in *Quadrophenia*; there are people to this day who complain about this or that. I remember being in New York at the Lincoln Center, and the first question after the film, this guy says, "I noticed a double yellow line in the Shepherd's Bush street scene. Double yellow lines didn't come out until a year later." You're expecting a compliment, so I said "what are you, a traffic warden?" The whole audience laughed. There were always people who complained.

PT: And that's not even a Mod detail about the clothing!

FR: I'd say to people, you mean you didn't enter the competition? There's ten mistakes in the film. Directors love accuracy too, of course. I don't want to make mistakes; I don't want the wrong car; I don't want the wrong bike or the wrong look. I want it to be authentic.

PT: And it feels authentic. You've said in an interview I read that you thought the film needed to work on different levels, as nostalgia, as a rock film, in its own right as a story, and as something with social and contemporary relevance. Did you have an ideal audience in mind when you were making it?

FR: If you're a producer or a marketing person you think like that. When you're a director or writer you don't think like that. I was just thinking I've got to make this emotionally authentic, socially authentic. I wasn't thinking in terms of it attracting a big audience or it being a success. I had no idea whether it would work or not; I was just in it, I was making it.

PT: I can see how it works for all sorts of people, but I think if I were you making it (which I was not!) I might have been thinking am I making it for Pete Townshend? Am I making it for sixteen-year-olds? Am I making it for Mods who were there at the time?

FR: I was just making a film; I didn't even think about the audience. I knew if it worked for me it would work for other people. And I'd just come from *Dummy*, which was very successful. And I thought what I was doing was trying to expand the margins of tolerance. Working in the BBC for several years and being around very serious and very interesting people you felt that you were part of people expanding the human experience. I didn't think whether old people would watch it, whether young people would watch it. I just thought I'm going to get this right. I'm going to show what it's like to be a young kid who's a bit of a loser. I wanted it to be different from some American films. I thought they're making films now where people succeed 99 percent of the time, whereas in my view people are failing 99 percent of the time. So I wanted to show people what it really felt like. You don't walk into a bar and beat up ten people. You walk into a bar and somebody gives you a slap.

PT: That seems to tie into the British vs Hollywood thing as well. *Quadrophenia* is an incredibly British film. Did you have a sense that you were speaking to a different tradition?

FR: But an interesting person is Nick Ray who did *Rebel Without a Cause*, and the films are very different, but there's a strange connection between them in that there's a little traumatized, inner turmoil with the character and things are not quite what they seem. The idea that you shouldn't pursue the things that people try and get you to pursue, that you should look at things as they really are. The getting of wisdom is really important—to me as an individual. It's very important for me to want the masses to have wisdom. With Trump and Brexit and Syria, you think "oh come on." I'm not a Christian, but the famous line on the cross "Father forgive them for they know not what they do." Again and again throughout history you see people making terrible decisions which are going to harm them. I wanted to show it—I wanted to show where it lies. Even though it's only a youth movie.

PT: I can understand why people might want a sequel, because if Jimmy gets wisdom at the end where does he end up? If it's a question of him rejecting everything he's been striving for, where is he left? Another question I have is about the women in the film. Leslie Ash as Steph is an interestingly strong character; she's just in it for a laugh. She's not the typical young woman you might get in a movie at the time.

FR: Yes, I turned that around. It's male nudity you get in the public bath, not female nudity. I wanted to flip it a bit. I felt that men's approaches to sexuality needed to expand. We had to start acknowledging men's attitudes toward romance.

PT: You were thinking about that at the time.

FR: When I look back now I was extremely conscious. Because I'd been working continuously doing documentaries for the BBC, because of my age, because of the age, because we'd come out of a political era. We were very concerned about the world politically, and all that had to be there. And I look at young people now, obsessed with selfies or how many likes they have on Facebook and worry that they've been duped into inactivity. I have two militant daughters, but they are militant vegetarians.

PF: What did your kids think when they saw *Quadrophenia*? What were their opinions of it?

FR: I have lots of children and they discovered it at different times. My eldest daughter was four months old when I was making it; my sixteen-year-old daughter was very happy to discover that it was her teacher's favourite film. My twenty-year-old daughter's boyfriend's granddad was talking about *Quadrophenia*, so I think it's a sense of pride. Martin Stellman (who wrote the film *Defense of the Realm* as well) and I were quite political. We wouldn't tell the film's producers about our politics and I hope we didn't stuff it down people's throats. I think we just integrated it.

PT: It's interesting to think it could have been more identified with punk if Johnny Rotten had actually gotten the roll of Jimmy. Could you have seen it being really different if you hadn't had Phil Daniels in that role?

FR: I think much of the success of *Quadrophenia* is down to Phil Daniels' performance. He's a really fine actor. He could have been Gary Oldman or Tim Roth; he chose to stay in England and do his stuff in the theatre. He's a brilliant actor, very sharp. Perfect in a weird sort of way.

The great thing about making films is that it is a collective art form. It was a lot of great people coming together and agreeing to in a certain direction. You create the bonding.

PT: What films and filmmakers or TV do you especially admire now?

FR: The thing I admire most at the moment is *The Young Pope*. Paolo Sorrentino—he directed *La Grande Bellezza* (The Great Beauty) (like a homage to *La Dolce Vita*). *The Young Pope* is extraordinarily bold—rips Catholicsim apart. I loved *Breaking Bad* and *Fargo*—beautifully made. And *House of Cards*. TV is eclipsing movies at the moment. I've seen a lot of extremely disappointing movies recently. When you want to take risks as a filmmaker it's difficult— I haven't made many films. If you're willing to accept middle of the road morality and politics then you can make movies all the time. If you want to do exceptional movies, you have to be very lucky and a few people get through and manage to make them. I always enjoy the Coen Brothers movies.

PT: One of the things that seems radical and interesting to me about *Quadrophenia* is that it's really about ordinariness and failure. It's incredibly sympathetic portrait of this ordinary guy who has desperate dreams but is not going to make it.

FR: If I think about it now I was very inspired by Truffaut in those days, and by Ken Loach. *Kes*—that was a beautifully sensitive film—and it was about ordinariness. And *400 Blows*. Those two films were very influential to me in the early part of my life. But also in the background were all the big westerns and adventure films I'd seen when I was younger so I had that as well. So I had a love of grand cinema, but I loved early Truffaut. One of my documentaries Mini is a homage to *400 Blows* in some sort of way, not consciously. When you make a film, I don't see any reason why it can't be a really memorable movie—one of the greatest movies ever made, if they don't get in your way—when people haven't gotten in my way (like *Quadrophenia* or *Aria*– they've been extremely successful. When they've started interfering—because I'm a polemic filmmaker—they fall apart. And a bit of my argument disappears.

PT: Something about the subculture has changed with the internet.

FR: Everything gets exploited immediately now. There was a great phase of Chinese movies with War Kai Wai. I can't always be bothered with the ordinary. It's ironic because the ordinary can be the most beautiful when it's done with great authenticity, but there are different kinds of ordinary.

PT: The Hollywood ordinary, where you know where it's going to go from the beginning.

FR: They used to say at film school that the difference between American and European films at the time was that with a European film you didn't know what was going to happen, but with American films you know what was going to happen it was just a question of when.
I like the sensitivity of *Kes* and *400 Blows*. These films really make you care about the wellbeing of the character. As you care about the wellbeing of people in the street or your neighbour. I read

a lot of all sorts of stuff including esoteric philosophy and I was reading some Jean Jacques Rousseau the other day and he said there is no greater wisdom than kindness, and I really believe that. I love intellectual pursuit but it comes down to kindness.

PT: I think that is true about *Quadrophenia*—it can be critical of Mod, but it's kind towards Jimmy, towards all of its characters.

FR: I think that was inbuilt in me from my mother. I hope it comes through my films. If you can make the audience care, you've expanded them. There's a messianic quality that I know I should slap down in myself, but I would like to change the world. As you get older you think, well I didn't get a chance, but when I was young I wanted to change the world.

The kindness thing—without being sentimental about that—if you embrace it you have to be generous, you have to be conscious, you have to be thoughtful. If you can get people to care—*Dummy*—it's a deaf and dumb prostitute—if you can care about her, it will affect your actions.

PT: I'm curious about how you felt when you knew there was going to be an academic conference on your film?

FR: When I looked at the Criterion Collection version I saw Howard Hampton's essay about the film—that really pleased me in the same way that the conference pleased me, that the content has got some validity. I think you can watch *Kes* now and still be moved by it; you can read Zola now and still be desperately moved, you can see Truffaut's *400 Blows* and still be moved, and you can still see *Quadrophenia* and it can still affect young people. It pleases me. The academic side—the fact that it can be a reference, that it can be useful is a wonderful compliment.

PT: I taught it to a bunch of students—they were critical of Jimmy, and of Steph, but the dilemmas still really make sense to them.

FR: It's interesting you can put something out there that resonates. People like Pete Townshend—they have that instinctively. There is a young man, a crazy guitarist, writing stuff because he understood the psychology of the young people. He got it—he knew it intuitively. A lot of the rock musicians—some of them are really great poets today too, like the Killers from the Southwest. They write stunning material.

PT: Do you still have fans coming up to you?
FR: It's strange because it's such a long time ago in one respect. Time is always moving on, but it's good. I'm glad that it made an impact.

CHAPTER 14

Interview with Ethan Russell

Pamela Thurschwell and Keith Gildart

Ethan Russell is a multiple Grammy-nominated photographer and director, who amongst other claims to fame, is the only photographer to have shot covers for the Beatles, the Rolling Stones, and the Who. His career as a photographer began in 1968, auspiciously, when he was invited to take some photos with a journalist friend who was interviewing Mick Jagger. His first work with Pete Townshend and the Who was for the album cover for *Who's Next*. Some of his best work can be found in the stunning photography booklet that accompanies the original album *Quadrophenia*. He graciously agreed to be interviewed via email for this volume.

The interview was conducted via email by Keith Gildart and Pamela Thurschwell

P. Thurschwell (✉)
University of Sussex, Brighton, UK
e-mail: p.thurschwell@sussex.ac.uk

K. Gildart
University of Wolverhampton, Wolverhampton, UK
e-mail: Keith.Gildart@wlv.ac.uk

PT/KG: Before working on the photo shoot for the album did you have a strong sense of the politics and culture of post-war Britain, or of Mod culture?

ER: I'm an American, of course, but one of my earliest memories, when I was eight years old, was watching the coronation of Elizabeth II. I had an English nanny and even at eight you could tell (very grainy b&w) this was something of vast importance. Whether that had anything to do with my eventual love of England I have no idea. As a matter of record, though, by the time I was photographing *Quadrophenia* I had come and gone from England, and in fact was living in Los Angeles when I got the call from Pete that I should come over and see what he was working on. (We had already worked together for the album cover *Who's Next* … something spontaneous that occurred on the drive back from a gig in middle England.) So I had some feel for post-war England, although the influences would've been peripheral and not at all linear. My father had been in the Royal Canadian Air Force, and my uncle (after whom I'm named) was lost over the English Channel the day after D-Day. But to be clear none of this adds up to a simple answer to your question. I absolutely do have a feel for post-war Britain (even stronger now than I did then), but there's not an obvious explanation for why.

The Mod question is a little easier to answer since I had absolutely no idea what a Mod was. I mean none. I had heard the word as an American university student who was as immersed in the so-called British Invasion as any one. The phrase "Mods and Rockers" was familiar. However, if you'd asked me to tell you what a Mod was my answer would've been along the lines of Brian Jones in his fluffy shirt. I visualized the conflict between "Mods and Rockers" as being between what would have been in English parlance a Teddy Boy and something like the young Rolling Stones, Beatles, longhair. So, no, I knew nothing.

But when I first came to England (entirely by chance in response to my father thinking it might be a good idea to get me out of San Francisco and the Haight-Ashbury) what I, of course, wanted to see was where all this phenomenal music was coming from. However, my experience was—when I got off the plane—that London was *nowhere* near as music-fueled as America and Haight Ashbury was at the time. I nevertheless loved England for reasons which were not entirely explicable beyond what I've noted above. I still feel incredibly at home there and always have.

PT/KG: Did Townshend give you ideas for the kind of images he wanted to have, or did you work directly from his story?

ER: My memory is of getting off the plane from America (now many years after my first trip) and going to sit down with Pete who felt (to me) extraordinarily under pressure already. He would never have given me anything like specific ideas for the images I don't think (although the picture with Jimmy lying in bed below a collection of naked women was specifically something Pete came up with in response to having seen a photograph somewhat like it at some point. I never saw that photograph for what it's worth but the idea was pretty great, I thought, and I used it.) I do recall thinking that what we would be trying do is tell the story of Jimmy visually and to create the world that he lived in. So, then I just embarked upon doing that.

As an aside, from the time of Dylan, leading to the Beatles, leading to the Stones, the thing that was arguably the most compelling to me was the singer-songwriter. I wanted to be a writer, photography was an afterthought but became, obviously, my primary career for a while. So, the idea of really bringing to life visually the nature of some of this great musical work just made sense. And of course Pete was a prime example. Other than the specifics of Pete's narrative, that really was the driving concept.

PT/KG: The black and whiteness of *Quadrophenia* seems key to its power, in contrast to the psychedelic colours of *Tommy*. What were you thinking when you chose black and white instead of colour for the photos?

ER: To be clear I'm not the kind of artist who sits down and surveys the landscape and makes a cerebral decision based upon doing something that opposed to something that occurred before. It's very much a feel thing. To me it was an homage to the early black-and-white films I saw prior to coming to England. There was also the work of an English photographer called Bill Brandt that I had admired for years. In fact, all of the work of *Quadrophenia* was for me a way to pay homage to that early sensibility. The movies were *A Taste of Honey*, *Hard Day's Night*, and *The Knack*.

PT/KG: The images seem to form a corrective to the mythology of a "swinging London." Was this intentional?

ER: Not intentional, but then I dismissed Swinging London within minutes of getting off the plane and going to Carnaby Street, way before I was in any way involved with the actual groups themselves or even working as a photographer. I was coming from San Francisco, after all, where these ideas (music and its revolution) were being taken very seriously. And Carnaby Street and Kings Road and all that always struck me as kind of trivial.

PT/KG: Battersea and its working-class youth had featured prominently in the work of novelists and filmmakers in the 1960s. Nell Dunn's *Up The Junction* and Ken Loach's subsequent television play/film are examples. Were you aware of the book and the film and did it inform your sense of working-class London?

ER: No I was not aware of them. My influences were as noted above. The whole idea of the class system was not particularly on my radar since I was an American.

PT/KG: Mod obsessives and fans of the album have tracked down many of the localities and spaces in the photos—how does that feel to you?

ER: Feels good, I guess. I'm proud of the work. It's really good work.

PT/KG: Did you listen to the songs on *Quadrophenia* before embarking on the photo shoot, or was the recording happening simultaneously?

ER: They were still working on the record that's for sure but, equally, I feel I had complete access to all of it. I certainly don't recall not having something I wanted. My manner of working was absolutely to immerse myself in the music as much as possible. I'm sure I listened to everything 50–60 times. And periodically to check in with Pete. And, as noted

	later, I was constantly working with Richard Barnes who Pete put in charge as the "content expert" if you will.
PT/KG:	The Who have often been depicted as a working-class band in terms of their core audience and this has been reflected on some of their album covers. The cover that you shot earlier for *Who's Next* features an old colliery "slag heap" in North East England. Was this a conscious decision to link the band to an industrial working-class Britain?
ER:	Over time people have tried try to attribute all sorts of intentionality to that cover. Everything about it was a completely spontaneous accident created out of basically thin air. I had been hired by Pete (this is mostly via my relationship with Glyn Johns who was producing *Who's Next* and who had become a friend of mine by that time and who bought me in) to come up with a cover. We were in a caravan of cars driving back from some gig when I saw these shapes (I had no idea whatsoever what they were; didn't really until many years later). When Pete, who drove maniacally fast, had to slow down for a roundabout, he turned and asked me if I had any ideas? My response was in effect "Well there's these shapes back there…" and Pete spun the car around and we walked out and in the midst of fooling around came up with that shot.
PT/KG:	In your published diary of the 1970s you said that it was the Englishness of the album that appealed. Can you say a bit more about this?
ER:	I think I alluded to it above. But when I arrived in England—well Central London—I felt like I belonged there. I had also by that point been extraordinarily influenced by the movie *Blow-up* (which in its own way was just added to my existing admiration for Bill Brandt, *Taste of Honey*, *Hard Day's Night* ethos). I walked all over London looking for that park. Never did find it. Now, of course, with Google maps I know where it is so perhaps one day I'll visit it. Very much a pilgrimage.
PT/KG:	You also co-wrote a proposed television play for *Quadrophenia* in 1973/4. Can you say a bit more about this? Was it similar to Franc Roddam's cinematic treatment in 1979?

ER: I was ahead of Franc Roddam to my knowledge. But my idea was actually for television, not film, and at its core it really tried to take the idea that I had now become very conscious about…which is that I wanted to bring the strength of the singer-songwriter to the screen. In the screenplay I co-wrote The Who would've performed the narrative of *Quadrophenia* only as a band—a musical performance which was to have (appeared to have) taken place within a grand ballroom on the pier, while the action was carried by actors. I spoke with Malcolm McDowell and he was interested. It would've been great, but the requirement from Who management at that point was that we get a prime time American broadcast. I was entirely naïve about the meaning of that, but if you consider that MTV was 1981 and this was seven or eight years before that, it was way too early for American commercial television.

PT/KG: Battersea Power station is almost as strong an image in the booklet as Brighton is. Did you have your own associations with Battersea when you chose to use it?

ER: Only viscerally. It's just an incredibly powerful as a piece of industrial architecture. And Brighton Pier was to me an entirely magical structure altogether. (A couple of years ago I was in Sussex with my then 12-year-old son and I planned to take him to see the pier only to find out it'd burned down, of which I was not aware. So that was a sad moment for me).[1] I think there was a related kind of influence which really was the Sgt. Pepper iconography. One of the last photographs I took of The Beatles (from their last photo session at John's house) was shooting through Victorian Sgt Pepper statues/heads. All of that was part of the same atmosphere which was appealing.

PT/KG: The domestic scenes such as the working-class family kitchen seem evocative of the social realist cinema of directors such as Karel Reisz, Lindsay Anderson, and Tony Richardson. Was their work or other filmmakers (or photographers) an influence on what you envisaged for *Quadrophenia*?

ER: No because I wasn't familiar with it. I love that I cast the female model whose entire work was doubling as Queen Elizabeth II as his mom.

PT/KG:	How much input did the individual members of the Who have on the ideas, scope and style of the photo essay?
ER:	Really regarding scope and style it was just me, checking in with Pete, and very specifically assisted by Richard Barnes who Pete brought into do exactly what I would have been unable to do as an American, which is to really know the specifics of what it meant to be a Mod. That was my education. It was kind of delightful really because who knew? And then to be subsumed into understanding that the collar had to be exactly like this and not a quarter inch wider, and the jacket exactly like that, and the scooter exactly like this. All of which was of course archetypal and universal, the kind of behaviour for all adolescents as they grow, it's just the specifics change. And they were a delightful set of specifics. But I relied entirely on Richard Barnes for them.
PT/KG:	Were there any photos that didn't make the final cut which with hindsight you would have liked to include in the album?
ER:	We—well I—had this, on the surface, rather obvious idea which was to create a face made up of all four members of The Who and that would be Jimmy on the front of the album. But I had no interest in replicating the sort of torn poster look that I'd actually seen used by other bands. I think maybe the band Spirit did something along those lines. The face I wanted would *not* have been initially recognizable as being made up of the four component members of The Who. And we shot the photographs for that, and I was working with the retoucher to do it. I can't remember the name of the retoucher but he was really the best. I became aware of his work because he had done and ad where Oxford Street had been filled with sheep, so I sought him out. By the time I was coming to the end of the project everybody—myself included—was incredibly wiped out. I think I lost 20 + pounds working on it. A great deal of it was just Chad—Jimmy—and me. We'd shoot in the day and then I'd work with the lab or the retoucher in every free moment late into the evening and then get up at 5 am and etc. The reason that shot wasn't used—I think today I might have made a mistake to let it pass so easily—was that the face for Jimmy (it was never entirely finished but it came quite far along and was

	really NOT recognizable as four faces of the Who) was just kind of—bland (not exactly the word but…) and so in the heat of the moment it got abandoned. Pre-Photoshop that kind of work was far from trivial. Then we got into a bit of tussle over what the cover *should* be. Jimmy riding his scooter with Battersea station behind him was one I wanted and Pete liked as I recall. And then there was one just of the scooter in profile and then the back shot of the album with the scooter in the sea. But Roger was really adamant that the Who would be on the cover and so ultimately the scooter and Jimmy were taken into Graham Hughes's studio where he did the shot that was used on the cover. I of course do not feel wonderful about that but equally I hadn't had that idea, which, while it was stylistically and artistically so different from what we were doing it was also pretty good
PT/KG:	Do you have one favourite photo? If so which is it?
ER:	I'd say there at least 8 to 10 photos off the top of my head that I think are pretty fabulous. I think the body of work in its entirety is fabulous. It was nominated for Grammy and I think we lost to Michael Jackson :-)
PT/KG:	Can you tell us something about shooting the train photo (which is echoed so closely in the film)? One of the essays in our collection compares it to the scene in the film, but also to a similar scene in *A Hard Day's Night*.
ER:	Very straightforward really, almost an illustration. One of the easier shots and in the book I think. I can't say I was "influenced" by anything just because it's so straightforward. Certainly didn't think of *Hard Day's Night*.
PT/KG:	For many Who fans the photos were as important as the music for conveying a sense of place, youth culture, locality, and feeling. Where would you place the importance of the photos in the canon of your work?
ER:	Oh, they're way up there. They really were an extraordinary proof of concept in my opinion of what you can do with visuals and music (and which is why I carried forward into the idea of doing television). Over the years, television started to take primacy in almost every culture and I really wanted to

	see the ideas and the values of the singer-songwriter brought forward. Wasn't to happen.

         I also have a very expensive 600 page book based on the Rolling Stones' 1969 Tour that took six years to do which is pretty spectacular. I'm the writer on that one as well.

PT/KG: Was there any disagreement between yourself and the members of the Who regarding the images you selected for inclusion in the album?

ER: Only around the cover as described above. There is also the moment when all 40 pages of the book (or whatever it is) were laid in front of Pete's feet and he looked at me rather plaintively and said I thought you said it was gonna be 12 pages. That sounds cavalier but it really wasn't. I wasn't trying to be irresponsible (didn't remember saying anything about 12 pages) and in the end the art just took over. Glad it did. It would never happen today, but I have (of course) more sympathy as an adult about what it must have meant for the bottom line.

PT/KG: Why do you think *Quadrophenia* still resonates with original fans of the Who and more recent consumers of their music and live shows in the way that it does?

ER: I of course don't know that since I can't speak for them, but it is my sense that the Who's music, the music of the Stones and the Beatles really are made of muscle and blood, they're analog, they have great spirit, and I think that continues to talk to people.

PT/KG: Have you revisited some of the original locations and what is your perception of youth culture in contemporary Britain?

ER: Well, I'm older, and I have a pretty standard grumpy old man response to much of younger culture. A less flippant response might be, about England in particular, that the class system kind of came home to roost. You know in America our royalty has always been talent of one sort or another since we didn't have royalty per se. So the early movie stars, or Hank Williams Sr., Elvis, or Muhammed Ali were royalty and so on. In England it was a different situation, but with global culture shifts the traditional class system was in its sights.

PT/KG: Do you think people are still doing interesting album or video art now? If so, who?

ER: Kind of a broad question. My observation is that in the music business in particular, it just dramatically shifted towards marketing, which is an entirely different universe than the one we were inhabiting. That was really the message of music video as well. A real answer would be very lengthy and would include changing from print culture to image culture to the Internet, so I'll just leave that there…

PT/KG: Any additional thoughts would be welcome. Thank you!

ER: Someone said in the BBC film on *Quadrophenia* that "As an American you were able to understand it because you were able to see it. You were able to see his room. You saw the life. It told you the story better than a movie, better than a video, it's all there…"[2] That is of course satisfying because that's exactly what I was trying to do.

Notes

1. Brighton's West Pier, pictured in Russell's book of photographs, closed in 1975, and suffered structural damage in a storm in 1987. It was further destroyed by fire in 2003.
2. Howie Edelson says this in *Quadrophenia: Can you See the Real Me?*

Index

A
Abrams, Mark, 17, 18
Absolute Beginners (film), 202–203, 206
Almost Famous (film), 58
Ash, Leslie (Steph), 25, 155, 207, 245
A Taste of Honey (film), 254, 255

B
Baba, Meher, 43, 102, 125
Balla, Giacomo, 212
Barnes, Richard, 36, 177–179, 181, 190, 191, 255, 257
Battersea, 86, 89, 96, 100, 104, 105, 107, 254, 258
  Power Station, 100, 208, 256
Beachy Head, 29, 221
Beatles, The, 37, 38, 46, 54, 55, 88, 137, 251–253, 256, 259
  Hard Day's Night (film), 137, 140, 254, 255, 258
  Harrison, George, 142
  Lennon, John, 87, 95, 139, 142
  McCartney, Paul, 139, 142
  Starr, Ringo, 137, 139, 142, 199

Bildungsroman, 3
Birmingham School, 6, 75, 174
Blow-up (film), 255
Bolan, Marc, 185
Bourdieu, Pierre, 2
Bowie, David, 35, 44–47, 93, 185
Brighton
  Aquarium, 36, 90
  Battle of Brighton, 14, 15, 23, 26–30
  Beach, 36, 77, 200, 206, 218, 224, 227, 229
  Trains, 42, 100, 131; Brighton Belle, 131, 136
British identity, 1, 2
Brown, Ken, 176, 179
Browne, Ken, 207

C
Clarke, John, 29, 39–41, 76
Clash, The, 230
  Strummer, Joe, 230
Cohen, Phil, 22, 23, 39, 141
Cohen, Stanley, 2, 23–26, 28, 39, 142, 240

Cohn, Nik, 37, 93, 158
Comte de Lautréamont (Isidore-Lucien Ducasse), 69
Cultural studies, 1–3, 6, 68, 69, 75, 89
Cultural turn, 68, 75. *See also* Cultural studies

D
Daniels, Phil (Jimmy Cooper), 5, 13, 140, 187, 206, 246
Dazed and Confused (film), 58
Deleuze, Gilles and Felix Guattari, 210, 213
Dunn, Nell, 86, 254
　Poor Cow (1967), 86
　Up the Junction (1963), 86

E
Embourgeoisification, 70, 76, 135
Emerson, Lake and Palmer, 59

F
Farson, Dan, 19
Feldman, Christine Jacqueline, 192
Fellini, Frederico, 21
　La Dolce Vita (1960), 21
Ferry, Bryan, 185
Fletcher, Alan, 7, 105, 132, 135, 140, 184, 189, 191
FM radio, 56–57
Fourier, Charles, 69
Freaks and Geeks (US TV show), 57, 59
Freud, Sigmund, 211, 217, 218

G
Gender and Sexuality, 2, 140, 174, 175, 192
　Gay/queer culture, 99, 173–192
　homosexuality, 182, 190, 191
　Sexual freedom, 155, 163–165
　Women in Mod subculture, 151–165
Glynn, Stephen, 39, 182, 185, 186, 221, 222
Grayson, Richard, 24
Green, Jonathon, 189
Greene, Graham, 16
　Brighton Rock (1938), 16

H
Halberstam, Judith, 174
Hall, Stuart, 6, 39, 41, 75, 76, 78
Haywood, Chris, 175, 192
Heath, Edward, 96, 97, 141
Heatwave (pamphlet), 67–69, 73–75
Hebdige, Dick, 2, 6, 19, 22, 23, 28, 41, 44–46, 77, 78, 134, 183, 201–204, 206, 207, 222, 240
　Subculture; The Meaning of Style, 2
Hewitt, Paolo, 156, 171, 185
Hoggart, Richard, 6, 75, 76, 91, 92, 99, 106
　The Uses of Literacy, 75, 92
Holder, Adrian, 186, 187

J
Jam, The, 3, 143, 221, 242
　Weller, Paul, 3, 221, 242
Jefferson, Tony, 39, 41, 76
Jephcott, Pearl, 18
Joyce, James, 229
　Portrait of the Artist as a Young Man, 229

K
Kelly, Roland, 179, 207
Kinglsey-Innes, Stuart, 165
Kinks, The, 23, 54, 60, 87, 94, 100, 101

Davies, Dave, 101
Davies, Ray, 87, 94, 95, 99

L
La Grande Bellezza (film), 246
Last Days of Disco (film), 58
Led Zeppelin, 53, 56, 61
Lester, Richard, 137
Levi-Strauss, Claude, 222
London to Brighton in Four Minutes (film), 136
Lyons, Jack (Irish Jack), 89

M
Mac an Ghaill, Máirtaín, 175, 192
MacInnes, Colin, 21, 70, 87, 201
　Absolute Beginners, 21, 70, 76, 78, 87, 97, 108, 201–203, 206
Manzi, Carlo, 160
Manzi, Eugene, 180
Marquis de Sade (Donatien Alphonse François), 69
Marx, Karl, 69
　Marxism, 70, 78, 99
McQueen, Roger, 157
Mods
　£75 cheque story, 26
　and Rockers, 2, 4, 14, 23–28, 36, 53, 55, 77, 94, 95, 140, 154, 155, 157, 185, 199, 201, 227, 240, 252
　beach fights, 41, 124, 220, 224. *See also* Mods and Rockers, Battle of Brighton
　beachniks, 20, 21
　drugs, 2, 13, 22, 25, 35, 42, 60, 77, 132, 133, 181, 203, 220, 221
　Fashion; Burton, Roger, 188; Carnaby Street, 21, 177–180, 190, 191, 254; English, Jack, 188; eye make-up, 140, 184–187; hairstyles, 13, 23, 41, 42, 76, 160, 183, 184; Levi's, 42, 179, 180, 188; parkas, 22, 25, 30, 41, 42, 183, 201, 208, 209, 211, 212; Stephen, John, 21, 177–180, 190; Vince's Man's Shop, 177
Modernists, 21, 68, 153, 154, 156, 158, 165, 201, 205
Sawdust Caesars, 2
Scooters; Lambrettas, 1, 13, 22, 183, 200, 201, 206, 207, 210, 212; Sportique, 206, 207; Vespas, 1, 7, 13, 22, 30, 38, 42, 77, 89, 183, 200–202, 205–210, 212–214, 220, 225

N
Newspapers
　Daily Mirror, 24, 26
　Daily Sketch, 26
　Evening Argus, 26, 27, 30
　New Society, 27, 33
　Sunday Times Magazine, 28
　Times, The (London), 20, 24, 28
Norman, Bill, 182, 191
Nostalgia, 37, 39, 106, 121, 135, 142, 143, 218, 220, 224, 244

P
Pennebaker, D.A., 55
　Monterey Pop (1968), 55
Pink Floyd, 61, 205
Prior, Barry, 30
Privilege (film), 92

Q
Quadrophenia, Can You See The Real Me? (BBC documentary), 9, 205, 232

R
Radcliffe, Charles, 69, 71–78
Rawlings, Terry, 158, 201, 206, 207
Ready, Steady, Go! (UK TV show), 155, 163, 179, 199, 200
Rebel Worker (magazine), 69, 71, 73, 75
Roddam, Franc, 3, 4, 8, 13, 53, 74, 85, 103–105, 132, 137, 140, 141, 143, 144, 163–165, 181, 182, 186, 189–191, 220, 256
Rolling Stones, The, 37, 46, 52, 54, 55, 88, 199, 251–253, 259
    Jagger, Mick, 251
    Jones, Brian, 252
Russell, Ethan, 4, 8, 42, 86, 89, 131, 139, 140, 142, 144, 204, 209, 219, 220, 229
Russell, Ken, 37, 143

S
Saturday Night and Sunday Morning (1958), 86, 91
Saturday Night Fever (1977), 59
Scala, Mim, 89
Sedgwick, Eve Kosofsky, 175
Segues, 217–234
Sex Pistols, The
    Rotten, Johnny, 230, 246
Shail, Gary (Spider), 187–189
Shindig! (US TV show), 54
Sillitoe, Alan, 86
Situationists, 6, 72, 73
    Debord, Guy, 72
    Lettrists, 72, 73; *Potlatch* (journal), 72
Small Faces, The, 21, 60, 162
    Stewart, Rod, 184
Smith, Cyril, 18
Soho, 21, 106, 162, 164, 176–179, 190, 201, 202, 205

Soul (music), 21, 35, 105, 181, 201
    Northern Soul, 96, 97, 105, 201
Springsteen, Bruce, 6, 119–129, 121
    Backstreets (song), 122, 125–128
    Born to Run, 119–128, 130
    Born to Run (song), 122–124, 126
    Jungleland (song), 122–126
    Night (song), 122, 127
    She's the One (song), 123, 125, 126
    Tenth Avenue Freeze Out (song), 124
    Thunder Road (song), 123–125
Sting (Ace Face), 5, 26, 141, 183, 189, 224
Subcultures
    beatniks, **20**, 27, 68
    disco, 58, 58–59
    glam rock, 5, 35, 39, 44, 45, 58, 97, 140, 185, 186
    hippies, 29, 55, 56, 58
    punk, 1, 5, 29, 38, 45, 47, 58, 59, 61, 105, 143, 157, 191, 222, 230, 241, 246
    skinheads, 29, 68, 96, 103, 105
    suedeheads, 97, 103
    Teddy boys, 19–21, 38, 67, 97, 102, 154, 252
Suicide, 8, 29, 40, 43, 44, 213, 218, 219, 242
Swinging London, 28, 93, 106, 107, 254

T
Teenagers
    affluence, 17, 18, 22, 23, 86, 87, 90, 107, 135, 203, 204, 208
    moral panic, 2, 23–25, 29, 39, 155
That '70s Show (US TV show), 58
The Knack (film), 254
Theweleit, Klaus, 7, 210–213

The Young Pope (film), 246
Todd, Selina, 17
Ton-Up Kids, 75
Townshend, Pete, 3–7, 35–47, 54, 56, 60, 61, 71, 73, 76, 85–95, 97–100, 102, 106, 118, 120, 121, 125, 131, 132, 137, 141, 143, 144, 173, 178, 190, 200, 205, 208, 219, 221, 223, 224, 226, 227, 230, 238, 241, 244, 248, 251, 253

V
Velvet Goldmine (film), 58

W
Weight, Richard, 1, 134, 176, 184, 191, 212
Wells, Simon, 1, 65, 233, 239
Who, The
  5:15 (song), 6, 42, 46, 100, 122, 131, 136, 137, 144
  Anyway, Anyhow, Anywhere (song), 88
  Baba O'Riley (song), 1, 53
  Bell Boy (song), 40, 95, 126, 203–204, 208, 224
  Curbishley, Bill, 60
  Cut My Hair (song), 39, 41, 90, 93, 122, 125, 128, 135, 228
  Daltrey, Roger, 30, 54, 55, 88, 174, 186, 208, 209, 214, 226, 228
  Dogs (song), 91
  Drowned (song), 44, 95, 102, 124, 200, 223
  Entwistle, John, 54, 88, 101, 208, 214
  Helpless Dancer (song), 46, 90, 98, 99, 103, 104, 106, 127, 174, 208, 226, 227
  High Numbers, The, 89
  I Can't Explain (song), 88
  I'm One (song), 41, 90, 94, 210
  Is It In My Head (song), 92, 127
  I've Had Enough (song), 28, 40, 41, 90, 127
  Jones, Kenney, 60
  Lambert, Kit, 54
  loudest band in the world, 56
  Love Reign O'er Me (song), 40, 43, 44, 125, 208, 219
  Meaden, Pete, 36, 54, 70, 89, 106, 212
  Meaty Beaty Big and Bouncy (album), 89
  Moon, Keith, 54, 59, 60, 88, 101, 126, 208, 214, 224
  My Generation (song), 1, 52–54, 88, 139, 222, 230
  Ramport Studios, 96, 205
  Sea and Sand (song), 39, 41, 76, 95, 122, 123, 128, 223, 224
  See Me, Feel Me (song), 1
  Stamp, Chris, 54
  The Dirty Jobs (song), 90, 97, 98, 104, 106, 126, 135
  The Kids are Alright (film), 52, 54, 60
  The Kids are Alright (song), 46, 226, 227
  The Punk and the Godfather (song), 4, 90, 92, 93, 225, 227–230
  Tommy, 1, 35, 37, 52, 54, 56, 61, 125, 143, 238, 253; *Lifehouse*, 37, 93
  Who's Next, 4, 224, 251, 252, 255
  Won't Get Fooled Again (song), 93, 118, 129, 234
Wood, James, 110, 233
Woodstock Festival, 55
Wilcox, Toyah (Monkey), 5, 155, 182
Wingett, Mark (Dave), 187, 188

Winstone, Ray, 22
Wyler, William, 21
   Roman Holiday (1953), 21

Y
Young, Hilary, 17

GPSR Compliance
The European Union's (EU) General Product Safety Regulation (GPSR) is a set
of rules that requires consumer products to be safe and our obligations to
ensure this.

If you have any concerns about our products, you can contact us on

ProductSafety@springernature.com

In case Publisher is established outside the EU, the EU authorized
representative is:

Springer Nature Customer Service Center GmbH
Europaplatz 3
69115 Heidelberg, Germany

www.ingramcontent.com/pod-product-compliance
Ingram Content Group UK Ltd.
Pitfield, Milton Keynes, MK11 3LW, UK
UKHW051328250126
10300UKWH00006B/15